Gender and the Labour Process

Edited by
David Knights
Hugh Willmott

Gower

Published by

Gower Publishing Company Ltd,
Gower House,
Croft Road,
Aldershot,
Hampshire,
GU11 3HR,
England.

Gower Publishing Company,
Old Post Road,
Brookfield,
Vermont 05036
U.S.A.

British Library Cataloguing in Publication Data
Gender and the labour process.
  1. Sexual division of labor   2. Women—
  Employment
  I. Knights, David   II. Willmott, Hugh
  331.4   HD6060.6

ISBN 0–566–00999–4

Library of Congress Cataloging-in-Publication Data
Main entry under title:

Gender and the labour process.

  Includes bibliographical references.
  1. Sexual division of labor—Addresses, essays,
lectures.   2. Women—Employment—Addresses, essays,
lectures.   I. Knights, David. II. Willmott, Hugh.
HD6060.6.G45   1985   331.4   83–21977
ISBN 0–566–00999–4

Printed in Great Britain at the University Press.   Cambridge.

Contents

List of Contributors

Harriet Bradley worked as an English teacher for some years before reading Sociology at Leicester University. She has taught at Durham University and is currently employed at Sunderland Polytechnic.

David Collinson has conducted research into shopfloor culture in the engineering industry and industrial relations in the printing industry. He has just completed a 2 year research project on sex discrimination in recruitment for the E.O.C.

Celia Davis was Lecturer in Industrial Sociology at Imperial College and subsequently Research Fellow in Sociology at Warwick. She has published articles on health professions and health policy and edited *Rewriting Nursing History* (Croom Helm, 1980). She is currently working with the statutory bodies in nursing on the future of nurse education.

Margaret Grieco is presently Researcher at the London Economic Policy Unit, Polytechnic of the South Bank and Transport Studies Unit, University of Oxford. She has researched and published in a number of areas; North Sea oil, family and employment, migration, health sector. She was previously Researcher at the University of Aston, and Phoenix Assurance Company.

David Knights is Lecturer in Management Sciences, UMIST and has research interests in management control, workplace industrial relations, discrimination and discipline. He is the joint organiser of the annual Labour Process Conferences.

Sonia Liff is currently carrying out research on the employment implications of new technology at the Technology Policy Unit, Aston University and is teaching at Hatfield Polytechnic. The article derives from her PhD, 'Occupational Sex-typing: Sexual and Technical Divisions of Labour', which was undertaken in the Science and Technology Policy Department, Manchester University.

David Podmore is a member of the Social and Technology Division, University of Aston Management Centre. His earlier research on the solicitors profession was published as *Solicitors and the Wider Community*, (Heinemann, 1980).

Jane Rosser is currently employed as a Research Officer in local government. Her previous work has all involved research into aspects of the National Health Service – most recently in Sociology at Warwick University, and prior to that in the Psychiatry Department of Manchester University.

Anne Spencer is at present Research Fellow (Senior Lecturer) in the Department of Management Studies, Sheffield City Polytechnic. She was previously Research Fellow in the Department of Sociology and Social History, and the Management Centre, at the University of Aston.

Richard Whipp first studied the relationship between gender and the labour process in his doctorate on the British pottery industry. He has published a number of articles and book chapters on this theme. Senior Research Fellow at the Work Organisation Research Centre, Aston University until September 1985, he is currently Senior Research Fellow at the Centre for Corporate Strategy and Change at the University of Warwick.

Hugh Willmott is Lecturer in the Management Centre, University of Aston. He is currently engaged in a joint research project on 'Corporatism and the Accountancy Profession' and in work on management control. He is the joint organiser of the annual Labour Process Conferences.

Anne Witz is a part-time Lecturer in Sociology at the University of Lancaster, where she is also an active member of the Women's Studies Research Centre. She is currently doing research into patriarchy and gender relations in the medical division of labour. She has a degree in Sociology from the University of Exeter and between 1977 and 1983 lectured at Manchester Polytechnic.

Introduction

David Knights and Hugh Willmott

Despite the 'heavy' determinism of *Labour and Monopoly Capital*, Braverman's concern to direct research attention towards the labour process within Western capitalist economies has generated a lively and appreciative, if not uncritical, response. An effective witness to this development is the recent proliferation of literature, empirical research and conferences with either a central or peripheral focus on labour process problems and controversies. Much of the earlier literature was dominated by general theoretical debates (Gorz 1976; Brighton Labour Process Group 1977; Aronowitz 1978; Burawoy 1978; Friedman 1978; Elger 1979). More recently, though, there has been a gravitation of interest towards more substantive empirical matters (Zimbalist 1979; Burawoy 1979; Wood 1982; Knights, Willmott and Collinson 1985). Within that interest the issue of gender in the labour process has also attracted a comparatively concentrated degree of research and conference attention (Gamarnikow et. al. 1983). Responding to these developments, the second UMIST-ASTON annual conference on the Organization and Control of the Labour Process in 1984 contained a series of papers on gender at work; a selection of which comprise this volume.

The interrelationship between research on gender and studies of the labour process is not merely one of empirical contingency. Yet the fact that women now represent 42 per cent of the labour force leaves no justification for the neglect that industrial sociology, labour economics and industrial relations have shown towards women and the problems of gender at work (Brown 1976; Hartmann 1979; Feldberg and Glenn 1979; Siltanen 1981; Thompson 1983; Siltanen and Stanworth 1984). Part of the explanation for this neglect relates to conventional academic divisions of labour where women's problems, whether in work or elsewhere, were assigned to sociology or economics of the family. In the context of labour shortage, the early studies (Myrdal and Klein 1956; Jephcott et al. 1962; Gavron 1970) presented a liberal progressive perspective concerning women's dual role and were optimistic about removing prejudicial obstacles to their increasing participation in employment (Beechey 1984). Conventional studies of work and employment, on the other hand, have remained oblivious to any problems concerning gender distinctions within the labour process. An unintended consequence of this is that they have assumed a 'masculine' model as the norm for the study of labour and workplace relations (Brown, op. cit.; Beechey ibid.). Furthermore, they have reinforced the prevailing tendency to locate women's activities and interests within the sphere of 'private', domestic family relations thus sustaining an artificial, gender-based division of labour within the social sciences and a false polarised stereotype between public man and private woman (Siltanen and Stanworth 1984).

One notable outcome of the development of labour process studies over recent years has been a reversal of this tendency for research on work to be gender-blind. Not that the inspiration to research gender relations at work is to be interpreted exclusively as a response to previous neglect or as a by-product of the framework and platform provided by the more radical approach of labour process theory. Much more is it a reflection of the intellectual and political impact of radical feminists. For it is they who, swimming against the stream of contemporary conservatism, have presented a most radical and resistant challenge to establishment inertia and complacency in regard to the role of women in modern culture.

Most recently, contemporary Western society has witnessed a comparative erosion of socialism as an effective political strategy at the same time as it has experienced the radicalising impact of an expansion and proliferation of feminist discourses and practices. There is hardly a single sphere of literature or politics that has been left unaffected by a radical reconsideration of the role of women and the relations between the sexes. Additionally, a measure of legitimacy to the feminist struggle for social and political change in the last decade has been provided by the various pieces of anti-discrimination legislation. Although limited because of the difficulties of enforcing or policing its regulations, the law does give credibility and support to the power of feminism to promote a re-examination of prevailing, and especially patriarchal, discursive and non-discursive practices.

In combination then, the historical expansion of women's employment, the renewed and uncompromising vigour of feminist discourse, and the limited assistance of anti-discrimination legislation give a tremendous impetus to theory and practice concerned with reconstructing gender relations both in and out of work. In turn, the studies of gender relations at work increase the impact of these three forces in continuing to constrain and disrupt 'comfortable' and 'self-satisfied' male-dominated interests and values. Moreover, what is especially interesting is that this impact has been felt not only in the patriarchal corridors of everyday life but also within those radical academic communities where one might least expect 'sexist' ideologies to be sustained. That is to say, critical or radical theorists, including academic Marxists, no less than conventional social scientists are now being challenged to re-think their analyses in the light of criticisms concerning the neglect of gender.

An effect of taking gender into account, and one that is well represented by some of the papers in this volume, is the questioning of traditional boundaries in the academic division of labour within and between say, sociology, psychology and economics. Once gender enters into the analysis, research that segregates studies of work from those of the family or which seeks to examine the sociology of the workplace independently of the economics and psychology of labour and of its domestic divisions becomes increasingly problematic.

As a consequence, gender studies of the labour process have contributed to rendering academic research more sensitive to the social and political issues of the day. So doing, they have shaken many students of work out of their gender-blind complacency as well as advancing further the breakdown of rigid and artificial internal boundaries within the social sciences. Most importantly, though, the introduction of gender into studies of the labour process has a potential to transform theoretical analysis in the direction of clarifying rather than obscuring the practical realities of everyday life.

As already intimated, theoretically one of the most important corollaries of gender research in the labour process is its power to question the adequacy of narrow Marxist perspectives that ignore conflicts and contradictions which cannot be readily subsumed under the category of class and the social relations of production. It is perhaps understandable if inexcusable that, when feminists focus attention exclusively on domestic and other 'non-productive' relations, Marxists dismiss their analysis as peripheral because it is concerned with super-structural matters lacking a determinative force. But the mere conflat-ing of the role of women in biological reproduction with their histori-cally specific contribution to the reproduction of male labour power is not an adequate response to the problem of this separation between Marxism and Feminism (Barrett, 1980: 27). Although it may force Marxists to take Feminism seriously, this is at the expense of a distinctive analytical focus upon gender. Fortunately, gender studies of the labour process are well placed to seek a reconciliation of the differences between Marxism and Feminism. This is because they involve a theoretically informed empirical focus on the relation of women to economic production and class reproduction as well as an analysis of the interdependence of this economic infrastructure with the sexual division of labour as a whole. Moreover, labour process researchers can draw upon and develop a feminist literature that has itself been engaged in a continuous debate with Marxism (Millett, 1971; Firestone, 1971; Leonard Barker and Allen, 1976; Molyneux, 1977; Beechey, 1977, 1978; Kuhn and Wolpe, 1978; Eisenstein, 1979; Hartmann, 1979; Amsden, 1980; Barrett, 1980; Coward, 1983). In identifying forms of domination, oppression and exploitation based both on gender and class, research has challenged Marxism to take account of patriarchal power and its relationship to capitalist production and reproduction. Also by insisting on empirical analyses, gender studies of the labour process are capable of advancing the theoretical debate beyond focusing upon patriarchy as an independent category (Millett op. cit., Firestone, op. cit; Bland et al; 1978). At the same time, the diversity and complexity of the empirical reality militates against subscribing to a simplistic Marxist-functionalism. Consequently, explanations of women's subordination exclusively in terms of its function for capitalism in sustaining the reproduction of labour and the continuous provision of a reserve army of female workers (Benston, 1969; Harrison, 1973; Reich, Gordon and Edwards, 1973; Seccombe, 1974; Gardiner, 1976; Eisenstein, 1979) are beginning to be treated with some scepticism (Barrett, 1980; Coward, 1983; Beechey, 1984).

Before the recent expansion of workplace ethnographies concerned with gender (Pollert 1981; Williams 1981; Cavendish 1982; Cockburn 1983; Wajcman 1983; Westwood 1984), current knowledge about women in the social and economic division of labour was seen as completely unsatisfactory (Leonard Barker and Allen 1976; Gardiner 1976; Beechey 1978; Kuhn and Wolpe 1978; Phillips and Taylor 1980; Barrett 1980; West 1982). And it has to be admitted that there are still numerous problems such as the explanatory status of patriarchy in understanding women's subordination (Coward 1983), the relationship between gender, class (and race) divisions (Barrett 1980), the conception of the 'family wage' in collective bargaining (Barrett and McIntosh 1980), the conditions and consequences of sexual relations at work (Hearn and Parkin 1983; Burrell 1984; Schneider 1984) and the construction of gendered subjectivity (Hollway 1984). Each of these problems can be seen as having some connection with the dualistic tensions which prevail in academic discourse between voluntaristic 'action' theory and structural determinism – tensions that reflect and reproduce a view of women as having their lives centred in private, domestic and apolitical relations by contrast with men's involvement in the public domain of economic production and engagement in socio-political practice (Siltanen and Stanworth op. cit.). While making no claim to having finally resolved any of these tensions and difficulties, the papers in this volume each address one or more aspects of the debate and, collectively, broaden the terms of labour process theory to fully incorporate a gender dimension.

The opening two papers address the problem of gender discrimination and inequality in the medical and legal professions respectively. In the first paper, Anne Witz traces the historical development of a number of patriarchal strategies within the medical division of labour. More specifically, she examines the gender-specific control, closure and demarcation of routes of access to technical skills and practical experience during the process of medical professionalisation from the sixteenth century onwards. Prior to the Medical Act of 1858, women had participated quite widely in medicine and indeed, in the Middle Ages, dominated the arts of healing. But the demise of women in medicine and their eventual exclusion from and/or demarcation within, the medical profession, Witz argues, has a patriarchal explanation. Because women's medical skills were often acquired through marriage to doctors and in any case only practised informally within the family and close neighbours, the power to resist guild and collegiate organisational restrictions of medicine as a domestic art were virtually non-existent. Witz was not surprised to find therefore that once, with the assistance of government legislation, professional closure occurred, patriarchal strategies excluded women not only from internal organisation and control of the occupation but also from all but certain marginal(ised) (e.g. midwifery) medical practices. The relationship between the male medical profession and female midwifery is examined in the final section of the paper to demonstrate how patriarchal closure is then supplemented and complemented by patriarchal strategies of demarcation. Witz describes three aspects of the demarcation. First, there is pre-emptive deskilling where midwives were restricted to the sphere of *normal* labour and all complications expropriated by male obstetricians. Second, pre-emptive incorporation where the male medical profession monopolised the use of specific surgical instruments (e.g. short forceps) thus precluding midwives from practising certain childbirth tasks. Third, pre-emptive closure was a patriarchal strategy employed by the profession to prevent midwives organising independently of male medical practitioners. Overall, Witz's contribution provides considerable historical evidence to conclude that the development of professional power within medicine was informed by patriarchal strategies of closure and demarcation which effectively excluded women from participating.

except marginally, in medical practice.

The second paper involves empirical research of the contemporary situation for women in the legal profession. In particular, evidence is produced on how women lawyers suffer the consequences of an internal dual labour market. Through interviews and documentary research, David Podmore and Anne Spencer demonstrate the significance of gendered segregation amongst both solicitors and barristers. Men are found to dominate a primary sector where income, prestigious types of work, career oportunity and stability of employment are considerably greater than in the secondary sector within which women are disproportionately represented. The major thrust of the paper is concentrated on the gendered division of legal labour in relation to the nature and type of work. Here the authors find that men are much more likely to be engaged in company/commercial and/or in criminal and litigation work, both of which are regarded as comparatively prestigious. In contrast, women are often restricted to matrimonial, wills, probate and associated 'desk bound' work. Where women barristers are involved in criminal work, it is typically minor not 'heavy crime' cases with which they deal. This pattern of work distribution is explained by Podmore and Spencer in terms of what they call 'pressure' and 'preference' theory. Women are pressured to work in those areas that are perceived by men to be appropriate to a stereotypical view of the 'feminine' character. At the same time, since many women have themselves internalised these so-called 'feminine' characteristics 'preference theory' suggests that they are genuinely attracted to tasks which have a 'helping' or 'caring' component. But the authors also point out that the gendered segregation of work itself has a self-fulfilling effect in so far as women might then actually prefer to remain in those areas comparatively free from the hostile competition of men. After a brief discussion of the 'poor' promotion opportunities and greater instability of employment for women in the legal profession, the authors conclude that despite this gendered inequality women lawyers are a comparatively privileged group. For gendered segmentation in the legal 'industry' as a whole is much more dramatic since, although representing 50 per cent of all personnel, only 2 per cent of women are 'fee-earners'.

The succeeding two papers are concerned specifically with the impact of technical change upon the sexual division of labour. Harriet Bradley's contribution involves a study of the relationship between gender and technological innovation in the hosiery industry through an analysis of historical documents by interviews with contemporary managers. She identifies the processes as dominating the history of technological change and employment relations in the hosiery industry.

Although particular employer and employee strategies have to be examined in relation to local conditions, product and labour markets, etc., the history of the labour process in hosiery can be seen as reflecting both the capitalist's continuous pressure to reduce labour costs and the determination of organised male workers to retain or restore traditional employment privileges. Bradley traces the history of these two processes in relation to their impact on women. In the context of the competitive pressure to reduce labour costs, new technology has generally resulted in de-skilling and a form of work degradation where women have been brought in to replace the men and jobs often redesigned to accommodate them. Organised male workers have at times resisted the influx of married women, which Bradley explains in terms of the economic impact of female labour in depressing wages. Overall, Bradley provides critical historical evidence to challenge the view that patriarchy and capitalism are entirely distinct systems operating to subordinate working women. The argument instead is that these systems of domination interpenetrate at the levels of managerial strategy and shop floor organisation to institutionalise a sex-segregated labour force.

This general theme is further explored by Sonia Liff who critically evaluates both the statistical studies of job segregation and the theoretical explanations of gender inequalities in the context of continuous technical change. After a brief description and critique of labour process theory accounts of technical change in relation to the employment of women, her paper concentrates its critical attention on current explanations of occupational sex-typing, focusing especially on the weaknesses in 'reserve army' analyses of the sexual division of labour. It is argued that the plausibility of such explanations of women's employment depends upon ignoring the continuous restructuring of the technical division of labour. In particular, historical comparisons of highly aggregated data is made problematic by the radical and continuous revisions in the classification of occupational groups. Census data, Liff suggests, must be used not as conclusive proof of job segregation but as suggestive of hypotheses which can be followed up through other, more intensive, empirical researches. Complementing Bradley's study, Liff observes that occupational sex-typing has remained fairly resistant to radical change, not least because of the opposition of male workers and their dominant position in trade unions. Further, she notes that although a breakdown of the sexual division of labour may be advantageous to capitalist production in the aggregate, individual competing capitalists are cautious of innovating for fear of resistance from organised male labour. Finally, Liff points to certain widespread labour market and labour process practices (e.g.

legal restrictions on shift work, effects of domestic responsibilities and career breaks on women's work, union involvement, training and progress) which seem to reinforce sex discrimination in employment. Some of these practices are examined in greater empirical detail in certain other contributions to this volume.

Celia Davies and Jane Rosser, for example, demonstrate how the psychological, social and managerial skills acquired by women in their domestic lives are exploited in the Health Service through a system where jobs become 'gendered'. A gendered job occurs where its unacknowledged informal responsibilities extend well beyond what the formal grading structure could demand, and are elaborated in a way that is dependent upon the gender and life-cycle stage of the job holder. Criticising previous labour process research for its peripheral treatment of gender, Davies and Rosser offer at least three reasons why this is unsatisfactory: first, the neglect of gender results in overlooking the way that male workers and unions as well as capitalists have contributed to reproducing an underprivileged, secondary labour market of predominantly female employment. Second, its omission leaves out of account the relevance of women's work to an understanding of the social construction of skill and, third, it ignores the importance of the family as the mediator of specific forms of wage labour. In their empirical analysis of administrative and clerical work in the Health Service, the authors draw on each of these issues to show that men have advanced their careers often with the assistance of women who occupy gendered jobs where formally recognised skill level and rewards are only tenuously related to actual practice. To a considerable extent, these gendered jobs are seen to be constructed and willingly occupied as a result of the traditional family commitments of previous generations of women. In conclusion, the authors predict that higher levels of education and shorter career breaks will result in a demand for increased recognition of the skill content of 'gendered jobs'.

The significance for the organisation of the labour process of women's experience and role in the family is also central to the contribution by Margaret Grieco and Richard Whipp. Using empirical evidence of both an historical and contemporary character, they observe how the fluctuating nature of capitalist production in industries as divergent as pottery-making, fishing and steel production often provides the conditions whereby working-class women, who are at the centre of family networks, act as informal employment brokers, trainers and managers of the labour process. In exploring women's position of influence within kinship networks, these authors provide an important counter to orthodox labour process studies where female subordination is described as completely determined by capitalist and patriarchal structures. Their empirical material challenges the conventional wisdom in four main areas. First, in terms of skill and the effects of new technology, women workers in the pottery industry were found to be occupying jobs incorporating a broad range of skills and were represented in every department. They were not just employed as helpers or 'attendants' as depicted in the textbooks. Also, in various industries, women at the centre of kin networks were found to determine employment location, skill acquisition and generally acted as an informal training and recruitment agency. Second, the authors found considerable evidence to suggest that, contrary to popular belief, men are not unambiguously in control of the wage packet and often only retain 'pocket money'. Third, women used their special position to provide pools of labour and skills in emergency and for temporary periods to extract informal concessions (e.g. leniency on absenteeism and lateness) from management. Fourth, partly because of the informal and discontinuous nature of female employment and the consequent under-recording of their participation rates, women's collective militancy has also often been disregarded. Yet, Grieco and Whipp argue, there is strong evidence of women exploiting their strategic position of providing additional, reserve labour during busy periods to exert considerable power and to defend their interests through localised collective action when necessary.

In providing solid evidence of women playing a much more significant role in the labour process than is suggested in earlier deterministic accounts of capitalist and patriarchal domination, the papers by both Davies and Rosser and by Grieco and Whipp show how women's direct or indirect participation in the labour process structures, as well as is structured by, the prevailing gendered social organisation of production. This theme is further explored and elaborated in the final contribution by Collinson and Knights. Their empirical data on gendered job segregation within an insurance office suggests that male-dominated management control and female clerical subordination are highly complex conditions and consequences of each other. The paper shows how job segregation arises and is reinforced through the actions of both men and women in their pursuit of whatever form of personal security is valued within the competitive context of the capitalist and patriarchal social relations of employment. Reviewing a cross-section of the literature on gender in the labour process, Collinson and Knights expose a structural deterministic slippage that they trace to the absence of a social psychology capable of mediating theories of capitalist and patriarchal domination, on the one hand, and observations of women's direct experience of the labour process, on the other. Drawing upon an intensive empirical case study of an insurance office, the authors explore how, in seeking to establish or maintain material and symbolic security through particular social identities, women as well as men contribute to the reproduction of relations of domination and subordination. In this study, managements' paternalistic power, embodying a refusal to 'risk' the employment of women in sales positions, and clerical women's defensive anxiety about the 'insecurity' of sales work were found to be mutually reinforcing, having the effect of institutionalising gendered job segregation. By examining employment practices in the context of management control and its impact on the labour process, Collinson and Knights reveal capitalist and patriarchal structures to be a consequence as well as a condition of employers' and employees' efforts to sustain and/or advance material and symbolic security.

Overall, this volume complements and extends recent 'post-Braverman' collections which have attended to a variety of issues, including forms of control and resistance at the workplace (Kelly and Clegg 1981), the degradation of work (Wood 1982), the historical development and comparative study of the labour process (Gospel and Littler 1983) and the design and structuring of work organisation (Knights, Willmott and Collinson 1985). The distinctive contribution of this volume lies in its collection of a diverse range of empirical studies that present sustained analyses of different labour process sites where capitalist and/or patriarchal power play their part in reproducing a gendered division of work. What unites them is a concern to assemble empirical data and develop theoretical arguments that further 'open up' and extend the debate so as to avoid the gender-blind analyses of much of the labour process literature (Cressey and McInnes 1980; Burawoy 1978, 1979; Stark 1980; Littler 1981; Littler and Salaman 1982; Storey, 1983). Their value resides in the provision of empirical and theoretical materials which, depending upon one's assessment of the strengths and weaknesses of Braverman's position, will contribute to the fleshing out, toning up or burial of the Marxian bones of the labour process perspective.

Acknowledgement
We would like to thank David Collinson for helpful comments on an earlier draft of this introduction.

References

Amsden, A.H. (ed.), (1980), *The Economics of Women and Work*, Harmondsworth: Penguin.
Aronowitz, Z. (1978), 'Marx, Braverman and the Logic of Capitalism', *Insurgent Sociologist*, **8**, 1, 126–46.
Barrett, M. (1980), *Women's Oppression Today: Problems in Marxist Feminist Analysis*, London: Verso and New Left Books.
Barrett M. and McIntosh M. (1980), 'The Family Wage: Some Problems for Socialists and Feminists', *Capital and Class*, **11**.
Beechey V. (1977), 'Some Notes on Female Wage Labour in the Capitalist Mode of Production', *Capital and Class*, **3**, 45–66.
Beechey V. (1978), 'Women and Production: A Critical Analysis of some Sociological Theories of Women's Work', in A. Kuhn and A.M. Wolpe, *Feminism and Materialism*, London, Routledge and Kegan Paul.
Beechey V. (1984) 'Women's Employment in Contemporary Britain', B.S.A. Conference Paper, Bradford, April.
Benston, M., (1969), 'The political economy of women's liberation', *Monthly Review*, **21**, 4.
Bland L. et al. (1978), 'Women Inside and Outside the Relations of Production', in Women's Studies Group (editors) *Women Take Issue*, London: Hutchinson.
Brighton Labour Process Group (1977), 'The Capitalist Labour Process', *Capital and Class*, **1** 3–26.
Brown R. (1976), 'Women as employees: Some comments on research in industrial sociology', in D. Barker and S. Allen (eds), *Dependence and Exploitation in Work and Marriage*, London, Longman, 33–46.
Burawoy M. (1978), 'Towards a Marxist Theory of the Labour Process: Braverman and Beyond', *Politics and Society*, **8**, 3–4.
Burawoy M. (1979), *Manufacturing Consent*, Chicago: Chicago University Press.
Burrell G. (1984), 'Sex and Organisational Analysis', *Organisation Studies*, **5**, 2.
Cavendish, R. (1982), *Women on the Line*, London: Routledge and Kegan Paul.
Cockburn, C. (1983), *Brothers: Male Dominance and Technological change*, London: Pluto Press.
Coward, R. (1983), *Patriarchal Precedents*, London: Routledge and Kegan Paul.
Cressey, P. and McInnes, J. (1980), 'Voting for Ford: industrial democracy and the control of labour,' *Capital and Class*, **11** 5–33.
Eisenstein, Z. (1979), 'Developing a Theory of Capitalist Patriarchy and Socialist Feminism', in Z. Eisenstein, *Capitalist Patriarchy and the Case for Socialist Feminism*, New York: Marketing Review Press.
Elger A. (1979), 'Valorisation and Deskilling', *Capital and Class*, 7, 58–99.
Feldberg R.C. and Glenn E.N. (1979), 'Male and Female: Job Versus Gender Models in the Sociology of Work', *Social Problems*, **26**.
Firestone, S. (1971), *The Dialectic of Sex*, London: Paladin.
Friedmann A. (1978), *Industry and Labour: Class Struggle at Work and Monopoly Capitalism*, London: Macmillan.
Gamarnikow, E., Morgan, D., Purvis, J. and Taylorson, D. (eds.) (1983), *Gender, Class and Work* London: Heinemann.
Gardiner, J. (1976), 'Political Economy of Domestic Labour in Capitalist Society', in D. Barker and S. Allen, *Dependence and Exploitation in Work and Marriage*, London: Longman.
Gavron, H. (1970), *The Captive Wife*, Harmondsworth: Penguin.
Gorz A. (ed.) (1976), *The Division of Labour: The Labour Process and Class Struggle in Modern Capitalism*, Brighton: Harvester.
Gospel, G. H., and Littler, C.R. (eds.), *Managerial Strategies and Industrial Relations*, London: Heinemann.

12　Gender and the Labour Process

Harrison, F., (1973), 'The Political Economy of Housework,' *Bulletin of the Conference of Socialist Economists*, Winter.

Hartmann, H. (1979), 'Capitalism, Patriarchy and Job Segregation by Sex', in Z. Eisenstein, (ed), *Capitalism, Patriarchy and the Case for Socialist Feminism*, New York: Monthly Review Press.

Hearn J. and Parkin P.W., (1983), 'Gender and Organisations: A Selective Review and a Critique of a Neglected Area', *Organisation Studies*, **4**, 3.

Henriques et al. *Changing the Subject*, London: Methuen.

Hollway W., (1984) 'Gender Difference and the Production of Subjectivity' London: Methuen.

Jephcott F, Sean B.N. and Smith J.H. (1962) *Married Women Working*, London: Allen and Unwin.

Kelly F.E. and Clegg C.W. (eds.) (1982), *Autonomy and Control of the Workplace*, London: Croom Helm.

Kuhn A. and Wolpe A.M. (eds.), (1978), *Feminism and Materialism*, London: Routledge and Kegan Paul.

Knights D., Willmott H.W. and Collinson, D. (eds.) (1985), *Job Redesign: Critical Perspectives on the Organisation and Control of the Labour Process*, Aldershot: Gower.

Leonard Barker J. and Allen S. (1976), *Dependence and Exploitation in Work and Marriage*, London: Longman.

Littler, C. and Salaman G. (1982) 'Bravermania and Beyond: Recent theories of the labour process,' *Sociology*, **16**, 2, 251–69.

Marshall, K. (1982), *Real Freedom*, London: Blackrose Press.

Millett, K. (1971), *Sexual Politics*, New York: Abacus.

Molyneux M. (1977), 'Androcentrism in Marxist Anthropology', *Critique of Antrhopology*, **9/10**.

Myrdal, A. and Klein, V. (1956) *Women's Two Roles Home and Work*, London: Routledge and Kegan Paul.

Phillips A. and Taylor B. (1980) 'Sex and Skill: Notes towards a feminist economics' *Feminist Review*, **6**.

Pollert, A. (1981), *Girls, Wives, Factory Lives*, London: Macmillan.

Reich, M., Gordon, D.M. and Edwards, R.C. (1980), 'A Theory of Labour Market Segmentation', in A. Amsden, *The Economics of Women and Work*, Harmondsworth: Penguin.

Schneider B.E. (1984), 'Approaches, Assaults, Attractions Affairs: Policy Implications of the Sexualisation of the Workplace', A.S.A. Conference, 26–31 August.

Seccombe, W. (1974), 'The Housewife and Her Labour under Capitalism', in *New Left Review*, **83**, Jan-Feb., 3–24.

Siltanen J. (1981), 'A Commentary on Theories of Female Wage Labour', in Cambridge Women's Studies Group, eds., *Women in Society*, London: Virago.

Siltanen J. and Stanworth M. (1984), *Women and the Public Sphere: A Critique of Sociology and Politics*, London: Hutchinson.

Stark, A. (1980) 'Class struggle and the transformation of the labour process: a rational approach' *Theory and Society*, 9, January, 89–130.

Storey, F. (1983), *Managerial Prerogative and the Question of Control*, London: Routledge and Kegan Paul.

Thompson P. (1983), *The Nature of Work: An Introduction to Debates on the Labour Process*, London: Macmillan.

Wajcman, J. (1983), *Women in Control*, Milton Keynes: Open University Press.

West, J. (ed.), (1982), *Work, Women and the Labour Market*, London: Routledge and Kegan Paul.

Westwood, S. (1984), *All Day Every Day: Factory, Family, Women's Lives*, London: Pluto Press.

Williams C. (1981), *Open Cut*, Sydney: Allen and Unwin.

Wood S., (ed.) (1982), *The Degradation of Work? Skill, Deskilling and the Labour Process*, London: Hutchinson.

Zimbalist A., (ed.), (1979), *Case Studies on the Labour Process*, London: Monthly Review Press.

1 Patriarchy and the Labour Market: Occupational Control Strategies and the Medical Division of Labour

Anne Witz

This paper considers the extent to which patriarchal power may be identified as a key resource in strategies of occupational control in the labour market and argues that patriarchal workplace or occupational organisations have played a key role in the structuring of sexual divisions in paid employment. First, two generic forms assumed by patriarchal control strategies in the labour market are identified as strategies of closure and strategies of demarcation, and I suggest on what grounds these may be described as patriarchal in form. Second, a more selective focus is adopted on the patriarchal structuring of the medical division of labour from the sixteenth century in order to identify some more specific forms that have been assumed by patriarchal strategies of closure and demarcation.

At a more general level, the discussion incorporates a conceptualisation of patriarchy which identifies male control over women's labour power as fundamental to patriarchal domination in relations of paid and unpaid work. Hartmann (1979) has argued for the centrality of the exercise of male control over women's labour power to patriarchy and that patriarchal control is maintained by denying women access to economically productive resources. Hartmann's argument is explored and developed here through a focus on women's access to medical skills and experience and on the ways in which this access has been subject to various modes of patriarchal control within the family and the labour market. The notion of patriarchal modes of control over women's access both to resources in the form of skills and knowledge and to opportunities to practise provides a crucial theoretical underpinning to the case study of female medical practice and its demise during the process of medical professionalisation from the sixteenth century onwards. By focusing on the changing forms of patriarchal control over women's access to medical skills and medical practice, I suggest how patriarchal control has assumed different and historically specific forms as men controlled and, subsequently, during the process of professionalisation of medical practice, closed off women's routes of access to medical skills and knowledge as well as their opportunities for legitimate practice.

Control over women's labour power is exercised in a variety of historically specific institutional contexts such as the household and the labour market. Within the household, male control over women's labour power is clearly more direct, and Delphy (1977) has argued that the patriarchal exploitation of women is located within the family where women, as wives, engage in productive activities and where men, as husbands, are able to appropriate women's labour power. In the labour market, however, patterns of male domination assume more opaque and arguably less direct forms.[1] It is, therefore, relatively more problematic to identify forms of male domination in non-familial labour processes and the major task confronting those who argue that patriarchal relations structure the sexual division of labour in the capitalist labour market is to identify more precisely how patriarchal power has been utilised as a resource in struggles around the division of labour, as well as how the exercise of this power has materially affected the position of both men and women. I argue here that one way in which patriarchal power has been utilised as a resource in struggles around the sexual division of labour has been in the form of strategies of closure and demarcation pursued within the context of occupational control strategies, and that workplace or occupational organisations have provided the institutional means whereby patriarchal power has been mobilised and patriarchal control maintained within the labour market.

Patriarchal control strategies in the labour market
I suggest here how an analysis of occupational control strategies may usefully proceed with categories of analysis derived from a theory of patriarchy, and argue that the notion of patriarchal control strategies has explanatory potential, in that it enables a focus on strategies of control pursued within the labour market which have implications for the structuring of the sexual division of labour. A minimal definition of occupational control strategies is one which defines them as modes of closure; as different means of mobilising power for the purposes of staking claims to resources and opportunities (Parkin 1974). To locate a discussion of strategies of closure within a theory of patriarchal relations involves investigating the extent to which patriarchal power may be used as a resource in staking claims to resources and opportunities within the labour market. A classification of patriarchal control strategies is offered here as a provisional means of investigating some more specific forms in which patriarchal power may be utilised within the labour market.

The conceptual groundwork done by Parkin (1974) and Kreckel

(1980) provides a useful starting point for considering modes of closure in the labour market. Parkin simply identifies two modes of closure: strategies of exclusion which represent the attempts 'by a given social group to maintain or enhance its privileges by the process of subordination i.e. the creation of another group or stratum of ineligibles beneath it, (Parkin op. cit.: 4); and strategies of solidarism which are defined as the defensive closure attempts of groups who are themselves subject to strategies of exclusion. Kreckel (1980) extends Parkin's two-fold classification into a three-fold classification of modes of closure by refining Parkin's notion of a strategy of exclusion. Kreckel distinguishes between strategies of vertical exclusion, directed at potential competitors in the labour market and involving a process of subordination, and strategies of horizontal demarcation which, whilst directed at potential competitors, involve processes of mutual differentiation rather than subordination. Kreckel retains Parkin's notion of a strategy of solidarism, but argues that these are not simply defensive closure attempts and are more likely to be effective the higher up the 'hierarchy of exclusion' a particular group is placed. For the purposes of the current discussion Kreckel's attempts to subsume demarcation strategies within the generic category of closure and to define these strategies in terms of the *absence* of any process of subordination are rejected in favour of adopting the notion of demarcation strategies as *itself* a generic category distinct from the generic category of closure. Thus, two generic categories are defined: *strategies of closure* and *strategies of demarcation*, and both may involve processes of subordination. The crucial difference between these two types of strategy is that closure strategies are primarily concerned with occupational control over the sphere of an occupational group's own labour, whilst demarcation strategies relate to those aspects of control that extend beyond the sphere of control of its own labour and touch upon related labour or occupations.[2]

Modes of closure have not been discussed specifically in relation to sexually structured labour markets, but it is argued here that such strategies may take the form of patriarchal control strategies when patriarchal power is mobilised in struggles around the division of labour. Hartmann (1979) has argued that patriarchal forms of workplace organisation have played a key role in generating and sustaining sexually segregated labour markets, whilst Cockburn's (1983) study of the changes in the printing labour process demonstrates how printing chapels have served to organise and maintain male power, which has provided a crucial resource in struggles around the division of labour. Walby's (1984) historical analyses of sexual segregation in the cotton textiles and engineering industries, and in clerical work, also identify workplace organisation and union strategies as patriarchal in their form and effect on the sexual division of labour.

Patriarchal strategies of closure describe those closure attempts where patriarchal power is mobilised for purposes of staking claims to resources and opportunities and which take the form of strategies of exclusion and strategies of solidarism.[3] A *patriarchal strategy of solidarism* describes the institutionalisation of male power in the form of the construction of the organisational means of occupational control as exclusively male organisations or as organisations where women are excluded from constitutional rights of government. The exclusion of women from the organisational means of controlling an occupation may be *de jure* or *de facto*, and the use of the term 'strategy' to describe solidaristic processes should not therefore be interpreted too literally. Rather, the notion of patriarchal strategies of solidarism directs attention to the fact that, as Hartmann (1979) has emphasised, men have been *able* to organise and have therefore been able to institutionalise male power within the capitalist labour market. *Patriarchal strategies of exclusion* may be identified as those where exclusionary practices are directed against actual or potential women practitioners or employees; it seeks to create women as a class of 'ineligibles'. A patriarchal strategy of exclusion may be pursued by an occupational group in its attempts to regulate the supply of its own labour where this takes the form of excluding women from routes of access to resources such as skills and knowledge as well as from opportunities to legitimate practice. It is one of the means whereby men are able to secure a competitive advantage over women in the labour market, but it is in no way the only means.[4] Analyses of patriarchal exclusionary strategies may provide some insights into the reasons for the conspicuous absence of women in many areas of paid employment.

Patriarchal strategies of demarcation relate to those aspects of occupational control that extend beyond the sphere of control over the supply of an occupational group's own labour and are concerned with the creation and control of occupational boundaries, attempting where possible to subordinate related or adjacent labour and occupations. Patriarchal strategies of demarcation describe those instances where patriarchy structures the division of labour and relations of domination and subordination between occupations through, for example, the sex-typing of tasks or the reproduction of patriarchal authority relations in non-familial labour processes. Patriarchal strategies of demarcation which have had considerable bearing upon the structuring of the medical division of labour have taken the form of what I term strategies of *pre-emptive closure, pre-emptive incorporation* and *pre-emptive de-skilling*. Pre-emptive de-skilling[5] refers to those processes of boundary definition where skills and tasks are 'creamed off' from an adjacent occupation, whilst pre-emptive incorporation describes the absorption of new techniques within the sphere of competence of one occupational group before they can be fully assimilated by another. Patriarchal strategies of pre-emptive closure describe attempts to subvert or pre-empt strategies of closure, particularly in the form of solidarism, being used by other female occupational groups, whose attempts at autonomous organisation are subverted. The notion of pre-emptive closure directs attention to the fact that, whilst women have acquired or maintained access to certain competences such as nursing, midwifery and radiography in the medical division of labour, nevertheless these occupational groups have been only partially successful in their attempts to secure closure; it directs attention to the possibility that occupational groups have been *prevented* from utilising strategies of closure.

Patriarchal control in the labour market may be realised within the context of struggles around the division of labour and specifically where occupational control strategies take the form of patriarchal strategies of closure or demarcation. Two forms of patriarchal closure strategies have been identified as solidarism and exclusion, whilst three varieties of demarcation strategy have been identified as pre-emptive de-skilling, pre-emptive incorporation and pre-emptive closure. This is not intended to be an exhaustive catalogue of forms of patriarchal control that may operate within the labour market, and indeed Walby (1984) has demonstrated the importance of patriarchal strategies of segregation in structuring gender divisions in clerical work. For the remainder of this paper, these strategies are brought to bear on aspects of the development of the medical division of labour, which provides a specific example of the restructuring of the sexual division of labour.

The patriarchal structuring of professional dominance: patriarchal control strategies and the medical division of labour

Selected aspects of the process of professionalisation of medical practice in Britain between the sixteenth and the nineteenth centuries are examined here in order to suggest some of the ways in which patriarchal domination and subordination have been sustained within the medical division of labour.

The 'strong thesis' of patriarchal domination in medicine

Prior to the professionalisation of medicine the arts of healing were practised throughout history mainly by women (Power 1921; Hurd-Mead 1937; Hughes 1943; Chamberlain 1981), and this has led some writers (Ehrenreich and English 1973, 1979; Oakley 1976) to argue that the professionalisation of medicine involved the wresting of control over healing out of the hands of women and placing it in the hands of men, thus securing male dominance in a sphere previously monopolised by women. This argument has taken the form of what I will call the 'strong thesis' of patriarchal domination, and rests upon the assumption that the patriarchal forces of the Church, State and nascent medical profession were united in the repression of female medical practice, which included midwifery, herbalism and other healing practices associated with 'wisewomen'. The strong thesis stands or falls upon the strength of its imputed connection between witchcraft and female healing practices (Verluysen 1980) which forms its central tenet, as it is the witch hunts in Medieval Europe between the fourteenth and seventeenth centuries which are cited as the means whereby the female monopoly over healing was broken. The strong thesis has been criticised on a number of counts: it amounts to a highly conspiratorial explanation of 'well-organised campaigns' against women healers; it ignores the fact that men as well as women were the practitioners of popular healing or 'empirics'; and it overlooks the fact that the Church was a declining force in the control of medical practice during this period (Doyal, Rowbotham and Scott 1973). The strong thesis is further weakened by the fact that women from all classes practised medicine, so medical practice was not confined to peasant women (Verluyzen 1980). Overall, the strong thesis of the suppression of female medical practice, whilst it is notable precisely because it locates an account of the decline of female medical practice within a thesis of male domination, is severely hampered by its almost exclusive focus on wisewomen and its neglect of other forms of female medical practice. It fails to appreciate not only the diversity of forms of female medical practice, but also the complexity of processes of patriarchal domination that characterised the emergence of professional control over medical practice between the sixteenth and the nineteenth centuries and brought about the demise of female medical practice. The witch hunts were one of the means whereby the female monopoly over healing was broken, but there were other significant shifts in modes in patriarchal control over women's routes of access to medical knowledge and skills, as well as over the different forms of female medical practice. It is important to recognise the gender-specific nature both of forms of female medical practice and of the ways in which women gained access to medical skills, in order to grasp the complexity of those processes that caused the demise of female medical practice.

Forms of female medical practice
Power (1921) distinguishes between three major types of female medical

practitioners in the Middle Ages: wisewomen of the villages 'who were skilled in the use of herbs and ointments, and sold medicines as well as charms'; noblewomen who practised medicine as a domestic art; and women who were engaged in 'something more closely approaching a professional practice of medicine and surgery' (p. 20). As Pinchbeck (1930) notes, it is difficult to determine the extent to which women engaged in professional as distinct from domestic or charitable practice, but women did apply for and were granted licences to practise in a wide range of medical specialisms. Hurd-Mead (1937) traces 66 licences granted to women after the passing of the 1511 Act[6] and James (1936) traces seven licences granted by the Archbishops of Canterbury to women between 1580 and 1775. There is evidence, then, that women engaged in something approaching professional practice, both as licensed and unlicensed practitioners, whilst Wyman (1984) has suggested that it was predominantly wives of independent traders and craftsmen who engaged in the professional practice of medical skills. The evidence further suggests that women of all social classes engaged far more extensively in healing practices but predominantly within the sphere of *domestic* relations, providing medical care for their families and frequently extending it to their neighbours.

Routes of access to medical skills

Overall, the evidence on female medical practice from the Middle Ages through to the eighteenth century points to the *gender-specific* nature both of *forms of female medical practice* and, most significantly, of their *routes of access to medical skills and knowledge*. Whatever the *form* of female medical practice, their knowledge was invariably acquired *informally* and by way of *marriage and family relations*. In their domestic practice of medicine, women acquired their knowledge chiefly from their mothers (Clark 1919), whilst for literate women there were also published works in English (rather than Latin) on medical matters, often written by women for a specifically female audience.[7] In their professional practice, women would frequently gain access to medical knowledge and skill through male relatives. Elizabeth Blackwell, who earned her living as a medical practitioner in the eighteenth century, initially studied anatomy and botany with her husband, himself a physician and apothecary (Hurd-Mead 1937). Husband and wife would sometimes practise jointly: eight women licensed after 1511 were married to medical men (ibid.); and in the eighteenth century the surgeon Catherine Bowles was married to a surgeon, as was the midwife Elizabeth Nihell (ibid.). Further, women were known to continue the practice of a male relative after his death: Mary Turberville, the sister of a seventeenth-century occulist, 'had all her brother's receipts and having seen his practice during many years, knows how to use them' (Clark 1919); and Mrs Read in the eighteenth century continued her husband's practice after his death, advertising her skills as an occulist gained 'by Several Years Experience' and her medicines as those previously used by her husband (Pinchbeck 1930). Jane Pernell, licensed to practise physic and surgery in 1685, claimed to have had over 20 years medical experience and both her husbands had been medical men, one a physician and man-midwife, the other a surgeon (Wyman 1984).

The importance of marriage and family relations in providing women with informal routes of access to knowledge and skills has been noted by both Clark (1919) and Pinchbeck (1930), whilst Pinchbeck has also pointed to the marriage contract itself as a route of access to the independent and legitimate professional and business practice of women:

> ... her marriage to a member of the Guild conferred upon a woman her husband's rights and privileges; and as she retained these after his death, she could, as a widow, continue to control and direct the business which she inherited from her husband.
>
> (p. 150-1).

The co-incidence of household and productive activities during the seventeenth and eighteenth centuries provided women both with informal routes of access to medical skills and knowledge, frequently by way of the marriage contract in the manner emphasised by Delphy (1977), and with a formal mode of legitimation of their independent medical practice:

> In some instances, wives and daughters of professional men appear to have been so closely associated with their work, that they were considered almost as partners, and after the death of husband or father, as the case might be, continued to practise independently.
>
> (Pinchbeck 1931: 302)

In conclusion, in both its domestic and professional forms, the medical practice of women was circumvented by domestic relations, in that marriage and family relations provided the institutional context for female medical practice, as well as the means of gaining access to the required medical knowledge and skills. But marriage and family relations are also constituted as patriarchal structures and thus at the same time provided the institutional means of *control* over women's access to medical skills and practice. As a means of regulating women's access, marriage and family relations would have become inappropriate when forms of occupational control became increasingly constituted as public organisational forms divorced from family and marriage relations. This suggests in turn, that the constitution of patriarchal control within capitalist relations of production was crucially dependent upon the ability of men to organise and pursue patriarchal strategies within the labour market, closing off women's former gender-specific routes of access, reconstructing gender-specific routes of access within the labour market, and excluding women from access to skills and experience through the same routes as men.

Patriarchal strategies of solidarism and exclusion in medicine

By the mid nineteenth century, women in Britain had been excluded from those branches of medical practice that had achieved professional closure through the passing of the 1858 Medical Act which had effectively placed the exclusive right to legitimate medical practice in the hands of men. Ironically enough:

> On paper the Medical Act of 1858 constituted no bar to the practice of medicine by women since it imposed no restrictions on candidates for registration other than having received a proper training. It had, however, failed to provide for the compulsory admission of women to universities, medical schools or qualifying examinations.
>
> (Manton 1965: 64)

Women were excluded from medical practice because the medical profession had legitimated only one route of access to medical knowledge: the formal university education system. Significantly, female medical practice had traditionally been based upon the acquisition of medical knowledge and skills by means other than formal education in university medical schools from which women had always been excluded (Lander 1922). What is signifcant here is that the 1858 Medical Act was premised upon the resolution of boundary disputes between organised male medical practitioners,[8] who had effectively established a professional/patriarchal *modus vivendi*, by organising to the exclusion of women; men had access to the *means* of organising and were thus able to institutionalise male power. It is significant that a branch of medical practice that did not achieve professional closure along with the physicians, surgeons and apothecaries was midwifery, traditionally a female sphere of competence. Midwifery was effectively marginalised because midwives had been unsuccessful in their attempts to incorporate themselves into a society and thereby establish the organisational means of closure over midwifery practice. Here, then, the notion of patriarchal strategies of solidarism has some explanatory power, in that men were able to organise in their own sectional interests, and further these interests at the expense of women through patriarchal strategies of exclusion in relation to women doctors, and through patriarchal strategies of demarcation in relation to midwives. The case of midwives and medical men is examined in the next section; for the moment the focus is on female medical practitioners within the tripartite division of labour between surgeons, physicians and apothecaries.

The tripartite division of labour of physicians, surgeons and apothecaries that characterised the emergent medical profession was significant in two respects. First, because patriarchal strategies of control *varied* between the three groups both in terms of the forms these assumed and in terms of their effect on female medical practice. In the case of surgeons and apothecaries who utilised guild forms of organisation, these strategies varied from city to city according to their locally constituted ordinances and regulations. Most significantly, however, patriarchal strategies of control varied according to the *form* of female practice that male practitioners sought to control and particularly whether this was regarded as an extenuated form of domestic practice, such as the healing activities of wisewomen, or as something more approaching professional practice. Women of the wisewomen category had commonly acquired their medical skills informally and extended their medical practice beyond the household or domestic sphere, invariably for payment of some kind. These women were regarded as a competitive threat by surgeons and apothecaries concerned to regulate *local* practice both because they offered an alternative to the services of local surgeons and apothecaries and because the popularity of wisewomen may have proved a disincentive to trained practitioners. Thus, references to wisewomen in the charters of city companies of surgeons and apothecaries may be distinguished from physicians' invectives against *all* women who dared to attempt the practice of physic, in that the former strategies were rather more specific and regulatory rather than purely exclusionary. The 1561 ordinances of the Barber-Surgeons Company of Norwich complain of the encroachments of 'sundry women' on the practice of surgery as:

> ... women giving over the good and profitable arts that they have been brought up with from their youths hitherto even for lucre's sake and idleness of life being unskilled and utterly ignorant of ... those things that they do minister.
>
> (cited in Pelling and Webster 1979: 212)

The objection is aimed at those women who gained access to their medical knowledge within the context of female *domestic* practice but who had extended their practice beyond the bounds of the domestic into something approaching, or encroaching on, professional practice, especially in so far as it was 'for lucre's sake'.

Guild control over female medical practice sought to restrict women's access to legitimate practice. On the one hand, some gender-specific routes of access to medical knowledge were denied legitimacy, particularly when women had gained their access to medical knowledge and their practical experience within the context of medicine as a *domestic* art, but then extended their medical practice beyond this sphere. These women healers were increasingly subject to strategies of *exclusion* from legitimate medical practice in so far as their practice was not legitimated and protected by guilds. On the other hand, women's route of access to medical skills was legitimised when it was through their husbands and it was therefore as wives, or more commonly, widows that their medical practice would be recognised and protected by guilds. As long as widows continued to inherit their husbands' rights and privileges as freemen, female professional practice and their distinctive modes of access to medical skills gained through the marriage/labour contract continued to be legitimised. Patriarchal strategies of control over female *professional* practice, then, took the form of regulation in the guise of *restricted or limited rights of access* to legitimate practice, premised upon women's restricted routes of access to medical skills *through their husband's practice*.

The division of labour between physicians, surgeons and apothecaries is significant in relation to female practice for a second reason, which is the dominance of physicians as architects of the tripartite division of labour (Pelling and Webster 1979). The physicians adopted a collegiate mode of organisation as distinct from the guild form utilised by apothecaries and surgeons (Berlant 1975). Physicians' strategy in the face of female practitioners differed from the outset: they sought to exclude women from the practice of physic, as well as to prevent women from exercising monopolistic control over medical practice of any type, particularly midwifery. They pursued a much more unambiguous exclusionary strategy in the face of the competitive threat of female medical practice, both in its domestic form and as something more approaching professional practice.

Physicians organised on an exclusively male basis,[9] which was inevitable as women were precluded from attending universities and obtaining degrees in medicine and would have found it quite simply impossible to satisfy the rules for fellowship of the college, which stipulated a doctorate in medicine as a requisite for admission as a candidate. On the other hand, however, although barred from a university education and the qualifying degree, women nevertheless utilised other routes of access to knowledge of physic. Thus, although barred from the university system and the organisational means of *control* of the practice of physic, women could apply for licences to *practise* as physicians. Physicians, however, sought to regulate the practice of physic through their powers of licensure and were clearly concerned to exclude women altogether from the practice of physic. Initially, then, their patriarchal exclusionary strategies were directed at discrediting and preventing female medical practice. In 1421 physicians had petitioned Parliament that no man be permitted to practise physic unless he had a university degree or doctorate in medicine and 'that no Woman use the practyse of fisyk' (Power 1921: 23). In 1511 the first Parliamentary Act relating to medicine was passed following a petition presented to Henry VIII by a group of London physicians concerned that physic and surgery should not be practised by 'ignorant persons' and again women were singled out indiscriminantly as among those who 'boldly and accustomably take upon them great Cures, and things of great Difficulty, in the which they partly use Sorcery and Witchcraft' (Clark 1964: 54). Nevertheless, after the 1511 Act, women as well as men were licensed to practise both as physicians and as surgeons. Of 66 licences traced to women, 4 enabled women to practise as physicians and surgeons, 2 as surgeons and midwives, and 31 as surgeons (Hurd-Mead, 1937). The Archbishops of Canterbury granted licences to women (James 1936), and the Bishop of Norwich licensed Cecily Baldrye to practise surgery in 1568 (Pelling and Webster 1979). Far more commonly, however, women practised medicine without a licence. 'Itinerants and old women' continued to be a particular cause of concern to the Royal College of Physicians in their attempts to stamp out unlicensed medical practice in London where, between 1550 and 1600, 29 women practitioners were prosecuted for practising medicine without a licence, and the ratio of female to male practitioners prosecuted between 1581 and 1600 was 21 to 78 (Pelling and Webster 1979).

More generally physicians' invectives against female medical practice were concerned to encourage the belief that women had no legitimate role to play in medicine both professionally and as domestic practitioners. John of Ardenne, a fourteenth-century physician, was scathing about the treatment meted out by women practitioners, despite the fact that his methods of treatment were virtually identical, and his motives for discrediting women's practice of physic are suggested by the fact that he described them as 'ladies bountiful' since they charged no fee (Chamberlain 1981). John of Mirfield, another fourteenth-century physician, wrote of the 'worthless and presumptions women [who] usurp this profession to themselves and abuse it' (Hughes 1943: 21).

John Cotta in the seventeenth century sought to discredit completely the medical and intellectual ability of women as well as their domestic medicines. Cotta was concerned that women's domestic medical practice posed an *alternative* source to that of the physician and that women 'persuade the sicke that they have no needs of the Physition' (cited in Chamberlain 1981: 46).

The invectives of physicians such as those above were directed at *all* forms of female medical practice, although physicians would have been particularly mindful of the competitive threat posed by women of upper-class households who would perhaps attempt to treat members of their households themselves instead of or prior to calling in a physician, and who may have acquired extensive knowledge of medicine, knowing enough to be extremely sceptical about physicians' claims to competence. Margaret Paston, for example, wrote to her husband in 1464 warning him of any medicines prescribed for him by London physicians (Hughes 1943). The domestic practice of upper-class women provided those few families able to afford a physician's services with an alternative source of medical treatment, and physicians indiscriminate invectives against the practice of physic by women may be better understood in the light of this; that it was not just the professional practice of medicine by women that they sought to discredit, but their domestic practice too.

Patriarchal closure

The suppression of female medical practice was an uneven and lengthy process rather than the 'well-orchestrated' campaign suggested by the proponents of the strong thesis. Women continued to practise medicine in both its domestic and professional forms well into the eighteenth century, and Chamberlain (1981) suggests that wisewomen survived in working-class communities even into the twentieth century. A survey of the literature which examines the extent of female medical practice from the Middle Ages to the eighteenth century suggests a number of reasons why the demise of the female medical practitioner should have been such a protracted process. First, it would appear that women's medical practice, in both its domestic and professional forms, was gender-specific and circumvented by patriarchal structures. Second, women's routes of access to medical skills were similarly gender-specific and particularly in so far as they were largely informal. Thus, in addition to circumventing the domestic and professional medical practice of women, patriarchal structures provided informal routes of access to medical knowledge and skills. The gender-specific nature of female medical practice meant that patriarchal strategies of control over female medical practice took a number of forms and were unevenly exercised, despite the ability of medical men to organise and construct emergent institutions of occupational control as patriarchal organisations, or in other words to pursue patriarchal strategies of solidarism. The city guilds of barber-surgeons and the Royal College of Physicians were aware of the competitive threat posed by female domestic practice not only because potential clients could consult women as domestic practitioners prior to consulting a medical man but also because women could extend their medical services beyond their immediate family, treating neighbours on a charitable or on a fee-paying basis. Attempts to exercise control over women's professional practice have been identified as exclusion from medical practice via the mechanism of licensing powers, and regulation of female practice by way of restricted access to guild protection. Finally, the fact that women did continue to practise well into the eighteenth century implies that they still maintained their gender-specific routes of *access* to skills and experience which enabled them to offer medical services of comparable efficacy to those of medical men, both in domestic and market arenas. Accordingly, it was the eventual exclusion of women from routes of access to medical knowledge that amounted to the most effective means of patriarchal closure.

The patriarchal structuring of professional dominance and subordination: midwifery and the male medical profession

Some aspects of patriarchal strategies of demarcation are demonstrated most vividly by examining the relationship between female midwifery practice and male medical practice.[10] First, there were attempts by members of the medical profession to renegotiate boundaries between midwifery and medical practice by fragmenting midwifery and incorporating certain aspects of midwifery into 'obstetrics' and by ensuring that midwives were restricted to the sphere of *normal* labour, seeking medical assistance for abnormal labour. These may be described as patriarchal strategies of *pre-emptive de-skilling*: the midwife's sphere of competence was narrowed and strictly bounded as aspects of midwifery practice were expropriated and placed within the exclusive sphere of competence of medical doctors. Second, a patriarchal strategy of *pre-emptive incorporation* was pursued in relation to the use of surgical instruments in childbirth, particularly the use of short forceps, and midwives were never able to incorporate these tasks within their own sphere of competence. Finally, strategies of *pre-emptive closure* ensured that midwives were unsuccessful in their attempts to organise on the same terms as physicians, surgeons and apothecaries despite attempts to do so in the seventeenth century.

Physicians and midwives: a case of pre-emptive closure

Midwives were unsuccessful in their early attempts to organise and were therefore unable to construct the organisational means of professionalisation, despite attempts to do so in the seventeenth century.

> The danger which threatened midwives by the exclusion of women from the scientific training available to men, did not pass unnoticed by the leading members of the Profession.
>
> (Clark 1919).

In 1616 midwives of the City of London petitioned the King for a Charter and for incorporation into a society so that:

> ... the skill of the most skilfullest in that profession should be bettered and none allowed but such as are meete which cannot be performed unless the said midwives be incorporated into a societye.
>
> (Cited in Donnison 1977: 13)

They also petitioned for lectures on anatomy, for regulations and for better education (Clark 1964: 236). The petition was received favourably by the King, but was then forwarded to the College of Physicians for comment, who immediately drew up a set of counter-proposals which, if they had been implemented, would have placed the powers of examination and instruction in the hands of the College. Most crucially, they appeared to have objected to the fact that it was *women* who were attempting to organise:

> The College recognised that many abuses arose from the unskilfulness of ignorant midwives; but it thought the plan of making them into an incorporated society to govern themselves new, unheard of and without example in any commonwealth.
>
> (Clark 1964)

This, together with the fact that the College of Physicians had the power successfully to pre-empt branches of medical practice such as apothecaries from organising autonomously, meant that the midwives' movement to organise was stalled for the time being. In 1634, once more without success, another move to incorporate midwives was made.[11]

In the latter half of the seventeenth century Mrs Cellier once again demanded the opportunity for midwives to receive better medical education and improve their skills (Aveling 1872). In 1687 Mrs Cellier appealed to James II to unite midwives into a corporation by Royal Charter:

> ... it is humbly proposed, that your Majesty will be graciously pleased to

unite the whole number of skilful midwives, now practising within the limits
of the weekly bills of mortality, into a corporation, under the government of
a certain number of the most able and matron-like women among them,
subject to the visitation of such person or persons, as your Majesty shall
appoint; and such Rules of their good government, instruction, direction
and administration as are hereunto annexed.

(Aveling 1872; Clark 1919).

Mrs Cellier recognised the necessity for organisation if the interests of
midwives were to be represented and their status as a profession
secured. The King agreed to her request but nothing was done.

London midwives appeared to be aware of the need to organise
midwifery practitioners and ensure some form of protection against the
encroachments of medical men. They also perceived the need for the
more systematic training in midwifery skills, and to construct some
organisational means of distinguishing between skilful and unskilful
midwives, in much the same manner as medical men were doing in their
guilds and college.

Obstetricians and midwives: pre-emptive de-skilling and pre-emptive incorporation

By the end of the seventeenth century midwifery still remained a
predominantly female occupation, but the crucial point to note here is
that whilst women continued to *practice* midwifery, *they had failed to
organise*. It was in the eighteenth century that male practice in
midwifery grew unabated:

> As the century wore on so the decline of the midwife continued – a
> cumulative process accelerated by the interested propaganda of a section of
> the medical profession, and in particular, of younger men anxious to capture
> the midwifery which gave the entrée to general practice.
>
> (Donnison 1977: 37)

Patriarchal strategies of pre-emptive de-skilling occurred as medical
men engaged in a gradual process of expropriation of midwifery
knowledge and skills and accumulated their knowledge of midwifery
largely by observing the practices of midwives themselves. Dr
Willughby, a famous seventeenth century man-midwife, makes
constant reference in his writings to midwives whose practice he had
observed (Aveling 1872). As part of their strategy of de-skilling and
narrowing the midwife's sphere of competence, medical men repeatedly
inveighed against any intervention by midwives in the process of
childbirth, thus attempting to reduce the role of midwife to that of an
attendant. At the same time, it was the use of instruments in difficult
deliveries that provided the lynchpin for the medical men's parallel

strategy of pre-emptive incorporation, and the monopoly gained by surgeons over the use of instruments proved of considerable advantage in pre-empting midwives from incorporating the use of instruments into their own sphere of competence.

Demarcation strategies pursued by medical men in relation to midwives reached their zenith in the last quarter of the nineteenth century during the protracted debate around proposals for midwife registration. This debate was essentially about the status of midwives, the precise nature of their sphere of competence and, most crucially, the terms of their subordination to the medical profession. Important disagreements emerged *within* the ranks of the medical profession during the course of this debate, which may be interpreted as dissension about which demarcation strategy to push through to its logical conclusion; that of pre-emptive incorporation or of pre-emptive de-skilling.

Sections of the medical profession who opposed the registration of midwives advocated the virtual abolition of midwives and were effectively arguing for the complete incorporation of midwifery skills within the sphere of competence of the medical profession; the physician's sphere of competence would be extended to incorporate not only abnormal but also normal labour. The patriarchal structuring of the medical division of labour is revealed in the abolitionists' argument that women should be restricted to a subservient role in the provision of health services and accordingly, that the role of midwife should be replaced by that of the 'obstetric nurse' who 'under the charge and supervision of a medical man, carries out that portion of attendance which is more suitable to a mere woman, the changing of sheets and the attending of the patient, and attentions of that kind' (Select committee on Midwife Registration 1892). Abolitionists were arguing for a strategy of incorporation that would not simply de-skill midwives by creaming off certain of their obstetric skills, but would incorporate all aspects of midwifery practice, not just the use of instruments, within the sphere of the medical profession.

The advocates of the de-skilling strategy, the most prominent of whom were members of the Obstetrical Society formed in 1858, were medical men concerned to *control* and *limit* the practice of midwifery by restricting the midwife's sphere of competence to that of normal labour and subordinating them to the medical profession. The de-skilling strategy involved the devolution of certain midwifery tasks onto midwives, who would operate within a strictly bounded sphere of competence and control. The advocates of the de-skilling strategy, because they did not advocate placing the midwife directly under the supervision of a doctor, had to ensure that the midwife did not transgress the occupational boundary between midwife and doctor. To this end, the Obstetrical Society took a lead in advocating the education and registration of midwives, as they sought to ensure that the midwife did not gain sufficient medical education to transgress occupational boundaries by dealing with medical matters surrounding abnormal labour. Midwives were to be educated 'to know their own ignorance' (Select Committee 1892). The Obstetrical Society's scheme for midwife registration also proposed that midwives' licences were to be renewed annually by the General Medical Council, who were also to have the power to strike off women who attended abnormal labours and did not seek medical assistance.

Midwives themselves were equally divided over the terms on which they wished to see the registration of midwives. Two midwives' organisations, the Female Medical Society and the Obstetrical Association of Midwives advocated registration as a method of achieving professional closure that would produce and reproduce high-status and well qualified midwives with a licence that would give them equal status to male medical practitioners and extend their sphere of competence to include abnormal as well as normal labour (Donnison 1977; Select Committee 1892). These organisations also proposed that there should be *two* classes of midwives, a subordinate class for the less qualified and a superior one for the highly skilled midwife with a more extensive medical education. The implication of this demand was that middle-class midwives wished to use some of the same means of occupational closure as medical men. However, they would have had to defeat the interests of male medical practitioners of their own class, who sought to preserve their professional dominance by means of patriarchal subordination. This poses an interesting and cross-cutting set of class and patriarchal dimensions in structuring the medical division of labour.

The sexual composition of occupations that have been subject to processes of pre-emptive de-skilling, pre-emptive incorporation and pre-emptive closure may therefore be seen to be of key importance in patterns of domination and subordination in medicine; the medical profession sought to subordinate and control the female practice of midwifery by means of patriarchal strategies of demarcation.

Conclusion

Patriarchal strategies of control in the labour market warrant attention because they constitute a key dimension of the patriarchal structuring of the sexual division of labour. I have examined some patriarchal strategies of closure and demarcation that have had direct implications for the sexual structuring of occupational boundaries in the medical division of labour. In the context of the medical division of labour, I have argued that patriarchal strategies of exclusion had the effect of closing off women's routes of access both to opportunities to practise and to those resources that constitute medical skills and knowledge. Patriarchal strategies of exclusion were premised upon the pursuit of solidaristic strategies, which describe the processes whereby men were able to organise to the exclusion of women. Finally I examined processes of boundary definition between medicine and midwifery, arguing that significant insights into the sexual structuring of occupational boundaries are revealed through the examination of patriarchal strategies of demarcation, which took the form of pre-emptive closure, pre-emptive incorporation and pre-emptive de-skilling. More generally, the importance of investigating patriarchal control over women's labour power as historically specific forms of control which extend beyond familial labour processes has been stressed.

Acknowledgement
Earlier drafts of this paper were presented to the Lancaster Regionalism Group and the Women's Research Group, both of the University of Lancaster. I wish to thank members of both these groups for constructive comments and criticisms, particularly Sylvia Walby and John Urry, as well as Brian Longhurst.

Notes
1. It is a moot point as to whether or not direct patriarchal exploitation exists within the labour market. Gamarnikov (1978), in her excellent paper on the patriarchal character of the sexual division of labour between the nursing and medical professions, argues that the sexual division of labour is 'a patriarchal ideological structure in that it reproduces patriarchal relations in extra-familial labour processes' (p. 21). Adopting a position similar to that of Barrett (1980), she thus argues that it is in the form of ideological representations that patriarchal relations are extended into areas where direct patriarchal exploitation does not exist, i.e. non-familial labour processes. Garmarnikov then permits herself to side-step the issue of the precise nature of the relationship between professional and patriarchal power relations, going only so far as to say that the former are 'over-determined' by the latter. But, whilst there have been attempts to establish the relation between professions and the class structure (cf. Johnson 1977; Larson 1977, 1979), there is little by way of analysis of professions and patriarchal structures except for Hearn's (1982) radical reconceptualisation of the process of professionalisation as a process of patriarchal domination.
2. Friedson (1977) has emphasised this dual nature of professional control and has defined a profession as 'an occupational monopoly with a position of dominance in a division of labour' (p. 24). Larkin (1978, 1983) also argues that the medical profession has been very much concerned with the skills and tasks of adjacent occupations in the health division of labour.
3. Here, Parkin's original two-fold classification of closure strategies is retained, but the notion of a patriarchal strategy of solidarism is not restricted to that of defensive

closure attempts by groups themselves subject to exclusionary strategies.

4. Although not discussed here, a strategy of segregation is yet another form of closure strategy. A patriarchal strategy of segregation provides yet another means whereby men are able to secure a competitive advantage over women, by fostering the sexual stratification of tasks *within* an occupational labour market. An example of a patriarchal strategy of segregation is provided by the case of radiographers during the 1920s and 1930s, as male radiographers sought to ensure that the competitive advantages enjoyed by female nurse-radiographers, particularly X-ray sisters, were not formally recognised and thus not legitimised. Instead, male radiographers sought to establish the superiority of 'technical' skills, largely through their mystification, and deny the legitimacy of 'nursing' skills in the radiographer's work.

5. Larkin (1978), discussing the professionally restrictive practices pursued by the medical profession in relation to radiographers, refers to a 'process of pre-emptive professional de-skilling' (p. 853), but appears to use the term rather more loosely than I do here, as encompassing a broader spectrum of professionally restrictive practices.

6. The 1511 Act was the first Parliamentary Act relating to the practice of medicine and stipulated that anyone wishing to occupy as a physician or surgeon within a seven-mile radius of the city of London had to be examined, appointed and admitted by the Bishop of London or Dean of St Paul's together with physicians. Provincial licensing was to be carried out by the diocesan Bishop, whilst the universities of Oxford and Cambridge still retained their powers of licensure (Clark 1964–72, Volume 1).

7. Examples of such publications are 'Nature unbowelled by the most exquisite Anatomizers of Her Choisest Secrets ... for the use of all infirmities, internal and external, acute and chronical, that are incident in the Body of Man' by Lady Arundell, 1655; 'Manual of Choice Remedies, or Rare Secrets in Physic and Surgery' by Elizabeth, Countess of Kent, in 1670; and a treatise on 'Physic and Surgery' by the Duchess of Newcastle (cited in Hurd-Mead 1937). Other books aimed at a specifically domestic female audience were 'The Ladies' Dispensatory' by Leonard Sowell in 1652 which contained 'the Natures, Vertues and Qualities of all Herbs, and Simples Usefull in Physick' (Clark 1919), and 'The English Housewife' by Gervase Markham in 1675 which contained advice on herbal remedies and surgical techniques (Wyman 1984).

8. Those branches of medical practice that successfully achieved professional closure with the passing of the 1858 Medical Act were the physicians, apothecaries and surgeons. Each of these branches of medicine had evolved the organisational means of securing closure, in that physicians and surgeons were organised as Colleges with Royal Charters whilst apothecaries had formed themselves into a Society. The end process of what has been an uneven and fraught process of professionalisation was the resolution of disputes between these three groups over boundary definition, where their respective spheres of competence and control were at issue. Physicians and apothecaries were repeatedly at loggerheads over the right to prescribe medicines and give medical advice, for example.

9. The Royal College of Physicians was created by a Royal Charter in 1581, and physicians were the first group of medical men to receive a Royal Charter. This granted the college the power of licensure over physicians and surgeons in London, whilst an Act of 1523 extended these powers throughout England (although they do not seem to have been widely used) (Clark, G. 1969).

10. For a fuller and more detailed account of boundary disputes between midwives and the medical profession between 1870 and 1900 see Witz (1985).

11. The Chamberlen family, who had achieved notoriety by an invention, a family secret, of the short forceps for delivery in childbirth, were allegedly involved in both attempts to incorporate midwives although their precise role in these events is far from clear. Both proposals involved granting Peter Chamberlen and subsequently

his son, also called Peter, the position of governor as well as a monopoly of licensing, instruction and attending difficult births. Their championship of the midwives' cause is variously imputed to self-interest (Donnison 1977; Clark, G. 1969) or to genuine concern about the lack of specialised training available to midwives (Hurd-Mead 1937; Clark, A. 1917), although it should be noted that accounts of their involvement in these events are contradictory. G. Clark, the official historian of the Royal College of Physicians, mentions the involvement of Peter Chamberlen the younger in the petition of 1633, but makes no reference to the involvement of his father in the petition of 1616. Clark also states that two midwives petitioned the College against Peter Chamberlen the younger in 1633, claiming that Chamberlen was solely responsible for petitioning the King a second time to incorporate midwives and that he did not represent their interests, but was solely intent upon securing a monopoly by obliging midwives to consult no one but him in their cases and by making himself governor. Donnison (1977) cites the number of midwives opposing Peter Chamberlen's 1633 petition as 60, whilst Hurd-Mead (1937) identifies the two midwives referred to by Clark as Hester Shaw and Mrs Whipp, but claims that they petitioned the College *for* incorporation. Aveling (1872), claims that it was the Peters Chamberlen who initiated both the 1616 and the 1633 petitions. However, in the midst of all the contradictory accounts and whatever the truth of the matter concerning the motivation and involvement of the Peters Chamberlen in the petitions of 1616 and 1633, there appears to be no evidence to contradict the claim that midwives themselves *were* involved in the attempt to incorporate in 1616, in spite of the fact that Peter Chamberlen the elder may have been out simply to line his own pocket. Furthermore, the fact that two or sixty midwives may have petitioned the Royal College of Physicians in 1633 against Peter Chamberlen may be taken to provide further evidence that midwives did seek to ensure incorporation for the benefit of midwives rather than an ambitious and self-serving physician.

References

Aveling, J. (1872), *English Midwives: Their History and Prospects*, London: J. and J. Churchill.

Barrett, M. (1980), *Women's Oppression Today: Problems in Marxist Feminist Analysis*, London: Verso.

Berlant, J. (1975), *Profession and Monopoly*, California: University of California Press.

Chamberlain, M. (1981), *Old Wives' Tales: their history, remedies and spells*, London: Virago.

Clark, A. (1919), *Working Life of Women in the Seventeenth Century*, London: George Routledge.

Clark, G. (1964–72), *A History of the Royal College of Physicians in London*, vols 1–3, Oxford: Clarendon.

Cockburn, C. (1983), *Brothers: Male Dominance and Technological Change*, London: Pluto Press.

Delphy, C. (1977), 'The Main Enemy', in *The Main Enemy: a Materialist Analysis of Women's Oppression*, London: Women's Research and Resources Centre.

Donnison, J. (1977), *Midwives and Medical Men*, London: Heinemann.

Doyal, L., Rowbotham, S. and Scott, A. (1973), 'Introduction', in B. Ehrenreich and D. English, (eds), *Witches and Midwives and Nurses: A History of Women Healers*, London: Writers and Readers Publishing Co-operative.

Ehrenreich, B. and English, D. (eds.) (1973), *Witches and Midwives and Nurses: A History of Women Healers*, London: Writers and Readers Publishing Co-operative.

Ehrenreich, B. and English, D. (1979), *For Her Own Good:150 Years of the Experts' Advice to Women*, London: Pluto Press.

Friedson, E. (1977), 'The Future of Professionalisation', in M. Stacey and M. Reid (eds.),

Health and the Division of Labour, London: Croom Helm.

Gamarnikov, E. (1978), 'Sexual Division of Labour: the case of nursing', in A. Kuhn and A. Wolpe (eds.), *Feminism and Materialism*, London: Routledge and Kegan Paul.

Hartmann, H. (1979), 'Capitalism, Patriarchy and Job Segregation by Sex' in Z.R. Eisenstein (ed.), *Capitalist Patriarchy and Socialist Feminism*, New York: Monthly Review Press.

Hearn, J. (1982), 'Notes on Patriarchy, Professionalization and the Semi-Professions', *Sociology*, **16**, (4).

Hughes, M. (1943), *Women Healers in Medieval Life and Literature*, New York: King's Crown Press.

Hurd-Mead, K. Campbell (1937), *A History of Women in Medicine*, London: Longwood Press.

James, R. (1936), 'Licenses to practise medicine and surgery issued by the Archbishops of Canterbury 1580–1775', *Janus*, **41**.

Johnson, T. (1977), 'Professions in the Class Structure', in R. Scase (ed.), *Industrial sociology: class, cleavage and control*, London: Allen and Unwin.

Kreckel, R. (1980), 'Unequal Opportunity Structure and Labour Market Segmentation', *Sociology*, **14**, (4).

Lander, K. (1922), 'The Study of Anatomy by Women before the Nineteenth Century', *International Congress of the History of Medicine, 3rd*, London.

Larkin, G. (1978), 'Medical Dominance and Control: Radiographers in the Division of Labour,' *Sociological Review*, **26**, 4.

Larkin, G. (1983), *Occupational Monopoly and Modern Medicine*, London: Tavistock.

Larson, M. (1977), *The Rise of Professionalism*, California: University of California Press.

Larson, M. (1979), 'Professionalism: Rise and Fall', *International Journal of Health Services*, **9**, (4).

Manton, J. (1965), *Elizabeth Garrett Anderson*, London: Methuen.

Oakley, A. (1976), 'Wisewomen and Medicine Man: changes in the management of childbirth', in J. Mitchel and A. Oakley (eds) *The Rights and Wrongs of Women*, London: Penguin.

Parkin, F. (1974), 'Strategies of Social Closure in Class Formation', in F. Parkin (ed.), *The Social Analysis of Class Structures*, London: Tavistock.

Pelling, M. and Webster C. (1979), 'Medical Practitioners', in C. Webster (ed.), *Health, Medicine and Mortality in the Sixteenth Century*, Cambridge: Cambridge University Press.

Pinchbeck, I. (1930), *Women Workers and the Industrial Revolution 1750–1850*, London: Virago.

Power, E. (1921), 'Women Practitioners of Medicine in the Middle Ages', *Proceedings of the Royal Society of Medicine*, vol. 15 (section on History of Medicine).

Select Committee on Midwife Registration (1982) P.P. XIV, Evidence.

Verluysen, M. (1980), 'Old Wives' Tales? Women Healers in English History', in C. Davies (ed.), *Rewriting Nursing History*, London: Croom Helm.

Walby, S. (1984), *Gender and Unemployment. Patriarchal and Capitalist Relations in the Restructuring of Gender Relations in Employment and Unemployment*, University of Essex, unpublished Ph. D. thesis.

Witz, A. (1985), 'Midwifery and the Medical Profession: sexual divisions and the process of professionalisation, 1870–1900', University of Lancaster: *Lancaster Regionalism Group Working Paper No. 15*.

Wyman, A. (1984), 'The Surgeoness: The Female Practitioner of Surgery 1400–1800', *Medical History*, **28**.

2 Gender in the Labour Process - the Case of Women and Men Lawyers

David Podmore and Anne Spencer

Introduction

A considerable body of literature in the sociology of the professions has portrayed professions as homogeneous and unified entities. Most of the classic and influential work on the professions has conveyed this view.[1] Differences between members of the same professions – in terms of status, rewards, the work activities they performed, etc. – were minimised, as were differences between types of professional practice. These accounts have tended to take for granted the professions' own evaluation of themselves, for example by accepting uncritically the so-called 'service' ethic or by taking as read the unity of interest amongst members of a profession. There are, however, important differences within professions. There is good evidence that, far from being homogeneous and unified, professions are characterised by a considerable degree of heterogeneity, diversity of interest, segmentation, etc.[2] The impact of social and technological change is likely to increase these tendencies and lead even to fragmentation[3] of professions.

One important source of diversity and segmentation lies in the increasing proportion of women recruited in recent years by traditionally male-dominated professions. In the English legal profession the increase has been considerable, though women remain a small minority. The number of practising women barristers rose from 64 (3.2 per cent) in 1955 to 641 (12.3%) in 1984 and of solicitors from 337 (1.9 per cent) in 1957 to 5,497 (12.3%) in 1984. Between one quarter and one third of all persons currently undergoing legal professional training are women, though a lower proportion of women than men actually enter the law after completing their training. The essentially 'masculine', male-dominated nature of the legal profession[4] is thus being challenged by the increased participation of women.

The penetration of women into the legal profession has been very uneven and a number of classic features of labour market segmentation can be found. A dual labour market (Reich et al. 1973) exists where a particular labour market is divided into two sectors, one characterised by 'good' jobs (the primary sector) and the other by 'bad' jobs (the secondary sector) (Loveridge and Mok 1979:5). These authors identify four features of a dual labour market – a division into higher and lower paying sectors; restricted mobility between sectors (the nature of the work in 'good' jobs being different to that in 'bad' jobs); readily available promotion 'ladders' in the higher paying job sector, but few promotion opportunities in the lower paying sector; relative stability of employment in the higher paying sector, whilst lower paying jobs are unstable.

In this paper we discuss the extent to which men and women lawyers[5] can be considered to occupy different sectors of the legal labour market. We pay particular attention to the second of the four features of a dual labour market mentioned above, the extent to which women and men lawyers do characteristically different kinds of legal work, and we go on to discuss some of the factors accounting for the work patterns found.

Lawyers' earnings
Data on the earnings of self-employed professional people are notoriously unreliable, but women lawyers clearly experience a 'deficit in rewards' (Coser 1981) compared with men. A survey carried out on behalf of the Royal Commission on Legal Services (1979: 444) found that the average income of women barristers was 50–60 per cent of that of men. This can be accounted for in part by women's under-representation in the high-prestige, high-reward areas of professional practice and in senior positions in the barristers' branch of the profession (these matters are discussed below). However, what is significant is that the survey found that when barristers *doing similar work* were compared, the average earnings of women were still only 50–60 per cent of those of men.

Information on solicitors' earnings is not available, but a number of the women interviewed told us that they believed that they earned less than their male counterparts. One woman said that, as an articled clerk ('apprentice solicitor'), she received only *one seventh* the salary of a man of similar status and seniority in the same firm!

The work of men and women lawyers
The main source of our data was interviews with 32 men and 32 women lawyers. The women were part of a larger group interviewed in a project investigating the position of women in the legal profession and the strains they experienced and accommodations which they made in their professional, domestic and personal lives.[6] The 32 women lawyers were

'matched' with 32 men, who were interviewed using a similar schedule, in order to ascertain how far their legal practice, career experiences and so on differed from those of the women. The 'matching' process was necessarily rather crude but the variables which were used to 'match' were:

> *type of work* (barrister in chambers or employed; solicitor in private practice or employed)[7]
>
> *date of qualification* (year, month)[8]

The work of solicitors

One of our central concerns was to ascertain how far men and women lawyers were involved in different kinds of legal work. Information on the type of work done by the private practice solicitors was obtained by presenting them with a list of ten types of legal work and asking them to mark the importance of each type of work in their personal workloads, on a seven-point scale ranging from 'extremely important' to 'not at all important' (Figure 1). It was made clear that 'importance' was to be judged in terms of the time spent on the various types of work. Scores

Figure 1 The work of the solicitor

	Extremely important					Not at all important
Matrimonial	:	:	:	:	:	:
Wills and probate	:	:	:	:	:	:
Estate duty, etc.	:	:	:	:	:	:
Company and commercial	:	:	:	:	:	:
European and international	:	:	:	:	:	:
Property/conveyancing	:	:	:	:	:	:
Tax matters	:	:	:	:	:	:
Personal injury	:	:	:	:	:	:
Criminal	:	:	:	:	:	:
Other litigation	:	:	:	:	:	:

were thus obtained for each of the types of legal work and the results for the men and women respondents are compared in Table 1. Property and conveyancing work was clearly the most important in the workloads of both men and women,[9] with an average score of 5·4 for men and 5·6 for women. It was rated at the top of the seven-point scale by ten of the thirteen women and eight of the men. The next most important types of work were matrimonial, and wills and probate. The table shows that men solicitors had higher scores in terms of importance

Table 1 The work of men and women solicitors in private practice*

Type of work	Men	Women
Matrimonial	3.5	4.2
Wills and probate	3.5	4.2
Estate duty	2.9	3.7
Company and commercial	3.8	2.2
European and international	1.7	1.0
Property and conveyancing	5.4	5.6
Tax matters	2.2	2.2
Personal injury	3.5	2.6
Criminal	3.5	2.5
Other litigation	3.7	3.0

* Average scores, where 7 is the maximum and 1 the minimum. Tests of statistical significance have not been applied because of the small numbers involved.

in their workloads for company and commercial, European and international,[10] personal injury, criminal and other litigation work, and women had higher scores for matrimonial, wills and probate, estate duty, and property and conveyancing work. Table 2 amplifies these

Table 2 Number of men and women solicitors in private practice rating types of work as 'very important' or 'not at all important' in their workload*

Type of work	'very important'		'not at all important'	
	Men	Women	Men	Women
Matrimonial	3	7	5	6
Wills and probate	2	5	5	5
Estate duty	1	4	5	6
Company and commercial	4	—	2	7
European and international	—	—	11	13
Property and conveyancing	8	10	3	3
Tax matters	—	1	7	9
Personal injury	4	1	5	7
Criminal	3	2	6	8
Other litigation	3	2	6	7

* Total number of respondents was 13 men and 13 women.

findings, by showing the numbers of respondents rating particular types of work at the extreme ends of the seven-point scale. There is clear evidence here that the men respondents tended to do rather different kinds of legal work compared to women. Men solicitors were more likely than women to be engaged in company and commercial work, one of the prestigious areas of legal practice, and in criminal and litigation work, which often involves frequent court appearances. (The men respondents appeared in court more regularly than the women. Three men solicitors appeared in court 'very frequently', compared with one woman; one man 'never' appeared in court, compared with six women.)[11]

Women solicitors, on the other hand, were more heavily involved than men in matrimonial work and such 'desk bound' work as wills and probate and estate duty. The types of work done by men and women solicitors in private practice are summarised in Figure 2. The work of the men tended to be in more prestigious areas of legal practice and to

Figure 2 The work of men and women solicitors

	Men's work	*Women's work*	
High prestige work	Company and Commercial	Matrimonial	*Low prestige work*
Mainly male clientele	European and international	Wills, probate	*'Caring' qualities required*
'Combative' qualities required	Criminal	Estate duty	*'Desk bound'*
Meetings with corporate clients, court appearances involved – implying much 'mobility'.	Personal injury		*High proportion of female clients*
	Other litigation		

Tax Matters

Property and Conveyancing
*('desk bound' – but a heavy load to be
shifted in most practices)*

involve adversarial work and court appearances. The work of the women typically involved an office-centred, 'desk bound' sphere of activity. These matters are discussed in the next section of this paper.

We now consider what some of the respondents had to say about the work which they did, since their comments throw light on the different work patterns of men and women. One woman assistant solicitor (i.e. salaried employee) who worked mainly on conveyancing, claimed that:

In this practice they don't like women doing commercial and company work, they prefer to keep them to the conveyancing and matrimonial.

Another described how she had been more or less pushed into specialising in matrimonial work, when the woman who had been doing this work left the practice. This respondent was the third successive woman to be responsible for this area of her firm's activities, a clear indication that this was regarded as 'women's work':

... she was leaving ... and so there was a gap there, they needed someone to deal with that particular side of the work, but it wasn't my choice.

This respondent's principals seemed to have clear ideas about the kind of work which women should do. Such ideas often manifested themselves early in a woman's career, when she was receiving training as an articled clerk. Several respondents mentioned that their training was rather limited, and that this 'closed off' possibilities to them after they had qualified:

I would like to have covered more general work in articles and then be able to do it now, but having done the work I did during articles it was very difficult after qualifying to branch into a different line.

It may be easier for men to break into different kinds of work, as one man told us:

... I was taken on (after qualifying) to do conveyancing and probate work ... the conveyancing market dipped off and I made a considerable effort to get contentious work.

Some women felt rather limited and frustrated by the restrictions placed on them by their seniors. One found that whole areas of the criminal practice in which her firm specialised were closed to her:

... the firm I was articled to had never had a woman before ... I found people very sceptical ... I found it terribly hard – they wouldn't let me see any of the rape files, the indecent assault files, and very rarely the murder files.

One of the men solicitors summed up attitudes which several others echoed:

... I think there are certain areas of work, particularly in the company and commercial field, where the clients might raise an eyebrow.[12]

He went on to say:

> I suspect in certain fields they (women) may more easily strike a *rapport* with
> the client. I think particularly obviously divorce work, where they're acting
> for the wife ... also in conveyancing which is, you know, moving house; to
> most solicitors, well, it's just another file, but for most women actually
> involved in moving house it's a fairly traumatic experience, and I think a girl
> lawyer is more readily able to appreciate it.

The work of barristers

Considerable differences were found in the work of the men and women
barristers. First, we will look at the type of chambers in which they
practised. Eight of the men were in 'general common law chambers'
where the work involved the mixed sort of practice which is typical of so
many barristers' chambers – a considerable amount of criminal and
matrimonial cases and general civil litigation. Such chambers averaged
in size from about 20 to 30 members and on the whole little specialist
work was undertaken. The remaining four men practised in chambers
which were mainly concerned with specialist work – these chambers
tended to be rather smaller in size. One of the specialist chambers was
heavily involved in commercial and shipping work, the second in
commercial law, the third specialised in restrictive trade practices and
monopolies matters. The fourth specialist chambers was small, only
seven members, where the members specialised in what the respondent
called 'intellectual property work', especially patents matters.

The women barristers, on the other hand, were concentrated in
general common law chambers. Only one of the 12 interviewed was in a
specialist set of chambers, which did a good deal of Chancery law work,
and Parliamentary, local government and ecclesiastical work.

Looking now to the work of the barristers themselves, we asked them
to estimate in percentage terms how much time they spent on different
kinds of work. Seven of the men spent a substantial amount of time (40
per cent or more) on criminal work[13] and one spent a substantial
amount of time on matrimonial work. The remaining four were
involved in specialist commercial law, practising in the chambers
referred to above. Five of the women spent 40 per cent or more of their
time on criminal work[14] and five were substantially involved in
matrimonial work. Only two women were involved in other general
'knockabout' work.[15] One was a senior member of the chambers which
specialised in Chancery work referred to above, and the second did a
good deal of specialist personal injury work. None of the women
mentioned commercial and company work as being at all significant in
their workloads. The pattern which emerges is thus of women barristers
being much involved in general 'knockabout' work, with men somewhat

involved in such work but also specialising in commercial work. What Kennedy (1978: 154) has observed was also true of our women respondents: 'There are still great difficulties facing a woman who wishes to practise outside the traditional fields of crime and divorce'.

These findings may be supplemented and illustrated from the interviews. Just as women solicitors seem to have been channelled towards particular kinds of work, so women barristers were pushed towards criminal work (usually minor crime) and matrimonial cases. The work which a barrister does depends very much on what the instructing solicitors and the barristers' clerks (who allocate 'briefs' within their chambers) believe to be suitable for that particular individual. Several women respondents felt that they had been forced to concentrate on these particular areas of work by the nature of the 'briefs' which came their way. One remarked:

> You find that most women at the Bar ... do get given a lot of matrimonial work, perhaps because ... the solicitors think that we're far too delicate to carry out the heavy criminal trials and that sort of thing ... I think a lot of us, simply because you want to keep in work, you've got to take what work you're given ...

Another, doing a lot of matrimonial work, said:

> It is in fact *foisted* on women who come to the Bar, as you probably realise.

Although many of the women barristers did criminal work, it was typically of a minor nature. One relatively senior respondent felt that she was being discriminated against because she did not get instructed in 'heavy crime' cases, where men barristers were almost always preferred:

> I was getting to the stage in chambers where I *ought* to have been doing what we call heavy crime, and I think if I'd been a man I would have been doing it. What I mean by heavy crime is robberies, arson, burglaries, wounding, rapes and murders if you were lucky ... and that used to worry me, that I wasn't getting into that sort of work ... I used to do quite a lot of lady shop lifters. I used to do a lot of juveniles ... because solicitors ... seem to think that you're more suitable for that sort of work.

This respondent has summarised neatly the 'men's work – women's work' segmentation at the Bar.

Discussion

In this section of the paper we consider some factors which contribute towards the marked internal segmentation within the legal labour market described above. These factors are numerous and complex – we have identified elsewhere ten different factors contributing to the marginalisation of women in male-dominated professions (Spencer and Podmore 1983). In order to simplify matters we will use the concepts of 'pressure theory' and 'preference theory' (Patterson 1973) to focus the discussion which follows.

'Pressure theory' suggests that the view is prevalent in society that the personal characteristics and qualities of men and women are quite different.[16] One of the consequences of this is the belief that certain types of work activities are best performed by men and others by women. When women enter occupations and professions 'best suited' to (and, of course, dominated by) men, they are pressured towards types of work considered to be most appropriate to their sex, towards segments of professional work:

> where a large measure of traditionally 'feminine' qualities are required; that is helping, caring, giving social and emotional support and so on – what has (been) called women's 'stroking' function.
>
> (Podmore and Spencer 1982a: 24)

This is a situation where women suffer the effects of 'the haunting presence of irrelevant statuses'[17] leading to their being channelled and pressured towards certain types of work,[18] work which is seen (by their men superiors) as being particularly suited to those with feminine qualities. So women lawyers find themselves pushed *towards* 'desk bound' and 'people-oriented' work, work which is relatively 'routinised' (Kanter 1978), and *away* from 'demanding' specialities. By a similar process, men are channelled in the direction of 'male-appropriate' segments of professional work, in accordance with the strong social expectations that men concentrate on 'instrumental' activities and women on 'integrative' activities, to use the Parsonian terminology which has played a not inconsiderable part in 'keeping women in their place'.[19]

We found a widespread belief amongst men lawyers that women were unsuited to some aspects of legal practice. One, a barrister, told us that the law:

> is a career based to some extent on competition and hustling and hitting people over the head and so on. Old-fashioned people like me tend to think that's more the masculine rather than the feminine role.

A solicitor remarked, similarly, that:

> Women just aren't tough enough. It's a competitive profession. Women can't cope with the hard bargaining that's involved.

This view holds that the legal world – particularly criminal work and advocacy, commercial and business negotiation, etc. – requires competitive, aggressive and extrovert qualities (a male barrister described advocacy as 'disposing of aggression in a controlled setting').[20]

Women are thus considered by the men who dominate the profession to be unsuited to important areas of the legal role and so must be channelled in the direction of more suitable ones.[21]

We argue, then, that women lawyers are pushed towards matrimonial work, where sympathy, tact and so on are believed to be the main qualities needed by the lawyer (and where, incidentally, the great majority of clients who file for a divorce in the first instance are women), and (in the case of solicitors) towards the conveyancing of property or wills and probate where similar qualities are thought to be necessary. This sort of work, as far as solicitors are concerned, is likely to keep them 'in the office' – it is largely 'desk bound' work.[22] What Bird (1971) characterised as 'inside – outside' division of activities between women and men is thus maintained. This pattern is, of course, very much a reflection of the position of women in the wider society – more constrained, less mobile and free than men.[23] When women *do* attempt to operate in areas which are seen as 'men's work', they are often subject to sanctions. One young woman solicitor doing a lot of criminal work said that she was irritated by the constant 'joshing' she received when visiting clients on remand in prison or detained in police cells, of the variety 'what's a nice girl like you doing in a place like this?'. We were told of the male head of a set of barristers' chambers who felt that the travelling involved in being a barrister 'on circuit' was too physically demanding for women, and so he would not even have them in his chambers.

'Preference theory' holds that women in the professions are genuinely attracted, by their interests, wants, etc., to the specialities in which they are found. 'Helping others' is often said to be one of the main things which women seek in their work (an extension of the traditional 'caring' role, of course). Several women respondents mentioned that the factor in their work which brought them most satisfaction was 'helping people'.[24] One said:

> One can help people, one feels one can give help to people in need and perhaps remove a trouble for them ...

None of the women barristers mentioned this as one of the satisfactions of their work; nevertheless, as we have argued, most were involved in this area of 'personal troubles', i.e. matrimonial and (minor) criminal work.

Our view, however, is that it is *socialisation* that dictates preferences, interests and wants;[25] this is what leads women towards particular areas of work which they have learned to believe they are best suited to perform.

We suggest that there is another factor which helps to explain why women 'prefer' to do certain types of work in male-dominated professions. There is good evidence that conflict and strain is markedly reduced when women 'choose' to work in the 'women's segment'. Male-dominated professions represent hostile milieux for women to operate in (Epstein 1974). Such 'discriminatory environments' (Bourne and Wikler 1978) can be made more tolerable by accepting situations as they are – by 'preferring' to do 'women's work' women minimise the extent to which they come into conflict and competition with men, and lower the tension all round. Moreover, by entering the 'women's segment' they can ensure a reasonable number of peers, who will provide support and comfort and act as 'sponsors' and 'role models'[26] and make life more bearable in a largely hostile environment. As Glancy has written of American women lawyers:

> Rather than fight the system some women restrict their aspirations . . . to less competitive 'women's fields'. (1970: 29)

Similarly, an American woman doctor interviewed by Quandango remarked:

> Maybe that's one reason why I'm interested in paediatrics. You know there are a lot of women in it . . . So maybe I'm just tired of having to battle. (1976: 450)

One woman barrister we interviewed who clearly did not 'prefer' to be instructed mainly in matrimonial work, was at least philosophical about the situation:

> It's more a case of 'Well, that's what I get so I better get interested in it'.

Our final comment is to note how the 'stacking up' of women in certain segments of professional work and their under-representation in others helps to create a self-fulfilling prophecy that the work which women do is 'women's work' and the work which men do is 'men's work'.[27]

Promotion opportunities
The third feature of a dual labour market is that promotion is more readily available in the 'primary' than in the 'secondary' sector. Our research suggests that women lawyers find promotion more difficult to

achieve than men. In an earlier paper (Podmore and Spencer 1982b: 352–5) we have described how a common theme in interviews with younger women assistant solicitors (salaried non-partners) was that they felt that they were regarded as a source of cheap labour. Their (male) principals expected women assistants to work for a few years only, before leaving to get married and have children. A number of the women we interviewed felt that they were not treated seriously – as not really wanting responsibility, promotion or a career. One woman assistant solicitor put it this way:

> I think they like having women work for them, because they think they will probably work harder (which they tend to) and work for less money (which they also tend to) and wouldn't be so keen on picking up a partnership, which is true as well.

Men partners viewed women lawyers as a 'risk' in terms of long-term commitment to their practices – some women, the interviews showed, recognised this and restricted their ambitions accordingly. Others felt increasingly frustrated.

If a woman decided she did wish to push for a partnership, she found more difficulties than a man:

> I think the disadvantage (of being a woman in a male-dominated profession) comes now, at the stage that I've reached, where you're talking about partnership ... if you were a man you'd automatically be offered some sort of future within a firm and I don't think it's so automatic for a woman.

A woman solicitor who had obtained a partnership felt that her status was inferior:

> I am a salaried partner, whereas if I was a man I would by now definitely be a profit-sharing partner.

These comments are supported by other evidence. A survey of West Midlands solicitors in 1975 found only one woman in a stratified sample of 125 partners in a private practice (Podmore 1980b: 144), whilst the Equal Opportunities Commission has commented on inequalities in opportunities for women in leading London firms specialising in presitigous company and commercial work (1978: 20–1).

The relative promotion prospects in the barristers' branch of the profession are more difficult to generalise about. Success at the Bar is gauged by the amount and quality of the work a barrister does and the fees he or she earns (the disparity in the earnings of men and women barristers has already been indicated). One outward and visible sign of advancement in the hierarchy of the Bar comes when a barrister 'takes silk' and becomes a Queen's Counsel, or when he or she is advanced to the Bench. Women QCs and judges are rare creatures – in 1980 only 13 out of 720 QCs were women and only 41 out of 1226 Appeal, High Court and Circuit judges and Recorders. As we have observed:

> The massive under-representation of women in the highest ranks of the barristers' branch of the profession is not wholly because there are few senior women barristers, though a high proportion of women *are* relatively junior in point of call. Kennedy (1978: 150) has shown that, in 1976, only 21% of women with more than 15 years practice since being called to the Bar had received a judicial appointment, compared with 53% of men of over 15 years call.
>
> (Podmore and Spencer 1982a: 21)

Stability of employment

Our research revealed only indirect evidence of women lawyers' employment being less stable than that of men. As already indicated, some women assistant solicitors felt that there was an 'expectation' that they would not want a permanent career within a firm after marriage and (certainly) after starting a family. A considerable problem for women was that of obtaining continuity in their careers between the 'academic' stage of their legal training and the 'practical' stage.[28] Many women experienced difficulties in obtaining places in solicitors' offices to fulfil their articles or in barristers' chambers to complete their pupillage. The (almost exclusively male) gatekeepers of the profession tended to be doubtful about taking on female 'apprentices' (Epstein 1970: 168–76) and many women reported a hostile atmosphere and prejudiced line of questioning at interviews when they were seeking articles or pupillage. Twice as many barristers as solicitors, when interviewed, felt that their sex had been a disadvantage at the stage when they were seeking a place. This is not surprising, because the Bar is without doubt much more of a male preserve, with its masculine ethos more sharply defined, than is the solicitors' branch (Kennedy 1978; Cheeld 1976). Kennedy has described how:

> Many chambers openly admit a 'no woman' policy ... (whilst others) hide their discrimination behind all sort of excuses. (1978: 151–3).

After completing their apprenticeship, the women lawyers we interviewed seemed to have had relatively few problems in obtaining first appointments as qualified barristers or solicitors. In most cases a place was made for the woman in the practice in which she had completed her apprenticeship. However, our interviews were with women who were established in legal practice. The number and proportion of women who have been unable to obtain a footing in the profession are unknown. Indirect evidence is available, in that only 33 per cent of women called to the Bar (that is, who passed the 'academic' stage) in 1975 had begun to practise four years later, compared with 50 per cent of men (Royal Commission on Legal Services 1979: 440).

Conclusion

Women lawyers suffer relative inequalities, compared with men, in terms of earnings, in terms of the work they do (to a considerable extent being restricted to 'women's work') and in terms of having fewer promotion opportunities.[29] There is some indication that women find continuity of employment less certain than do men between the 'academic' and 'practical' stages of their professional training. Women lawyers thus experience some of the classic attributes of secondary labour market employment. These are only *relative* inequalities, of course. In this paper we have considered segmentation within a profession which itself is obviously – to use Loveridge and Mok's terminology – one of the 'good' jobs. The inequalities and disabilities experienced by women lawyers are, it may be argued, unimportant compared with those of women hospital workers, cleaners, shopworkers, etc. Indeed, women lawyers are a privileged group compared with other workers in the legal 'industry', which is characterised by a three tier segmentation – professional, para-professional and clerical-secretarial.

There is a marked gender effect in this segmentation of the internal labour market of the legal 'industry'. The lowest tier of the hierarchy, clerical-secretarial, has become almost wholly feminised. Sachs and Wilson (1978: 178) have estimated that about half of all people employed in the law are women, but only 2 per cent are 'fee-earners' – that is, doing work which is 'responsible' enough to earn fees directly from clients. This is a clear indication that gender-based segmentation in the legal 'industry' as a whole is much more dramatic than that within the ranks of legal professionals.

Acknowledgement

The support of the Economic and Social Research Council is gratefully acknowledged.

Notes

1. See, for example, Parsons (1968); Goode (1957); Barber (1963).
2. This has been a neglected field, but see Smith (1958); Bucher and Strauss (1961);

Podmore (1980a); Child and Fulk (1982: 180–3).

3. A term used, but not fully explored, by Johnson (1977).
4. For discussion and illustration of this, see Sachs and Wilson (1978); Pearson and Sachs (1980); Spencer and Podmore (1983: 23–35).
5. We are concerned with qualified solicitors and barristers, excluding from the discussion para-professionals such as legal executives and managing clerks, and non-professional staff such as secretaries, etc.
6. A total of the 76 women lawyers were interviewed, in 1979–80, 48 solicitors and 28 barristers. The solicitors were a one in two sample of women practising in the West Midlands and worked in a number of different environments – partners in private practice, salaried assistants in private practice, in local government, statutory bodies, business and industry, and higher education. The barristers were either practising members of the Midland and Oxford circuit (based in the Midlands or in London), or practising employed barristers, working in industry, higher education or as magistrates' clerks.
7. Of the 32 men and 32 women lawyers, 17 were solicitors and 15 were barristers. Thirteen of the solicitors were in private practice and four were employed elsewhere; 12 of the barristers were in chambers and three employed. The work of the men and women solicitors and barristers employed outside private practice was not markedly different and the discussion in this paper concentrates on the 25 men and 25 women privately-practising solicitors and barristers.
8. That is, of admission as a solicitor or call as a barrister. This information was readily obtainable from the annual publications *Solicitors' Diary and Directory* and *The Bar List*. The dates of admission of the solicitors ranged from July 1958 to April 1978 and the dates of call of the barristers from February 1957 to July 1977.
9. Conveyancing is, of course, by far and away the single most important category of work in virtually all solicitors' practices and most solicitors themselves, except for those in large, specialised practices, spend a good deal of time doing this kind of work. It has been estimated that 50–60 per cent of the time of the average English solicitor is spent on conveyancing work, with wills and probate, and litigation work, next in importance (Johnstone and Hopson 1967: 372). For a fuller discussion of the work of solicitors, see Podmore (1980b: 33–7).
10. Only two of the 26 solicitors (both men) rated this work as other than 'not at all important'.
11. Respondents were asked to tick off a card which presented the question: 'How often do you make appearances in Court and before Tribunals?'

    ☐ *Very frequently* (4 or 5 or more appearnaces each week, on average)
    ☐ *Frequently* (2 or 3 appearances each week, on average)
    ☐ *Sometimes* (1 appearance each week, on average)
    ☐ *Seldom* (1 appearance each month, on average)
    ☐ *Never*

12. The 'clients might not like it' argument is frequently used as an excuse for excluding women (and members of other minority groups) from full participation in the professions (on this, see Novarra 1980, especially pp. 13–14). A woman barrister, noting how women get channelled into the less prestigious ares of legal work, recognised the problem when she commented, 'I feel it's more difficult for a woman to get on with Chancery (trusts, bankruptcies, etc.) commercial, tax (work) because I think people will trust you with their marriages or their liberty, but not with their money.'
13. Three of these spent a further 30 per cent of their time on matrimonial work. Just as conveyancing work is the 'staple diet' of most solicitors' practices, so criminal work (virtually all legally-aided, of course) and matrimonial work (often legally-aided) are the mainstays of the average set of barristers' chambers.
14. Three spent a further 30 per cent of their time on matrimonial work.

15. The term used by one woman to describe the mixed bag of common law work of her chambers.
16. The work of Broverman et al. (1972) suggests that this view is, indeed, widely held.
17. Merton, quoted in Cole (1979: 81).
18. The American literature refers to this process as 'tracking'.
19. Such stereotypes not only create prejudice in that women are *expected* to behave in certain ways, they also lead women *actually* to behave in these ways. And, if women do not conform to 'feminine' stereotypes then they are likely to be criticised as 'unfeminine' (see Prather 1971; Chapman 1978).
20. A woman solicitor told us that, in doing divorce and conveyancing work, she found that women solicitors 'on the other side' were much more likely to compromise than men. Men solicitors, she said, always wanted '100 per cent or nearly' for their client. Men litigation solicitors tried 'to bash everyone into the ground'. However, negotiation, compromise and adjustment are also important features of the legal role (see Podmore 1980b: 33–5). The very qualities attributed to women in the stereotype of femininity (sensitive, intuitive, compromising, etc.) would therefore seem to render them particularly suited to performing successfully as lawyers!
21. A number of writers have shown how women in other male-dominated professions are channelled towards 'appropriate' specialities and away from 'inappropriate' ones. American hospital doctors interviewed by Quandango (1976), for example, saw paediatrics and psychiatry as requiring 'feminine' traits, and surgical specialities as requiring 'masculine' traits. Kosa and Coker (1965) similarly found that women were heavily over-represented in these specialities, which are congruent with the traditional female 'caring'/'expressive' role. Women were also over-represented in the American public health service; the authors argued that this was because government service is much less 'competitive' and 'entrepreneurial' than is private practice.
22. A similar segmentation of activities was found by Epstein (1980), even in Wall Street firms in New York where women had gone a long way towards gaining acceptance as equals with men.
23. For two interesting discussions on this theme see Weitzman et al. (1972), who point to important differences in the ways in which boys' and girls' lives are presented in children's books, and Lever (1976), who shows how the different games and leisure patterns of children lead to the development of different social skills in adults.
24. This is one of the reasons why semi-professions such as social work and teaching are so appealing to women, according to Simpson and Simpson (1969: 203) – the semi-professions appeal to the heart rather than the mind and attract those who want to work with people and be of service, i.e. women rather than men.
25. We accept the conclusions of King's (1974) extensive review of the literature – that there is a large overlap between men and women in terms of capacities, abilities, personality, interests and values.
26. For a fuller discussion of these considerations, see Spencer and Podmore (1983).
27. This was also the conclusion of Cole (1979: 255–6) in his study of women in American science.
28. Most entrants to the legal profession now have a degree (usually in law) and all must attend an approved 'academic' training course; most do so before completing a compulsory period of 'practical' training.
29. As do British graduate women generally (Chisholm and Woodward 1980), and women hospital doctors (Elston 1977) and academics (Blackstone and Fulton 1975) in particular.

References

Barber, B. (1963), 'Some problems in the sociology of the professions', *Daedalus*, **92**, 669–88.

52   Gender and the Labour Process

Bird, C. (1971), 'The sex map of the work world', pp. 39–57 in M.H. Garskof (ed.), *Roles Women Play*, Belmont, Calif.: Brooks-Cole.

Blackstone, T. and O. Fulton (1975), 'Sex discrimination among university teachers: a British-American comparison', *British Journal of Sociology*, **26**, 261–75.

Bourne, P.G. and N.J. Wikler (1978), 'Commitment and the cultural mandate: women in medicine', *Social Problems*, **25**, 430–40.

Broverman, I.K. et al. (1972), 'Sex-role stereotypes: a current appraisal', *Journal of Social Issues*, **28**, (2), 59–78.

Bucher, R. and A. Strauss (1961), 'Professions in process', *American Journal of Sociology*, **66**, 325–34.

Chapman, J.B. (1978), 'Male and female leadership styles – the double bind', pp. 97–123 in J.A. Ramaley (ed.), *Covert Discrimination and Women in the Sciences*, Boulder, Colo.: Westview Press.

Cheeld, D. (1976), 'The rise of an angry young woman', *Law Society's Gazette*, **73**, 634–5.

Child J. and J. Fulk (1982), 'Maintenance of occupational control: the case of professions' *Work and Occupations*, **9**, 155–92.

Chisholm, L. and D. Woodward (1980), 'The experiences of women graduates in the labour market', pp. 162–76 in R. Deem (ed.), *Schooling for Women's Work*, London: Routledge and Kegan Paul.

Cole, J.R. (1979), *Fair Science: Women in the Scientific Community*, London: Collier-Macmillan.

Coser, R.L. (1981), 'Where have all the women gone? Like the sediment of good wine, they have sunk to the bottom', pp. 16–33 in C.F. Epstein and R.L. Coser (eds.), *Access to Power: Cross National Studies of Women and Elites*, London: Allen and Unwin.

Elston, M.A. (1977), 'Women in the medical profession: whose problem?', pp. 115–38 in M. Stacey et al. (eds.), *Health and the Division of Labour*, London: Croom Helm.

Epstein, C.F. (1970), *Women's Place: Options and Limits in Professional Careers* Berkeley: University of California Press.

Epstein, C.F. (1974), 'Ambiguity as social control: consequences for the integration of women in professional elites', pp. 26–38 in P.L. Stewart and M.G. Cantor (eds.), *Varieties of Work Experience*, Cambridge, Mass.: Schenkman.

Epstein, C.F. (1980), 'The new women and the old establishment: Wall Street lawyers in the 1970's', *Sociology of Work and Occupations*, **7**, 291–316.

Equal Opportunities Commission (1978), *Women in the Legal Services*, Manchester: Equal Opportunities Commission.

Glancy, D.J. (1971), 'Women in law: the dependable ones', *Harvard Law School Bulletin*, **21**, 23–33.

Goode, W.J. (1957), 'Community within a community: the professions' *American Sociological Review*, **22**, 194–200.

Johnson, T.J. (1977), 'The professions in the class structure', pp. 93–110 in R. Scase (ed.), *Industrial Society: Class, Cleavage and Control*, London: Allen and Unwin.

Johnstone, Q. and D. Hopson. (1967), *Lawyers and their Work*, Indianapolis; Bobbs-Merrill.

Kanter, R.M. (1978), 'Reflections on women and the legal profession: a sociological perspective', *Harvard Women's Law Journal*, **1**, 1–17.

Kennedy, H. (1978), 'Women at the Bar', pp. 148–62 in R. Hazell (ed.), *The Bar on Trial*, London: Quartet Books.

King, J.S. (1974), *Women and Work: Sex Differences and Society*, London: HMSO.

Kosa, J. and R.E. Coker (1965), 'The female physician in public health: conflict and reconciliation of the sex and professional roles', *Sociology and Social Research*, **49**, 294–305.

Lever, J. (1976), 'Sex differences in games children play', *Social Problems*, **23**, 478–87.

Loveridge, R. and A.L. Mok (1979), *Theories of Labour Market Segmentation: a Critique*, The Hague: Martinus Nijhoff.

Novarra, J. (1980), *Women's Work, Men's Work: the Ambivalence of Equality*, London:

Marion Boyars.

Parsons, T. (1968), 'Professions' *International Encyclopaedia of Social Sciences*, **12**, 536–47.

Patterson, M. (1973), 'Sex specialization in Academe and the Professions', pp. 313–31 in A. Rossi and A. Calderwood (eds.), *Academic Women on the Move*, New York: Russell Sage.

Pearson, R. and A. Sachs (1980), 'Barristers and gentlemen: a critical look at sexism in the legal profession', *Modern Law Review*, **43**, 400–14.

Podmore, D. (1980a), 'Bucher and Strauss revisited: the case of the Solicitor's profession', *British Journal of Law and Society*, **7**, 1–21.

Podmore, D. (1980b), *Solicitors and the Wider Community*, London: Heinemann.

Podmore, D. and A. Spencer (1982a), 'The law as a sex-typed profession', *Journal of Law and Society*, **9**, 21–36.

Podmore, D. and A. Spencer (1982b), 'Women lawyers in England: the experience of inequality', *Work and Occupations*, **9**, 337–61.

Prather, J. (1971), 'Why can't women be more like men: a summary of sociopsychological factor's hindering women's advancement in the professions', *American Behavioural Scientist* **15**, 172–82.

Quandango, J. (1976), 'Occupational sex-typing and internal labour market distributions: an assessment of medical specialities', *Social Problems*, **23**, 442–53.

Reich, M. et al. (1973), 'A theory of labor market segmentation', *American Economic Review* **63**, 359–65.

Royal Commission on Legal Services (1979), *Final Report*, Volume II London: HMSO (Cmnd. 7648).

Sachs, A. and J.H. Wilson (1978), *Sexism and the Law*, London: Martin Robertson.

Simpson, R.L. and I.H. Simpson (1969), 'Women and bureaucracy in the semi-professions', pp. 196–265 in A. Etzioni (ed.), *The Semi-Professions and their Organization*, New York: Free Press.

Smith, H.L. (1958), 'Contingencies of professional differentiation' *American Journal of Sociology*, **63**, 410–14.

Spencer, A. and D. Podmore (1983), 'Life on the periphery of a profession: the experience of women lawyers', *Paper presented to B.S.A. Annual Conference, April 1983*.

Weitzman, L. et al. (1972), 'Sex-role socialization in picture books for preschool children', *American Journal of Sociology*, **77**, 1125–50.

3 Technological Change, Management Strategies, and the Development of Gender-based Job Segregation in the Labour Process

Harriet Bradley

'You can imagine how boys would feel about being a machinist!' The traditional masculine horror expressed in this comment by the manager of a Leicester knitting factory, a subsidiary of Courtauld's, in 1983, echoes the fear expressed in 1868 by A.J. Mundella, Nottingham hosier and liberal reformer. 'It would be an awful thing to have only women and boys employed in a trade.' (Royal Commission on Trade Unions 1868:82) But machismo is only one of a variety of elements involved in the hardening out of a segregated job structure. In the following discussion I hope to trace the way the sexual division of labour originated in pre-industrial household structures, but arrived at its present state as a result of complex negotiations consequent upon two conflicting drives: the competitive pressure on employers to cheapen their labour costs, and the determination of organised male workers to retain traditional forms of employment.

I have argued elsewhere that three processes must be taken into account when studying the development of any 'labour process'. The first of these is the long-term trend towards the 'degradation' or 'real subsumption' of labour. What is involved here is an attempt by employers and managers to reduce labour to its most basic form, easily manipulated and easily replaced, as part of the drive towards increased efficiency, increased productivity and profits (see Wright 1978 for a similar conclusion). This, in turn, generates resistance, as sections of the labour force which possess still-needed skills retain a strategic position in the complex division of labour, or, because of tight and militant union organisation, fight against the degradation of their jobs. The conflicts and negotiations involved will often result in a second process, that of resegmentation, whereby these powerful groups succeed in hanging on to positions of privilege, retaining old 'skills' or monopolising new ones. Third, in addition to these 'global' tendencies, there exists a repertoire of strategies used by employers and managers in response to specific problems of control and efficiency. These will be highly variable in response to context: they are influenced for example, by extremely localised labour market conditions, by local industrial tradition, by the product market, by state legislation, and so forth. The attempt to typologise and periodise such employer strategies, a central concern of the 'labour process' literature, is perhaps a rather futile exercise. Such a categorisation can certainly not be achieved on a historical basis (any given strategy can usually be traced back to the early industrial period, albeit in a modified form); if it has to be done at all, I have argued (Bradley 1984) that this should be done on the basis of what type of problem is addressed by the strategy. Following Braverman (1974) and Cressey and MacInnes (1980), I would argue that there are two inherent sources of tension in any capitalist enterprise. First, the indeterminacy of the reward/effort bargain has to be addressed by the tightening-up of work organisation, that is by taking away from the workers any space which they can use to exercise their own autonomy, thus altering the 'contract' in their own favour. Strategies with this objective I call 'restrictive' strategies. But, as Cressey and MacInnes (ibid.) show, there is also a tension between the employers' desire to tighten this control and their need for the co-operation, or at least compliance, of the workforce, to ensure, for example, that goods of high quality are produced in sufficient quantity when and as needed. The labour/capital relationship, that is to say, is one of antagonism *and* interdependence. (See Bradley 1984 for a fuller elaboration of these distinctions.) Strategies to cope with this problem involve the yielding and conceding of space and autonomy to workers to gain their consent; thus, I call them 'pacificatory'.

I have briefly outlined the elements of a general theory of the labour process, but such a theory is clearly without value, unless it sheds light on the development of any concrete labour process. Accordingly, in this paper, I want to show the working out of these processes in the case of the East Midlands hosiery industry and, in particular, how they have helped to shape the sexual division of labour in the industry.

Feminisation, unions and employers

Processes of degradation and resegmentation have, of course, been very intimately linked with shifts in the sexual division of labour. In hosiery, as elsewhere, technological change has been closely associated with a policy of introducing female labour, which Humphries in a recent paper has seen as a manifestation of a long-term process of 'female proletarianisation' (Humphries 1983). Although the term 'female substitution' has been used for this tendency, it is important to note that women in such cases rarely perform exactly the same tasks, under the same conditions, as the men formerly performed: inherent in this 'feminisation' process is the *transformation* of jobs, sometimes involving deliberate redesign of tasks and machinery or creation of new forms of work organisation to accommodate the use of women.[1] 'Degradation', then, quite frequently involves an attempted switch to female labour power. However, in hosiery, as elsewhere, feminisation has been fiercely resisted by male trade unionists, seeking to defend their jobs, living standards, and long-established 'trade customs'. Over time their resistance has been successful enough to ensure that in 1984 'women's jobs' and 'men's jobs' are more strongly demarcated than ever.

In a recent article Walby (1983) has claimed that such exclusionary practices by male workers demonstrate a contradiction between the demands of capital and of patriarchal authority, thus challenging the argument of Hartmann (1976) and others, that job segregation should be seen as the result of an interaction between capitalist and patriarchal interests. Thus, at a certain point, Walby claims, the erosion of male dominance becomes too much for male workers to tolerate, threatening both their status as major wage-earners and their domestic comfort, so that a wave of female substitution is likely to be followed by an exclusionary backlash. Although this push-pull phenomenon fits rather well in the hosiery example, as I shall hope to show, I believe it is a mistake to view patriarchy and capitalism as analytically separate systems with different 'system needs'. As Barrett (1980) argues, capitalist production has evolved within the context of a specific form of sex-gender system (patriarchy) and vice versa: the two have thus combined together in a complex and often contradictory unity, which manifests itself, for example, in the curiously inconsistent set of attitudes held by men about women as workers, both in the nineteenth century and today. The development of the capitalist labour process, therefore, must be seen as inextricably linked with the construction of sex-typed jobs. The choice of contextual strategy, too will be heavily influenced by the sex-composition of the workforce, and although I shall not be able to expand on this point as fully as I should like, I hope to show that the presence of women in large numbers in the industry has helped to promote a strong paternalist tradition which, combined with the piece-rate system, has enabled employers over time to get high levels of productivity from their female workers with little resistance.

Hosiery production: the domestic system

The domestic system in hosiery had two special features which made it particularly exploitative of the workforce. First, since the stocking frame was not invented until 1589, the industry was not covered by the

1563 statute on the restriction of apprenticeship. Although the 'Worshipful Company of Framework Knitters' was granted a Charter in 1664, this body was highly ineffective, and the knitters never managed to achieve any degree of monopolistic control. From the beginning, then, the industry was seized upon by capitalist entrepreneurs. Second, these entrepreneurs controlled not only raw materials and markets but also the machinery which they hired out to the stockingers: their profits were, thus, not solely from production but also from the frame rent they charged. Consequently it paid them to spread work out thinly over a large number of frames, since rents were paid whether or not the workpeople were fully employed, or indeed working at all. In these circumstances there was an incentive to use female or boy labour, since output would be reduced but the full frame rent would be paid.

From the beginning of the nineteenth century, then, there are accounts of women engaged in what was primarily viewed as 'men's work', operating the frames, although the more traditional household division of labour was still the norm: men worked the frames, wives and daughters did the finishing jobs (seaming and stitching), and boys wound the yarn on to the frames. A second charter of 1745 had forbidden women to work the frame except for widows, who under rule 29 'upon being admitted members, may exercise the trade during their widowhood'. In fact, women other than widows could and did operate the frames, although witnesses to the 1845 Royal Commission on the framework knitters claimed that the numbers were few in the early part of the century, because of the availability of alternative forms of employment. An Anstey villager claimed that in 1810 'women got their bread by spinning and handknitting'. During the Luddite period the men were still fighting this growing tendency, and machines worked by women as well as those worked by 'colts' (unapprenticed boys) were attacked. 'When they found a frame worked by a person who had not served a regular apprenticeship, or by a woman, they discharged them from working and if they promised to do so they stuck a paper on the frame with these words written upon it "Let this frame stand the colts removed"', reported a magistrate (Aspinall 1949:118). The fight against women's employment as knitters *in their own right* (as opposed to as a man's assistant) was from early on a part of the struggle to retain a modicum of craft control.

By 1845, however, considerable numbers of women worked on frames. It was estimated, for example, that 25 per cent of frames in Leicester were operated by women and young people and in villages it might rise to 50 per cent. Individual employers stated that two-thirds of their frames were worked by women. (1845 Royal Commission.) A recent study by Levine using 1851 census data shows that in one village, Shepshed, 22.6 per cent of the stockingers were women (Levine 1977). Employers claimed that they were especially found in branches such as the wrought hose branch, where work was lighter, while men had shifted to the better-paid areas such as gloves. Women were said to achieve around two-thirds of a man's output; but one thing they could not do was maintain the machine or alter it to perform different operations, which was an integral part of the stockinger's craft: 'Every man is familiar with his own machine and can take it to pieces to repair it or alter it. He is clever at expedients and schemes many contrivances.' (Gent 1893:5).

Their exclusion from technical knowledge and knowhow significantly prevented women from being able to substitute completely for men. Where groups of women were employed together in a workshop a male overlooker would have to be responsible for machine maintenance. This presumably helped to confirm the idea of women as *subsidiary* to men, and in most instances their subsidiary role was clear. Most would still be working at home with their husbands, sometimes knitting, sometimes seaming. Their work was firmly embedded in the context of a collective family endeavour, in which the earnings potential of every family member could be realised as fully as possible (see discussion in Anderson 1980)[2] Women, obviously, had to combine their work with household responsibilities, and seaming was highly compatible with domestic duties. As John Cooper told the 1863 Children's Employment Commission, 'It fills up the intervals of household work' (p. 290).

Children were taught to sew as young as $2\frac{1}{2}$ or 3, and sent out to work from 5 or 6. Girls might be sent to a neighbour to 'nuss and seam', to 'seaming school' where they might pick up a little reading while donating free labour to the schoolmistress, or to labour in teams under 'driving mistresses'. The burden of the family enterprise weighed particularly heavily on the women and children, especially in view of the men's habit of 'shacking' on Monday, and often on Tuesday too, which meant that at the end of the week to get the quota done in time the women and children habitually had to sit up sewing into the small hours. One witness to the 1863 Commission spoke of sitting up all night after working all day in the factory, another of working straight through 48 hours until she 'was exhausted'.

This division not just of labour but of effort within the family was little resisted by the women who seemed to bear it with a stoical resignation. 'It's very hard work, sir, but there's a many has to do it', said Sarah Mabe in 1863 (1863 Children's Employment Commission: 284). The child labour which horrified the middleclass observers was also seen as normal. As the Leicester sisterhood of spinners had said of spinning in their 1788 petition, domestic industry which provided employment for the 'children of the poor' was beneficial not only in increasing the family budget, but also in habituating children to 'habits of industry at an early age'. Nearly 100 years later Mrs Fray of the Seamers' Union expressed the same idea: 'If they have one that is old enough, of course it is a mother's duty to teach her to work as early as possible after school hours.' (1876 Commission on Factory and Workshop Acts: 384).

Such attitudes must have been grounded in the stark economic necessity that perpetually confronted the knitting families in the first half of the century. A perpetual surplus of labour (augmented continuously by redundant agricultural workers), periodic trade recessions, and lack of any alternative sources of employment kept the stockingers on the brink of starvation, and under the threat of the hated workhouse. All family members were dragged into the struggle for survival. Levine's study of Shepshed emphasises how important having a family was to a young stockinger: the prospect of making an independent living was possible only if he had a wife and children to perform the subsidiary tasks. The inducement to early marriage and early child bearing was strong. William Jones commented, 'The seaming is most of it done in the house when my wife is well, but she is at this time bad, or else that would be 10½ pence.' (Royal Commission 1845:242). The way in which family initiative, economic viability, male ambitions and romantic emotions were interwoven could not be better expressed than by the ironic ballad, 'The Love of Thomas and Mary' which appeared in the *Hinckley Journal* in 1859.

> 'I'm promised a three legger soon, a nice house I've found and shop. But without you're willing Mary, all this happy plan must stop. For I want you, that is Mary,' – Thomas here began to stutter – 'If I get the legger working, will you come to be my footer.'

In one or two cases the male stockingers echoed the idea, commonly voiced by middle-class commentators, that female employment was destroying the home and eroding traditional female domestic skills. One knitter saw it as a 'detriment to domestic comfort' as well as to the trade. But on the whole women's employment was seen as a fact of life. Male attempts at exclusion must be seen, then, as representing economic more than patriarchal motives, in a context where alternative male employment was virtually non-existent. But the division of labour and of effort in the home, plus the preference to keep women in the subsidiary roles, were clearly also dictated by patriarchy. The whole system of domestic production rested on a recognition of the authority of the head of household. 'We consider every head of a family in our village to be head of his work. We have always been very independent in that respect', said Storah Wise of Anstey (1842 Royal Commission: 180). Thomas Adcock in 1915, looking back to Leicester in the old days, confirmed this view of the paterfamilias: whatever the subservience of a man in other areas, 'as a father of a family he was monarch of all he surveyed. His word was law' (Leicester Co-operative Congress Souvenir 1915:81).

Possibly this view of patriarchal responsibility lies behind the limited involvement of the women in formal trade union activity of this period. This appears curious in view of the extremely strong local tradition of female political involvement. The aforementioned all-female spinners' union, the 'sisterhood' in their 1788 petition explained how the women had been instigators of the recent outbreaks of rioting and machine breaking. 'A certain manufacturer of worsted threatened a sister of ours that he could get all his jersey to spin at the mill ... She having more spirit than discretion stirred up the sisterhood and they stirred up all the men ... to go and destroy the mills erected in and near Leicester.' At that period, as elsewhere, women had also been leaders in food riots.

In the 1779 riot at Nottingham, after the rejection of the first framework knitters' petition, women and boys led the attack on the houses of the 'obnoxious hosiers' (Henson 1831). Another demonstration in 1812 featured 'Lady Ludd' drawn through the streets on a chair. Women were active participants in many demonstrations such as those of unemployed stockingers. Leicester women marched at the head of a column of 2,000 who smashed machinery being taken out of Leicester in 1825: later they took a notably active part in the GNCTU, of which Leicester was a stronghold, forming all-female lodges. Nottingham had a very active Female Political Union, and in 1856 in Leicester there was 'an extraordinary meeting at the Town Hall composed exclusively of women to consider the laws relative to the gentler sex' (Hewitt's Chronology of Leicester). All this is perhaps predictable where women's employment is the norm and they are not so firmly debarred from the 'public sphere'. Yet women members are only recorded in one of the many early attempts at union organisation, the 'Seven Years Union' initiated by a middle-class sympathiser, the Rev Robert Hall in 1819, which was run on the lines of a friendly society; the 1812 petition was prefaced by the declaration 'all of the men in the trade may sign, but none of the women' (Thompson 1963). Rather than purely seeing this as an effect of male sectionalism, I suggest that the answer may be that the male unionist saw himself as not simply representing himself as individual but as the representative of his whole family.[3] Where a clash of male and female interests, though latent, was still not clearly perceived by all the knitters, a man might have been justified in the belief that he was acting for the collectivity, not just for himself; only where numbers were needed on the streets to convince the hosiers of the unity of their employees would there have been seen a need for female participation.

The transition to factory production

As we have seen, in this early period 'women's work' was quite clearly defined although 'men's work' less completely so. The subsidiary role of women in the division of labour was maintained by their subjection to the patriarchal authority of the head of the household. The following period, in which production moved from the cottage to the factory, saw an intensification of the drive to feminisation, posing a greater threat to the 'sanctity' of 'men's jobs'. This led to a growing political rift between the men and the women, as male union activity was more and more concentrated on the issue of keeping the women out. In addition, a new element was added as for the first time the women became directly subjected to a new source of male authority external to the home: supervisors and managers. What independence from the authority of their husbands women might have gained by the expansion of employment opportunities outside the home was offset by the success of the managers in habituating them to male control at work.

Women were involved in factory production from early on. The first experiments at factory organisation had used adult males, and had failed because of their refusal to accept regular hours and discipline. Two brothers explained the problem to the 1845 Commission. 'They would laugh at us and say they did not like being obliged to work and being shut up so that they could not see anything that occurred in the course of the day. They preferred working at a less price at home.' 'They would fill their pipes and jugs and all sorts of things in the factory if they were not constantly looked after.' Thomas Collins, however, who had established a successful factory with 55 rotary machines by 1845, employed mainly girls aged 13–17, and claimed to have turned away streams of applicants. With male outworkers, however, he still had problems: 'They are so insolent and so saucy no one knows how to deal with them; they have no gratitude about them.' (1845 Royal Commission: 70, 211, 215).

As the factory system developed and home knitting became non-competitive, the men were forced out of their resistance, but modernisation also meant that women were pulled into the labour force in large numbers. In 1861 only 31 per cent of hosiery workers were women; by 1901 it was 73.5 per cent. The majority were employed in specifically 'female' jobs in warehouses, seaming, folding, pressing, mending, embroidering, etc. Single women especially worked here, as many of the married women found it easier to continue seaming and stitching at home, while caring for their children. Women were, however, also employed on knitting machines, especially in the villages. The employers preferred to use women both because of their cheapness, and as a way of opposing the union and its defence of established trade customs. In the towns, the union was able to exercise some degree of control, but among the scattered country workers organisation was very low. In the last quarter of the century the union officials estimated that at least one firm a year was moving out to the country. Between 1883–6 15 firms left Nottingham. For example, Pool, Lorrimer, and Tabberer moved their factory to Foleshill after a dispute about women working on machines in Leicester. 'A woman can work the machines by power just as well as a man; of course when we moved them to Foleshill, we put women on the machines and employed men to look over them.' (1892 Commission on Labour: 95) Women were also used by employers, as the Union Minutes record, to force increased working loads on the men, and in attempts to institute a set wages system instead of the piece rates preferred by the unions: in their terminology, which explains their motivation, a shift from working 'on one's own time' to working on 'the employer's time'.

In Nottingham in 1871 there was a general strike over the employment of women on knitting machines. Yet by the early 1890s women in the town were operating most of the circular machines, although rotary machines, especially Cotton's Patents, were almost all worked by men. The Leicester union secretary in 1913 confirmed this when he complained that 'men have nothing left now but Cotton's Patents, and if women are to have them then the men are done'.

The objective of the men in opposing women's work was clearly an economic rather than a domestic one. James Holmes, the Leicester secretary, did complain in 1892 that outworking tended 'to turn the home into anything but a home and has a demoralising influence' (1892 Commission on Labour: 55). But his campaign against the employment of married women was based on the grounds that they were able to work for below subsistence wages, undercutting both men and single women, and thus depressing wages and hampering union attempts to resist price reductions.

In their campaign over Cotton's Patents, men were trying to hang onto their remaining monopoly on the most complex machines, partly to keep up wages, but also to retain jobs for themselves in an industry to which they displayed a curiously stubborn commitment. The former objective was clearly expressed in a letter written to Ramsay MacDonald at the peak of a campaign involving a firm, Stretton's, which had persistently banned the union and used women on Cotton's Patents. When they started working on Government contracts, the union attempted to use the Fair Wages Act against them:

> We have no objection to the employment of women, what we object to is that women are receiving less for the work than men. If Strettons . . . care to put women on the machines in preference to men that is their business, but we claim that they should be compelled to pay the rates of prices for this kind of work. But the War Office states that the women's work is not comparable with that of men, as they receive some help from men in adjusting their machines.

> (Note the continuing problem of women's lack of mechanical knowledge.)

The women, in the meantime, were making their own stands in their own way. Particularly striking is the immense determination they showed to carry on working in whatever conditions. The 1876 Factory Acts Commission reported wide-scale evasion of the Acts in Leicester and Nottingham. One employer, W.H. Walker, who admitted infringing the Acts by employing women in his factory up to 52½ hours per week, explained how he and the School Board had been surprised to discover how many unsupported women with children there were in Leicester; such women wanted to work as many hours as possible, often preferring the informal organisation of small workshops, which fell outside the legislation, despite the lower wages: it is arguable that the Factory Acts were forcing women into low-paid, segregated areas of work.

The fact that the employers had forced women and men into confrontation was reflected in union organisation. The Leicester Union and the Nottingham Rotary Union by the 1880s become aware of the need to organise the women, but had little idea of how to do it efficiently. They voiced the familiar grumbles about the apathy and lack of participation of the women as union members: they were difficult to organise, they joined at crisis points but dropped out, they wouldn't come to meetings. 'It is impossible to get a woman to serve on the executive committee, so accustomed are they to having everything done for them,' said Holmes. His attitude to women is neatly encapsulated in the fact that when two young girls were reported to be working on set wages in one factory, he resolved to go and visit *their father* to get *them* to join the union.

In fact, as is so often the case, the women were often at the centre of industrial disputes, in which they demonstrated considerable militancy and determination. Women, for example, were active in the violent strike in Leicester in 1886, leading the mob in smashing factory windows, and they were the initiators of a long, bitter strike in 1913 in Fleckney Village, finally destroying the paternalist grip of the firm of W.H. Walker against which the union had hopelessly struggled for years.

The men often failed to take account of the very real pressure applied to women by male managers and supervisors. There *are* reports of women who had the courage to strike against such bullying (two for example, in the 1913 union minutes), or to protest against workmates disciplined for petty offences such as singing. But more numerous are the reports from women who had been bullied, victimised and dismissed for involvement with the union. A classic case was the dismissal of two girls aged 19 and 16 from Buchler's: they were sacked for trying to organise their workmates. The other girls had quickly chickened out in face of the employer's threats, and though the union managed to make some fine propaganda from the case, it was some months before the girls found re-employment in another factory.

During this period women did show more initiative in organising to further their own interests. Two all-female unions, the Stitchers' and Seamers' and the Menders' Unions were founded in Leicester, and affiliated to the WTUL, and there was another in Nottingham, and also in Hinckley. The Seamers' Union was the most successful: it had 3,000 members at its peak, but was overdependent on its organisers, Mrs Mason, Mrs Matthews and Mrs Fray who had to tramp miles between isolated villages to reach the scattered homeworkers. After Mrs Mason's death it lost its dynamism and was merged with the men's union. However, by now the men were working more sincerely to organise the women: by 1920 there were 9,000 female members as opposed to 3,000 men, and there was one woman on the Executive Committee.

A certain social unease characterised relations between the two groups. Girls from the Co-op who refused to join the union in 1909 grumbled about 'not being asked properly'. The baffled men had to enlist female support in organising the women, co-opting the fiery Lizzie Willson from the women's boot and shoe union, and borrowing a female organiser for the GFTU (General Federation of Trade Unions) in 1930. They tried to woo the women by combining recruitment meetings with dances (although they did not always find the audience as attentive as they hoped). By the time they appointed their own female organiser in 1934 (not without male resistance) the need for integration was fully appreciated.

In the earlier period, however, women had received little help from the union in coping with the authoritarianism of managers and supervisors. The employers found it relatively easy to intimidate the women, especially in the villages, where jobs were scarce. Some more progressive employers in the towns, however, were concerned to establish good relations with a loyal workforce. Rather than strict supervision, such employers as Corah's and Walker's in Leicester, Hine and Mundella, and Morley's in Nottingham, turned to the techniques of paternalism. The laying on of parties, feasts and carnivals, the provision of libraries, rest-rooms, social clubs, charitable gifts and benefit funds was a clear predecessor of the canteens, sports grounds, pension schemes, hardship funds and medical services that these same firms were providing by the twentieth century. Although the provision was aimed at both sexes, the historical link between paternalist practice and the employment of women has often been noted (see, for example, Nelson 1975 and Joyce 1980). Paternalism is often initiated when the workforce is defined as being in need of care and protection: women, children and young people. Young girls in particular are often viewed as irresponsible children who must be looked after carefully, and this attitude was reflected in the moral panics over factory girls and vice that sprang up in Leicester and Nottingham in the early days of the factories. One old framework knitter refused to let his daughters work in factories as he considered them 'perfect hellholes as to morals', and suggested, like others, that the low wages forced girls into prostitution. The behaviour of benevolent father-figures like Samuel Morley and the Corah family must have done much to allay such anxieties in parents, and by the twentieth century, 'Get them into Corah's and they'll have a job for life' was received parental lore in Leicester. Such factories became bastions of respectability.

In playing strongly on family imagery (John Cooper told the assembled workforce at the opening of Corah's famous St Margaret's Works that he looked on the workpeople as brothers and sisters) paternalism resonates specifically with women's own life experience and interests (Webb 1948:48). Employers who continually stressed the continuity of family involvement in the family enterprise, and who encouraged the workers to recruit their sons and daughters into the firm with them, emphasised that their priorities were not dissimilar to those of their workpeople. Older women were particularly likely to respond to these, and such women often formed the stable and loyal core of a workforce. There is a strong theme in the history of the industry of women supporting and praising benevolent employers and expressing gratitude for service and favours. An early example was the letter sent to Samuel Morley when he lost his Parliamentary seat on a charge of election malpractice, along with a Bible and handworked bookmarks:

> The females in your employ would ask your acceptance of this present as a
> token of their great esteem. We deeply sympathise with you in the trouble,
> anxiety and disappointment it has been yours to endure. To show the great
> love and respect we feel towards you, we present you with a copy of the Holy
> Scriptures.
>
> (Hodder 1887:169)

It seems obvious that such employees, if Morley had wished it, would
easily have been dissuaded from joining a union! Paternalism was a
most effective way of persuading women to work their utmost for a
company.[4]

Modernisation

Increased prosperity and widened opportunities outside the home
improved women's position in the latter part of the century, and
observers noted that women now had a heightened sense of self-respect,
more leisure, better health and greater independence from their
menfolk. They were still, however, subject to male authority in their
working lives as well as in the home, at the same time as their increasing
employment threatened to destroy any continuing notion of 'men's
work' and thus to erode the dignity and status of the male workers
(some of whom, of course, would have been their husbands), although
the growth of the boot and shoe and elastic web industries was
producing a welcome diversification in Leicester industry.

The more pacificatory role that the union was beginning to adopt
towards women is perhaps demonstrated in the fact that substitution
processes in the First World War were harmoniously carried out. Men's
employment decreased by 23.5 per cent between July 1914 and
November 1918 and women's increased by 13 per cent in the same
period. Agreements had been made on the usual lines between
employers and unions. Women were to be trained by men at special
rates, once trained were to receive men's rates, and were to be
withdrawn at the end of the war. Women were taken on to all knitting
machines, and into another male preserve, countering and trimming.
The unions seem to have been surprisingly unworried by these
developments, partly perhaps because of the excitement and optimism
generated by the boom in membership at this time. The only slight hitch
was at the end of the War when it was reported that many Leicester
women were reluctant to leave their jobs, although the union claimed that
girls on the heavier machines were relieved to be off them. In all events, by
April 1919, 3,000 of the lost male jobs had been regained and everyone,
according to the union secretary, had been re-accommodated in 'some
department or other'.

But the union optimism was soon lost as membership fell off, and the employers, faced with recession, returned to their policy of seeking cheap female labour. For example, there was a prolonged struggle at a Bedworth factory where the management took on women as counterers and trimmers, and compelled the women to leave the union by telling them if they were members the union would force them to give up their job. The union managed finally to reassure them and cajoled them into rejoining, thus averting a strike by the men: the price management paid was an agreement that any new trimmers should be men.

The Second World War followed the pattern of the first, but things altered afterwards. Once again the unions increased their strength, and had the sense to consolidate that strength by amalgamating. The local unions merged to form the National Union of Hosiery Workers in 1945. It started out full of militant self-confidence, demanding among other things that the new national agreement should include the clause, 'male persons only should operate the knitting machines'. But this clause disappeared during the fierce and long-drawn-out hostilities that followed over the more central demands for a minimum wage and an end to night work.

However, things had changed in the trade. It was no longer going to be easy for employers to use women to undercut wages, and there was now a huge labour shortage in the industry. Between 1939 and 1945, 10,418 women left the industry, large numbers entering engineering. Life in engineering and munitions factories seemed to them more relaxed and agreeable, claimed the Leicester Corporation, than the 'concentrated' and 'stressful' conditions of hosiery production, with its fevered pace. Female employment in hosiery declined 42 per cent (*Leicester Corporation Handbook* 1946). According to Hinckley District Union, Leicester employers exacerbated this problem by employing women in 'jobs that are more suitable for men, because in the past female labour was cheaper than men could compete with' (*Hinckley Times*, 13 December 1946).

Employers sought labour elsewhere: Corah's started several branches outside Leicester, and other firms, too, moved to the North or to East Anglia, seeking 'green' (and of course cheaper) labour that was now unavailable in Leicester. Others tried to attract local women back into the industry: Corah's, for example, started up a training school.

The labour shortage may have been one factor leading to the abandonment of the employers' old policy. There are occasional references in the records of the later 1940s and 1950s to the issue of substitution (there was a long and bitter defence of countering as an all-male job throughout the 1950s, for example) but these were not widespread enough to threaten the men in the same way. By the 1970s a stable job-segmented structure had emerged. This may also be seen as a result of the vastly improved relationship between the union and the employers, mediated through the continuingly active Joint Industrial Council. In the 1950s and 1960s both sides boasted of industrial peace and of their own moderation and good sense: a 'spirit of co-operation' was agreed to have replaced the hostility of the past. This may have been because employers did not wish to antagonise the union negotiators over the knitting jobs which now represented only a small core of the total jobs in the industry, as knitting technology increased productivity dramatically. In the sock industry of today, for example, one man tends 18 machines where once he operated one.

In hosiery factories today, in Leicester at least, men are the knitters and women do the making up. Of six firms interviewed in 1983 only one employed female knitters. This firm was, significantly, the only one on a single-shift system. Arguably the Factory Acts have been as significant as union negotiations in pushing women from the knitting job. At one firm only were males, both white and Asian, to be found operating sewing machines, and the managing director himself seemed slightly surprised that men would undertake such a 'cissy job'. Countering has now become a mixed job, although there are tendencies towards segregation in any firm or department. At firm C, for example, men did countering in underwear, girls in socks.

The division of labour clearly favours men. Knitters' wages are reasonably high, ranging between £100–£200 per week at the six firms visited, and averaging around £150. Women's rates are extremely variable, owing to the range of jobs and piece-rates, but machinists at the six firms were said to earn between £50 and £100. The average is probably around £65, but considerably lower wages may be earned in the small, less reputable factories, and of course, by outworkers. The union estimates that 60 per cent of women earn less than £75 per week, 8 per cent less than £50. (*NUHKW Journal*, August 1983).

As well as male financial interests and government legislation, employer attitudes act to maintain segregation. All six managers interviewed were of the opinion that knitting is a 'suitable' job for men, sewing for women. Trimming, said Manager B, 'is a rough, tough, hard work, unsuitable for women'. This attitude appears to rest partly on ideas of attributes of jobs (strength and dexterity), partly on tradition ('these things tend to grow up in firms and also in families,' said Manager D) and also there is some feeling that work group relations are more satisfactory when segregated. 'If I were a woman, I'd want to be in a garment factory with lots of other women,' said the manager of Firm F, a fabric factory. It is clear that most managers felt uneasy about working with women themselves, despite an awareness of new attitudes on sex discrimination. 'You can't have a logical argument with a woman', said the youngest of the six.

The managers' comments mirror expectations and attitudes about men's and women's work found generally in Leicester, and which are not particularly challenged even by the militant women in the union, who seek merely to improve the rewards and status of women's work within the segmented structure. 'I do not want to be disrespectful to our male members when we speak of equal pay for work of equal value, but there are highly skilled jobs performed by our female members which men cannot do,' said Ms Inglis at the 1983 Annual conference.[5]

Possibilities of change, however, cannot be ignored as advanced technology makes a belated appearance in the industry. Electronic cutting machinery has now been followed by electronically-controlled knitting machines. At £30,000 a piece, these are still too expensive an investment for many small firms, but are making their appearance in the large firms. The manager of Firm B, a subsidiary of Courtauld's, made it clear that knitting is now a job which requires no mechanical or technical knowledge, and that it could be done by women were it not for the shift system: while Manager A, the employer of the male machinists, claimed that the use of the new machines could be picked up quickly by people of 30-plus, formerly too old to learn the skills. He believed that in future he would probably be using more unskilled (cheaper) labour, and more older women (always preferred by managers to young girls who are seen as shiftless, undisciplined, lazy and prone to leave). Although this has not happened yet, pressure to cut labour costs in a highly competitive and extremely unstable industry may well push employers into another attempt at feminisation, although factory legislation, an institutionalised form of discrimination, remains a crucial barrier.

As stated above, it seems unlikely that a challenge to segregation will come from within the unions. However, despite the fact that women are still as under-represented as ever in the union hierarchy (one woman full-time official out of 33), there are signs of a great awareness of women's rights and needs. The greater involvement of young women with militant ideas in the union has led to a growing interest in 'women's issues'. At the 1982 conference there was for the first time a resolution for a minimum flat rate increase, as opposed to a percentage increase, and at both the 1982 and 1983 conferences protests were made about the four-fifth payment rules, whereby women working temporarily on a new job are paid four-fifths average earnings. In 1983 a resolution was passed demanding improved equal pay legislation, and calling on the NEC to produce positive policies to ensure the full involvement of the union's female membership at all levels. However, the activist women themselves opposed a resolution calling for a Women's Advisory

Committee; 'I do not think we are denied a voice at Conference, and if we are then it is the women's fault,' said one woman, and another commented on her visit to the TUC Women's Conference. 'If the women who attended were active in the TUC itself, by God, the TUC would have a shock. It really would. It would rock on its foundations. That is where they should be active, not in a separate TUC. It divides us.' These arguments are, of course, long-standing ones in the feminist debate over separate organisations, but their use seems to indicate that for these female activists class solidarity is still a more important objective than female solidarity.

If women are beginning to fight back in the union, there is less sign of change on the front of male authority at work. Edwards (1979) argues that where women or other 'secondary' groups of labour comprise the majority of the workforce, there is a likelihood that forms of 'direct control' will still be used, and this seems to fit the hosiery case. As Edwards and Scullion (1982) point out in their study of a hosiery firm, management control is tight, with firm supervision, and a very fast pace of work. Piece-rates, highly set, are perhaps the most important mechanism of control in the industry (see Brown 1964 for a similar view). The older women are self-motivated to work as hard as they can to achieve high wages, and there is not much evidence of high levels of pace-setting and output restriction. As managers admit, there remains a discipline problem, especially with young women, which they seek to control by efficient supervision. If women still resist, it seems it is often individually rather than collectively (see also Collinson and Knights, this volume). Turnover rates are very high, especially among young girls, and this remains the major management problem in many firms. (See Edwards and Scullion op. cit.).

While restrictive strategies of strict supervision and tight piece-rates are used to keep effort levels high, most firms seek to solve the problem of turnover by building up a stable core of long-serving married women, and here a pacificatory strategy is needed; this frequently takes the form of a modified paternalism. Central to this are arrangements for flexible hours, permitting the women to tie their work in with family requirements. Although this may cause managers some problems over planning and co-ordination of production, it is presumably validated by the gratitude it invokes. An employer who makes these concessions is seen as a 'good boss', and women may develop a clear sense of personal loyalty to him and his firm. During the worst period of the recession in Leicester recently, at least three cases are on record of women workers agreeing to wage cuts to help such 'good bosses' (*Leicester Trader* 12 March 1980, *Financial Times* 18 August 1980). Since the family remains the central life interest of these women (see

Brown 1964), concessions to family requirements, plus the continued use of family imagery, seem to work very effectively in securing commitment to the job, especially as the family firm tradition, and that of family recruitment, are still strong in the industry.[6] The interests of employers and employees, it is stressed, are one and the same: family loyalties, not class loyalties are the crucial ones.

Conclusion
This paper has been an attempt to show how, in an analysis of a specific case, some general or 'global' theory of labour process development, as well as consideration of contingent or 'local' strategic choices, can be helpful. But I hope I have also demonstrated how processes of degradation and resegmentation are often intricately linked with the development of sex-typed jobs within a patriarchal division of labour.

Labour should *not* be taken as a genderless category. Female labour is both viewed differently and used differently by employers and managers. Different control strategies, both restrictive and pacificatory, are deemed appropriate for use with male and female labour, different patterns of hierarchical and authority relations are developed, and technology is deployed differently. All these considerations, as well as the 'cheapness' of female labour power (see Beechey 1977), lie behind the process of feminisation which is so often part of technological development.

In light of this, it seems that discussion of gender must be central in further contributions to the labour process 'debate'. In particular, two issues which I have not been able to investigate fully here appear of crucial relevance: first, the social construction of skill as a male monopoly, and the consequent downgrading of the skills, techniques and knowledge involved in women's work, and second, the related question of the differentiated relationship of men and women to machinery and to scientific and technical knowledge. The salience of these issues has been demonstrated in the exciting work of Cynthia Cockburn (1983, 1984) in looking at contemporary technological advances. Historical research, too, must focus on these issues, including, it is to be hoped, work carried out by male researchers. The development of the capitalist labour process cannot be satisfactorily analysed without consideration of the development of sex-typed jobs: the social division of labour is also a sexual one.

Acknowledgements
I would like to thank Warwick University Sociology Department for encouraging comments on an earlier version of this paper, and Sonia

Liff for her perceptive criticisms of the version presented at Aston, some of which have been incorporated into this final draft.

Notes

1. For example, in hosiery the employment of women on steam-powered machines involved the creation of a new work hierarchy: male overseers were employed for machine maintenance and technological adjustments. See p. 62.
2. See Bradley (1984) for elaboration of the significance of the 'family project'.
3. See Alexander (1984) for a similar analysis. Alexander claims that male heads of household, speaking *on behalf* of the community as a whole, constituted the 'political subject' of the 1830s and 1840s.
4. See Westwood (1984) for a fascinating account of the continuation of paternalist practice and of the paternalist ethos in a contemporary hosiery factory.
5. It is clear that, in this industry, women's jobs have always been classified as 'semi-skilled' merely because they are *women's* jobs.
6. See Chapter 6 in this volume by Grieco and Whipp for confirmation that it is not in the hosiery industry alone that the interpolation of family relations into work is a key feature.

References

Alexander, S. (1984), 'Women Class and Sexual Difference,' *History Workshop Journal*, 17, 125–56.

Anderson, M. (1980), *Approaches to the history of the Western family*, London: Macmillan.

Aspinall, A. (1949), *The early English trade unions*, London: Batchworth p. 118.

Barrett, M. (1980), *Women's oppression today*, London: Verso.

Beechey, V. (1977), 'Some notes on female wage labour in capitalist production', *Capital and Class*, 1, 45–67.

Bradley, H. (1983), 'From butties to robots: controlling the labour process', *Economy and Society*, 12, (4), 499–519.

Bradley, H. (1984), 'Gender, authority and the division of labour in the workplace', unpublished paper presented to BSA Annual Conference.

Braverman, H. (1974), *Labor and monopoly capital*, New York: Monthly Review Press.

Brown, R., Kirby, J. and Taylor K. (1964), 'The employment of married women and the supervisory role', *British Journal of Industrial Relations*, 2 (1), 23–41.

Cockburn, C. (1983), *Brothers: Male Dominance and Technological Change*, London: Pluto.

Cockburn, C. (1984), 'Women and technology: opportunity is not enough', unpublished paper presented to BSA Annual Conference.

Cressey P. and MacInnes J. (1980), 'Voting for Ford: industrial democracy and the control of labour,' *Capital and Class*, 2, 5–35.

Edwards, P. and Scullion, H. (1982), *The Social Organisation of Industrial Conflict*, Cambridge: Cambridge University Press.

Edwards, R. (1979), *The contested terrain*, London: Heinemann.

Gent, T. (1893), *Robert Finch*, London: Simpkin, Marshall, Hamilton, Kent & Co., p. 5.

Hartmann, H. (1976), 'Capitalism, patriarchy and job segregation by sex', *Signs*, 1 (3), 137–68.

Henson, G. (1831), *History of the framework knitters*, reprinted Newton Abbott: David and Charles.

Hewitt (1863), *Chronology of Leicester*, Leicester: Hewitts.

Hodder, E. (1887), *Life of Samuel Morley*, London: Hodder and Stoughton.

Humphries, J. (1983), 'The "emancipation" of women in the 1970s and 1980s', *Capital and Class*, **20**, 6–28.

Joyce, P. (1980), *Work, society and politics*, London: Methuen.

Levine, D. (1977), *Family formation in an age of nascent capitalism*, New York: Academic Press.

Nelson, D. (1975), *Managers and workers*, Madison: University of Wisconsin Press.

Thompson, E. (1963), *The making of the English working class*, London: Gollancz.

Walby, S. (1983), 'Women's unemployment, patriarchy and capitalism', *Socialist Economic Review*, 99–114.

Webb, C. (1948), *Corahs of Leicester*, Leicester: Corahs.

Westwood, S. (1984), *All day, every day*, London: Pluto.

Wright, E. (1978), Race, class and income inequality, *American Journal of Sociology*, **83** (6), 1368–97.

Parliamentary Reports

Report of the Commission on the Condition of the Framework-knitters 1845, xv.

Report of the Commission on the Employment of Children 1863, xviii.

Royal Commission on Trade Unions 3rd report 1867–8, xxxix.

Report of the Commission on the Factory and Workshop Acts 1876, xxx.

Report of the Commission on Labour 1892, xxxvi.

4 Technical Change and Occupational Sex-typing

Sonia Liff

This paper is concerned with the impact of technical change on occupational sex-typing. More specifically, it asks under what conditions could we expect the sex-typing of jobs to break down? Current labour process theory and debates *cannot* be said to have ignored either technical change or women workers. However, they have addressed these issues in a very specific way which has precluded examination of the questions raised here. The paper proceeds in four parts. First, it briefly outlines the way technical change and women workers have been considered within labour process work and the limitations of this. Second, it examines the rudimentary understanding of occupational sex-typing within labour process theory and some of the evidence which makes such an explanation problematic. Third, the paper turns to another major body of theory – reserve army of labour theories – which have often been invoked to interpret these issues. In examining the limitations of this approach the paper moves on, fourth, to point to developments which need to take place within labour process debates.

Labour process theory and studies have taken the 'de-skilling' of craft workers as the central issue in their analyses of technical change. They have been concerned to define de-skilling, its role within the process of capitalist accumulation and the extent and success of craft unions' opposition to the process. While these are clearly very important issues there has been a tendency to ignore the many other ways in which technical change can affect the labour process. I have discussed these in detail elsewhere (Blackburn, Green and Liff 1982) and so will only point to a few examples here. These include automating all or part of the labour process; altering the product in ways that transform the production process (for example, the switch from electro-mechanical to electronic components in many goods); the use of electronic work monitoring to reduce the porosity of the working day; the greater use of an international division of labour facilitated by developments in communications and transportation technologies; and of course the role played by technical change in the development of new products.

Lack of attention to these wider issues has contributed to the problems labour process work has had in understanding the political struggles around technical change. Thinking about the de-skilling of craft workers leads to a focus on a certain type of struggle between capital and labour at the point of production. Yet the broader forms of technical change described above often lead to far more radical restructuring of employment. Workers in one firm may be made unemployed while at the same time employment is created in another firm often in a different geographical region, another country or even in a different industrial sector. Similarly a loss of employment opportunities for craft and unskilled workers may be accompanied by new opportunities for those with technical skills.

These aspects of technical change make it clear that we are not talking solely about a restructuring of capital-labour relationships but also about changes within capital and within labour. This should further alert us to the ways in which conflicting interests over the outcome of technical change are likely to emerge within the workforce. This has recently been apparent in a number of areas, most obviously among print workers. Yet this is nothing new. Craft workers, who have tended to be seen as the defenders of working-class interests in struggles over technical change, derive their strength in no small part from their past exclusionary practices. Their gains have often been made at the expense of less skilled or less well-organised sections of the workforce.

This aspect is also one that those labour process writers interested in women workers have been reluctant to take up. While there are increasing numbers of studies of women workers, including ones which analyse technical change, few studies have attempted an analysis of the technical division of labour sensitive to gender. By this I mean that they have tended not to look at the relationships between men and women in the workplace and the way this relates to the construction of jobs and the sex-typing of occupations.

Labour process analyses of the effects of technical change on men and women workers therefore retain many contradictory aspects. Marx's writings on the development of the capitalist labour process stressed the role of technical change in increasing the division of labour in a way that, he believed, would lead to an increasing homogenisation of the labour force. One feature of this was the anticipated absorption of women into the workforce. Thus technical change 'de-skilling' and the substitution of female for male workers have become very closely associated tendencies in labour process debates, particularly within analyses of nineteenth-century changes.

Such an approach seems to suggest that technical change which has very damaging effects on male workers is a good thing for women since it creates de-skilled jobs which they can take up. This analysis – presumably based on the assumption that women are better off in this type of job than in the home – fails to address the reasons for women's original and continued exclusion from the 'better' jobs in the labour market.

The revival of labour process analyses initiated by Braverman has continued these trends. It has also considered longer-term changes whereby some occupations have been 'feminised' – that is they have changed from being sex-typed as 'men's jobs' to being sex-typed as 'women's jobs'. The relationship between the theoretically predicted trend – homogenisation, and the observed trend – feminisation, is never explicitly dealt with in mainstream labour process literature. If pressed, however, most non-feminist theorists revert to a dual labour market explanation. This sees women workers as having a range of distinct and desirable characteristics – most notably cheapness – and relegates any explanation of this to their domestic position.

The long-term and broad nature of these trends do not make them amenable to the short-term, factory-level studies that have dominated empirical work within a labour process perspective. This may in part explain why writers have noted widespread technical change throughout the economy but have generally failed to ask why some jobs have been retained by men and others have been opened up to women. Yet surely the theoretical perspective should at least make us surprised that so few of the contemporary studies of de-skilling in male jobs contain any reference to the likelihood of these jobs being opened up to women.

We are left with a body of theory which is highly ambiguous in its treatment of the sexual division of labour. Its analysis would suggest that occupational sex-typing is closely related to the nature of the work and that periods of technical change, by altering the work, would prove highly destabilising for such definitions. Yet the empirical data is very unconvincing on this point. It therefore becomes necessary to look to different sources of information and types of explanation.

Anyone who has visited a range of workplaces can testify to the pervasiveness of occupational sex-typing. Yet data which demonstrates this or allows one to analyse changes is not readily available. The major source of occupational data appears in the census. Hakim (1978, 1981) has made the most concerted effort to examine job segregation from this data. She uses Census data from 1901 to 1971 and supplements this with data from the Labour Force Survey for 1973, 1975, 1977 and 1979. She is not primarily concerned with changes within particular occupations but rather with changes in the over or under-representation of women in 'female' and 'male' occupations. Such occupations are defined as those where the proportion of workers of each sex is different from that expected from their overall proportion in the workforce.

Hakim uses the data to produce indices of both horizontal and vertical segregation. Horizontal segregation refers to a situation where men and women are most commonly working in different types of occupation, and is the main focus of this paper. Vertical segregation refers to men typically working in higher grade occupations than women. There are internal problems with the data relating to changes in the basis of classification and to different forms of collection of the two data sources. There are also broader problems relating to their adequacy as measures of occupational segregation. The classification involves putting together a range of jobs to produce occupational groups. These often involve aggregating jobs which are sex-typed differently. Thus these measures tend to underestimate the extent of segregation which would be seen with more detailed analyses.

Nevertheless the data produces some interesting results. The main finding is a remarkable degree of stability in occupational segregation. The 1978 article, which deals only with the Census data, uses a variety of measures to explore horizontal segregation. She first looks at the percentage of men and women working in occupations where they are disproportionately represented to varying degrees: This shows that the ratio of the percentage of men in occupations which had at least 90 per cent male workers to the percentage of women in equivalent occupations has increased between 1901 and 1971. Hakim concludes that 'male inroads into women's preserves have not been counter-balanced by women's entry into typically male spheres of work' (p. 1255).

There are many reasons for being slightly wary about this conclusion. It may well tell us as much about occupational classifications as it does about occupational segregation. For example the figures show that since 1921 an average of 24 per cent of men have worked in occupations which were 100 per cent male. The equivalent figure for women workers is 0.1 per cent. This does not accord with anything we know about the structure of the workforce. One likely reason for this is to be found in the fact that disproportionately female occupations account for only around 25 per cent of all occupations throughout the century despite changes in occupational classification. This means that the occupations in which women are concentrated are much less finely defined than those in which men are concentrated. Thus evidence for the more extreme aspects of occupational segregation is more likely to be missing in female occupations.

The main measure used in the article is also problematic. This is a measure of the under or over-representation of women in occupational groups relative to the proportion that would be expected from their degree of participation in the labour force overall. This shows that in 1901 the ratio of the observed percentage of women to the expected in disporportionately female occupations was 2.7. In 1971 the equivalent ratio was 2·0. A similar calculation for women in disproportionately male occupations shows the ratio to have changed from 0·18 in 1901 to 0·27 in 1971. These figures suggest again that women's under-representation in 'male jobs' is far more marked than men's under-representation in 'female jobs'. It also suggests that the situation has been gradually improving over the century. However this finding is not standardised for women's increasing participation rates over the period and this in itself may account for much of the change.

Hakim's 1981 paper which uses a different source of data is more optimistic in tone, although it is difficult to find the basis for this in the material presented. The ratios in 1979 show a slight improvement for women in disproportionately female occupations (down to 1·95) and a slight worsening of the position in dispropotionately male occupations (down to 0·24). The figures vary considerably over the period showing significant improvements up to 1977 – which she attributes to equality
*legislation; before a reverse – which she attributes largely to the effects of recession.

Hakim notes that studies at company level show much higher degrees of occupational segregation (particularly for vertical segregation not specifically referred to above) than do her national figures, (e.g. Hunt 1975; McIntosh 1980 and we might add any labour process study such as Cavendish 1982). But she argues against the usefulness of such studies on the grounds that 'monitoring changes in job segregation is more reliable at the national level than at company level, where the pattern of change might be almost invisible' (p. 527). This conclusion seems rather perverse in view of the qualifications she makes earlier about aggregated data.

This data should make us doubt the validity of a simple reading of labour process theory's analysis of the effects of technical change on occupational sex-typing. However it is not very helpful in suggesting what to put in its place. While reasons are suggested for the recent changes there is little attempt to situate the longer-term changes within any broader analysis. In addition the aggregated nature of the data means we get no sense of which particular jobs are showing a significant degree of change. This makes it difficult to assess the relative importance of general trends such as women's rising participation rates and the entry of a few women into previously totally segregated occupations as against more radical changes such as those brought about by technical change.

There is another theoretical approach which has been relevant to the analysis of job segregation by sex. This is an approach derived from Marx's notion of a latent reserve army of labour. Analyses based on this approach do not overcome problems mentioned above relating to the level of aggregation. Nevertheless they do give a theoretically informed account of the type of broad labour market trends discussed above. As such they are a useful addition to the debate.

Marx used the example of agricultural workers in the nineteenth century to show the ways in which a group who were under-employed and had some independent form of subsistence could become an important source of labour; being easily drawn in or repelled from wage labour at a relatively low cost to capital. The existence of a reserve source of labour has the additional advantage of holding down wage levels of those in employment. A number of feminists have adopted this approach as a way of describing the position of, at least married, women workers.

In this vein, Beechey (1977) highlights two characteristics of married women which may currently make them a preferred reserve of labour:

(i) married women comprise a section of the working class which is not predominantly dependent upon its own wage for the costs of production and reproduction of labour power;

(ii) married women are a section of the working class which is not heavily dependent upon the welfare state, which refuses to recognise married women as individuals in their own right (e.g. denying them social security benefits if married or cohabiting). (p. 57)

The consequences of being a labour reserve are taken to be that a group will be preferentially drawn into and expelled from the labour force as demand changes. To fulfil this function a group needs to be readily available and dispensible and be competitive with the 'core' labour force.

There have been a number of wide-ranging critiques of the use of reserve army theory totally to characterise women's employment position and Beechey (1983), herself has recently expressed doubts as to its usefulness. Here I want to concentrate much more narrowly on those problems and developments within this theoretical approach which relate to occupational segregation.

The key question from this perspective is the extent to which women have been real competitors for men's jobs. Unless one can demonstrate the possibility of substitution of women for men and men for women then it is difficult to see in what sense women can be said to be functioning as a reserve. Two aspects of the contemporary British situation make the competitive criterion problematic.

The first aspect refers to macro-level changes. While it is undeniable that large numbers of women entered the labour force in the post-war boom the overwhelming majority went into the service industry or into service occupations within other sectors. That is they entered new or expanding areas of the economy rather than as substitutes for men in traditional jobs. At this level it is also difficult to find evidence of women's preferential expulsion from employment in periods of recession. The statistical arguments will be reviewed below but the fact that women's employment continued to grow in the 1970s, while male employment fell, suggests that the argument will not hold at this macro-level.

The second aspect refers to the lack of more detailed examples of substitution. Some early discussions used examples drawn from the wartime utilisation of female labour in traditionally male jobs to argue that substitution of women for men could occur (e.g. Beechey 1978). However this is now generally accepted as a very exceptional situation. Other studies of the 1930s depression (e.g. Milkman 1976) have found no evidence for the substitution of men for women. Similarly in the current recession, while there may be political calls for married women to return to the home to make jobs available to men, there is little evidence of men queueing up for women's low-paid, often part-time, jobs.

There have been a number of responses to these problems – none of which have been to reject the usefulness of the notion of women as a reserve army of labour! Much of the literature has side-stepped the issue trying instead to empirically demonstrate the greater insecurity of women's employment *vis-à-vis* men's. Thus it is argued (e.g. Connelly 1978) that the existence of low-paid women in insecure jobs can act indirectly to hold down wage levels and impose labour discipline on workers by the possibility of substitution at a group level even though occupational segregation prevents individual women entering 'male' jobs.

Attempts to demonstrate the volatility of women's employment have become statistically complex. In an early attempt to test empirically the hypothesis, Bruegel (1979) looked at different possible interpretations for the changes that occurred in Britain between 1974–8. She argues that at a macro-level the hypothesis could 'be taken to imply that women's employment opportunities, taken as a whole, deteriorate relative to men's in times of recession' (p. 16). At this level the hypothesis is false since this period saw an increase in female employment of 145,000 jobs while numbers of men at work fell by

361,000. Arguing that this result derives from women's more favoured position within service sector employment, Bruegel moves to a more detailed hypothesis. This states that 'any individual woman is more susceptible to redundancy and unemployment than a man in an equivalent situation would be' (p. 16).

The reason for taking this hypothesis is clear. Women's industrial concentration within the services, at a time when these industries were not experiencing the decline of manufacturing, is seen as distorting the overall position. Hence the attempt to look at men and women in similar circumstances. The way the hypothesis is tested by Bruegel is nevertheless confused by her lack of attention to occupational segregation. She considers this hypothesis to be substantiated because 'in every industry employing a substantial number of women and where employment declined between 1974 and 1977, the rate of employment decline was greater for women than for men' (p. 16). A note relating to this analysis highlights a difficulty with the approach:

> Unfortunately, data on occupational groups are not available on an annual basis. Such information would have been very helpful for the analysis because the jobs (occupations) women do within an industry tend to be very different from those of men. In theory, the higher rate of job loss for women within each industry could be due to the particular vulnerability of the jobs that women do, rather than the vulnerability of women in any particular area of work. (p. 22 note 15)

She goes on to say that analysis of more detailed occupational data available for the electrical engineering industry suggests that this is not the case. Some of the difficulties with occupational statistics have already been discussed. What is important to note here is that while all later writers have followed Bruegel in analysing employment by industry (as the only realistic option given the statistical data) they have argued that it is precisely the jobs women do which explains their vulnerability. This is not to abandon any notion of the specificity of women in the labour market since it is still necessary to explain how women come to be doing these jobs. The argument becomes that women function as a reserve by undertaking the least secure jobs available in any sector – thus giving men preferential access to the more stable ones. This of course relates to occupational segregation in that it suggests some rationale for determining which jobs are likely to be among those undertaken by women. (The theory does not of course rule out some men also undertaking insecure jobs because of the relatively high proportion of such employment.)

Armstrong (1982) gives an interesting example of the insecurity of women's jobs in two factories. He argues that women become concentrated on labour-intensive processes and men on capital-intensive ones. This arises primarily from a combination of the desire to make maximum use of expensive equipment and the inability or unwillingness of women to work shifts or nights. Armstrong argues that labour-intensive work is inherently more insecure both to short-term changes in demand and to long-term pressures for automation.

Rubery and Tarling's analysis (1982) is the most developed attempt to demonstrate women workers' greater vulnerability in terms of a dual labour market approach. Their methodology involves regressing the percentage change in female employment on the percentage change in total employment. This provides a test for the hypothesis that the rate of change in female employment is more cyclically volatile than that for total employment. Using figures for the UK over the period 1960-80 they found some contradictory results.

These suggest that the hypothesis is true only within those industries where women form a significant but not dominant proportion of the workforce. They explain this finding as follows. First, in areas dominated by male employment women are mainly employed as clerical workers. These types of jobs have tended to be more secure (during the period in question) than employment generally within manufacturing. Second, in areas where women are a significant but not dominant proportion of the workforce women tend to be concentrated in secondary jobs (in the sense of vulnerable to employment loss) and men in primary jobs. This category includes industries such as electrical engineering and food, drink and tobacco. Third, in areas dominated by female employment, women form the bulk of both the primary and secondary workforce. This category includes industries such as clothing and footwear. While being interesting in its own right this is not very enlightening from an occupational segregation point of view since it is not clear why industries should have different proportions of women in the first place.

Humphries (1983) has refocused the debate in an interesting way. She argues that feminists have confused short-term cyclical changes with the longer-term trends inherent in the notion of a latent reserve. Going back to the example of displaced agricultural workers, she argues that they lose their characteristics as a reserve over time and become absorbed into the main body of the labour force. Using American data she attempts to show that the same is happening to women. The consequences of this are assumed to be that women workers will lose any distinctive characteristics such as greater cyclical insecurity of employment *and* occupation segregation.

Humphries argues that:

A direct confrontation of the substitution hypothesis involves an analysis of the distribution of the growth in female employment. If women are simply responding to an increased demand for female labour within already feminised industries, we would expect to find a major part of the growth in female employment concentrated in the latter kind of industry. Alternatively substitution of women for men within the industrial structure would involve a high proportion of the increase in female employment being concentrated in industries initially dominated by men. (pp. 23–4).

Her results are presented for manufacturing only and while suggestive are far from conclusive. Certainly the increase in women's employment has not gone into industrial groups that are already predominantly female.

However, since these are mainly mature, labour-intensive industries such as clothing this is hardly surprising. She argues that 'women were increasing their representation in relatively male dominated industries at a rate which denies that they were doing so as non-production/clerical employees' (p. 24). However she gives these increases in the form of percentages which may well look highly significant when they are increases on relatively small initial numbers. It is therefore difficult to know whether this is the case or not.

This finding appears to contradict those suggested by Hakim's work. Hakim argued that men's entry into women's jobs was much more pronounced than the trend Humphries identifies, women's entry into men's jobs. Both approaches are subject to the problems of classification and data availability which have been mentioned throughout this paper. In addition Humphries' starting point is the growth in female employment rather than redistribution within the labour force between occupations. As such she does not have anything specific to say one way or the other about the movement of men between occupations.

Nevertheless the thrust of Humphries' theoretical approach suggests that the entry of women into non-traditional areas is the active element in breaking down occupational sex-typing, and this is what her data seems to show. In contrast Hakim has no specific explanation of her findings. While this may make Humphries' findings intuitively more appealing it is obviously no guarantee that they are correct. On the other side of the balance, Humphries' use of American data and of industrial rather than occupational data may make us doubt its relevance to the current British situation.

There is one further level of detail within occupational statistics which we can examine. The Census identifies a set of occupational groups (relating broadly in the 1961 and 1971 Census to industrial classifications) and within these major occupations by numbers of men and women within each group. By identifying particular groups of jobs this data source could be expected to shed more light on the nature of any changes which are occurring. This data source has not been used much by researchers and the reason is again the problems surrounding classifications. In Britain, the post-war period has seen two major revisions in the classification system, for the 1961 and 1981 Census. Both these changes were sufficiently radical to make comparison across the period 1951–81 very difficult.

The need for such frequent and wide-ranging changes should in itself make us think again about the assumptions behind the studies discussed above. The focus on substitution inevitably creates an image of men and women workers being redistributed within a relatively unchanged occupational structure. Changes in classifications suggest in contrast that we cannot separate changes in the sexual division of labour from a restructuring of the technical division of labour. The role of technical change in this process is difficult to disentangle. Some occupational titles remain relatively unchanged over periods when industry level studies show significant technical change. In other cases technical change seems to lead to the emergence of a new occupational category. The latter case is extremely frustrating for those trying to understand changes in occupational sex-typing since a revision in the classification system produces new occupational groupings strongly sex-typed in one direction or the other without any way of telling how these emerged.

There are other specific problems about this data source. Again the figures are highly aggregated referring to groups of jobs which may well differ in terms of sex-typing. The figures also do not cover all workers but only those in occupational groupings over a certain size. For this reason, although the titles of occupational groups appear to relate to industries, they do not accurately reflect the proportion of men and women in each industrial group.

Despite these reservations the data is worth examining in more detail because it can suggest hypotheses which could be followed using other forms of investigation. Below figures are presented for the proportion of men and women in five occupations within the occupational groups 'Food, drink and tobacco workers' and 'Electrical and electronic workers' for 1961, 1971 and 1981. The figures for 1981 are not strictly comparable because of revisions in the classification system. Nevertheless they appear to be close enough to merit inclusion. The two groups have been chosen because they derive from significantly different industrial situations. Food, drink and tobacco has traditionally employed substantial numbers of women although it has never been dominated by 'women's jobs'. Women now represent a substantial minority of workers within the electrical and electronic engineering sector. However traditionally few women have been employed within engineering. The occupational category within which most women appear first appeared in the 1961 Census and has no precedent in 1951 classifications.

Both industrial sectors have seen output growth over the period but this has taken rather different forms. In the food sector this has largely taken the form of productivity induced 'jobless growth' and product diversification. Electrical and electronic engineering saw employment growth in the early 1960s and the development of new or radically redesigned products. Four of the five occupations have been chosen because they are the most strongly sex-typed male and female jobs within the group. The reasons for the inclusion of an additional group, food processors, will become clear in the later discussion.

Sexual division of labour in selected occupational groups in 1961, 1971 and 1981*

'Male occupations'

	Year	Proportion of men employed
Butchers and meat cutters	1961	96.1%
	1971	93.0%
	1981	91.8%
Linesmen, cable jointers	1961	99.9%
	1971	98.9%
	1981	95.4%
Food processors n.e.c. (1981 figures refer to foreman only. Figures in brackets for 1961 and 1971 give nearest comparison)	1961	59.7% (75.5%)
	1971	55.4% (78.8%)
	1981	(75.9%)

'Female Occupations'

	Year	Porportion of women employed
Tobacco preparers and product makers	1961	69.4%
	1971	70.3%
	1981	56.9%
Assemblers (electrical and electronic)	1961	80.6%
	1971	84.2%
	1981	77.6%

Source OPCS Census 1961, 1971 and 1981 Economic Activity (10% sample)
*Note 1981 Categories are differently labelled and not strictly comparable.

It is interesting that the two most strongly sex-typed occupations in these two groups are both long-established jobs with strong craft links. Butchers' and linesmen's jobs are overwhelmingly carried out by men and show little signs of changing. Technical change has occured but has not radically changed the boundaries of the job or the way it is done.

The two occupations predominantly performed by women present a rather different picture. The tobacco industry is largely made up of highly routinised low-skill operations (see Pollert 1981). In addition the sector has seen a dramatic decline in employment and rapid automation particularly in the latter period. The occupational title is very broad and is 'product orientated'. That is workers are defined in terms of the end product rather than in terms of its method of production. There appears to have been a fairly substantial growth in the proportion of men undertaking this work between 1971 and 1981. Classification changes make it difficult to be certain about the exact size of this shift. Nevertheless it seems likely that automation has led to the disappearance of significant numbers of machine-assisted 'assembly' and packing jobs (traditionally areas of women's employment). The number of men in this occupational group was almost unchanged in the 1971–81 period while the number of women dropped by a half. It seems likely that the changing ratio of men to women in this group is a result of the disproportionate effect of technical change on women's jobs rather than the entry of men into previously female areas of work.

In contrast the other disproportionately female category, electrical and electronic assemblers, seems to be undergoing little change. This is a 'process orientated' category in that it refers to the way work is done rather than to the final product. As has already been said, assemblers appeared as a significant occupational group only in 1961. At that time employment was growing fairly rapidly although it has been in decline since 1967. The tasks are highly routinised and have been subject to automation almost as soon as they emerged.

The emergence of such a strongly female sex-typed occupation is interesting particularly since it is in such marked contrast to the other occupations classified for electrical and electronic workers. In no other area do women operatives represent even 5 per cent of employment within the occupation. Thus women's growing importance within the sector is almost entirely dependent on the growth of the assembly area. It also seems significant that it was a *new* type of work within the sector rather than simply an area of employment growth. The occupational group 'electrician' has also expanded greatly in this period yet women operatives still make up less than 5 per cent of this employment.

Food process workers have been included since it includes

disproportionately male jobs. These de-skilled jobs were created through the effects of technical change on craft-based jobs. For example, mixing and cooking processes once involved moving large quantities of ingredients and craft knowledge about recipes and cooking techniques. In larger firms, at least, this area of work is now highly automated. This applies both to the transportation of materials and to mixing and cooking processes. Recipes are standardised and often under computer control. Factory level studies show that this is still a strongly sex-typed area of work. The figures documented in the table do not show this since the occupational group includes a large number of jobs done by women such as preparing fruit and vegetables for canning. Nevertheless the figures do seem to show a high degree of stability.

These five occupations present an interesting range of situations from which to re-examine approaches to occupational sex-typing. The two occupations overwhelmingly carried out by men – butchers and meat cutters and linesmen and cable jointers – seem to suggest that once a job becomes sex-typed it is unlikely to change in the absence of any radical restructuring of the area of work or the way it is carried out. In contrast the case of the electrical and electronic assemblers shows that radical changes in production methods and product ranges can lead to the emergence of an occupation sex-typed in opposition to the rest of the group. This suggests we need to consider whether the factors which determine the original sex-typing of a job are different from those which maintain this definition in an established job. This suggestion is strengthened by the case of the food process workers. Here the way the work has been carried out has changed radically. Much of it now conforms to the 'simple, clean and light' characterisation of women's work. That these jobs have not been taken over by women seems to show that it is possible for a *job* to retain its original sex-typing regardless of changes in the *work* required to carry it out. We could further argue that women tobacco workers lost their jobs because the work no longer required any human labour and there was therefore no job to be retained as 'female'. However this would be something of an over-simplification. Automated equipment requires monitoring and maintaining. We need to ask why women apparently failed to establish a claim to these jobs.

We could look at a wider range of occupations in an attempt to strengthen the evidence for these suggestions. Such an investigation would probably lead to them being refined if not substantially revised. However studies at the level of occupational statistics can never be more than suggestive. We can note the common factors in certain situations where changes in sex-typing have or have not occured. But to

find out whether these factors were important and if so in what ways w‹
need the type of detailed examination that only labour process studie›
can provide. It is rare to find a labour process study that addresses thes‹
questions yet it seems likely that many researchers could think o‹
examples from areas they have studied which would at least clarify th‹
issues.

Attention to questions of occupational sex-typing would also lead t‹
different types of studies being carried out. It would be illuminating t‹
have studies which compare sex-typing in firms producing similar item›
particularly where different technologies are being used (see Cockbur‹
1984), old and new factories, or traditional versus 'green field' sites›
Technical change remains a potential time of change in the sexua‹
division of labour. We need studies which approach it from thi›
perspective, looking at the way decisions are reached about changin‹
the division of labour particularly the circumstances under whic‹
questions of sex-typing are considered. Such studies may well need t‹
be longer-term than many currently carried out and take a broade›
perspective on the changing way tasks are divided into jobs and th‹
consequences of this for occupational segregation.

Conclusion

The foregoing discussion can do slightly more than just suggest ne‹
lines for labour process research. It can also point to fallacies in labou›
process theory's approach to occupational sex-typing. We have enoug‹
evidence to say that a simplistic reading of labour process theory, whic‹
sees the manufacturing sector developing, via technical change and th‹
introduction of women, towards a goal of a largely unskilled›
unorganised, undifferentiated and cheap workforce, has little basis i‹
fact. We might instead argue that whatever the 'abstract' advantages fo›
capital in reversing occupational sex-typing, such an occurrenc‹
appears to be the exception rather than the rule and seems to require ‹
particularly radical form of change.

The most obvious reason for such a divergence from the expecte‹
path is that the theory has failed to take account of the ability of mal‹
workers to oppose such changes. The stability of the sex-typing of 'mal‹
jobs' may represent the strength of organised male labour. Critics o‹
'mechanical' Marxist models of capitalist developments have alread‹
argued that we need to take account of the strength of organised labou›
in affecting the direction taken by capital. We could take this a stag‹
further and argue that the context within which the capitalist mode o‹
production operates also includes labour organised to defend mal‹
interests over the allocation of work and a social organisation of th‹
reproduction of labour power which is heavily dependent on a sexua‹

division of labour. Further, as Phizacklea's (1983) study of migrant women workers showed, we need to also consider exclusionary practices based on race. It is clear that the directions taken by producers within such a context will vary from those predicted by a purely economic theory.

Such a perspective also underlines the importance of another development within labour process theory. That is, the recognition of the need to differentiate between a generalised notion of capital's interests and the interests and actions of individual capitals. In a hostile environment changes which might be beneficial for all firms in a sector if implemented throughout, may well prove disastrous for any particular firm trying to initiate them.

Some labour process studies do seem to illustrate this. Lazonick (1976) gives examples of situations where the long-term interests of the textile industry seemed likely to be served by breaking the power of particular occupational groups, but where individual capitalists who tried to pursue these aims suffered damaging strikes and in some cases went out of business. Similarly Cockburn's (1983) discussion of the history of the printing industry shows capital goods producers specifically developing and marketing machinery for use by women workers. While some printing establishments did change working patterns in this way the practice was vigorously opposed by male workers and never became generalised. These studies seem to show that *short-term* competitive pressures *between* capitals can favour compromise within the status quo rather than radical reorganisation.

But if male workers have been so successful in defending their jobs where does this strength come from and how do they exercise it? Labour process theory would lead us to expect that their strength derived from craft-based control over their jobs and that they exercised it by overt point-of-production struggles or the threat of such struggles. And indeed the two examples given above seem to substantiate this approach. The entry of women into *new* jobs rather than *changed* jobs seems to lend further weight to the argument. If an area of work is sufficiently disrupted such that new jobs are created in new plant with very different production methods or moved from one sector of industry to another then we could expect point of production struggles to be fairly unsuccessful.

Yet we can note male craft workers' ability to organise in a hostile way against women (and indeed unskilled men) when their interests are directly challenged and still feel that there are other processes at work. If managers were continually considering it in their interests to introduce women into 'male jobs' and were prevented only by the threat of industrial disruption, we would expect the sexual division of labour to be a very live issue both for management and unions. There is little evidence that this is the case. Asking management why a certain job is done only by men, one is often met by incomprehension. It does not appear to be a question to which they have ever given much thought. One is often told, 'This has always been a man's job' or 'We've never had a woman apply to do it'. Such statements may be followed by an attempt to justify the sex-typing of a job in terms of the nature of the work and the different characteristics of men and women. These justifications may be extremely contorted and unconvincing but they are significant in demonstrating that female and male workers are not seen as undifferentiated substitutable groups.

This should hardly surprise us since we live in a society where beliefs about the different characteristics and abilities of men and women are deeply rooted and are institutionalised in terms of a sexual division of labour in all walks of life. Yet it is something that labour process theory has failed seriously to take account of. By adopting such a perspective, labour process theory could usefully switch from its focus on explicit conflicts between male and female workers to one that analyses the factors that prevent these conflicts occurring in the majority of cases. This would also involve developing an analysis which was far more specific about the conditions under which men's interests are likely to be threatened. On this latter question we can go further and point to the need for more studies like Milkman's (1983) comparison of the electrical and car industries. This shows that even when men's interests are challenged the circumstances under which this occurs may mean that strategies based on the exclusion of women workers are not seen as viable and that the threat is contained by strategies which are aimed at raising the wages and conditions under which women work.

We can summarise the implications of these points by returning briefly to the comparisons made earlier between the five occupational groups. An attempt to analyse these different situations could usefully be carried out at three levels. First we could focus on the ways in which widely held views about the correctness of a sexual division of labour at home and at work make it unlikely that women will gradually 'drift' into unchanged male areas of work such as the craft occupations as a result of equal opportunities legislation.

Even in occupations which are affected by technical change it would appear that it is possible, as in the case of the food process workers, to retain the original sex-typing of the job. From the very limited evidence we have (food process workers versus electrical assemblers) it would appear that changes in the nature of the work are less threatening than changes in the focus or location of jobs. This suggests that it is jobs rather than types of work which are sex-typed, although we might wish to argue that *original* sex-typing is more strongly work-related.

This brings us, second, to more specific reasons for these different outcomes. Most obviously we should note that retaining the focus of a job allows the perpetuation of trade union organisation based around that particular occupation. Thus the analysis should develop a better understanding of the ways male workers organise, not just against management but also against other groups of workers, in this case women. Such an analysis should not merely consider the different trade union practices of male and female workers. It also needs to consider whether there are characteristics of the jobs men currently do which facilitate the development of these forms of organisation. For example the breadth of craft jobs has clearly been an important factor in allowing men to redefine what their jobs involve and thus hold on to them through periods of significant technical change. In contrast, for most women who work in very narrowly defined jobs, comparable technical change, as for example seen by women working in the tobacco industry, can be devastating.

We therefore have some ideas about the broad social values supporting the perpetuation of a sexual division of labour and maintaining established sex-typing. We have also looked at the forms of trade union activities which men have developed to defend these positions when threatened. But there is also a third level where we need to understand practices within both the labour market and the labour process which contribute to the maintenance of sex-typing, and hence to the relative lack of conflict over occupational sex-typing.

Such factors have been investigated most fully by those trying to find ways of improving women's opportunities at work. Thus positive action programmes have pointed to a range of factors which, while not explicitly discriminatory, *de facto* exclude women from many areas of work.

Such factors often rest on the interaction between differences in men and women's working patterns and the design of jobs and job opportunities. Women's working patterns are affected by legal restrictions on their hours of work; the immediate effects of domestic responsibilities on hours of work, union activities and so on; the longer-term effects of domestic responsibilities such as breaks in employment and the likely lower degree of interest in training and career development. Women also enter the labour market with different skills and expectations from men, derived at least in part from the experience of an educational system which itself perpetuates sexual stereotyping.

These features mean that a factory job being worked on a shift basis is almost invariably a male job. If a second job is only open to someone

who had previously done the shift-based job then this would also ensure
that it was a male area of work regardless of the actual hours worked. In
these and many other ways, including recruitment practices and
training provision, the competition between men and women workers,
which labour process theory predicts, fails to materialise. These factors
are often very poorly understood so that managers who positively want
to encourage women to apply for particular jobs or training courses
often fail because they do not know how to make these opportunities
genuinely available to women. These factors also throw further light on
the distinction between changed jobs and new jobs. In jobs which
change but that nevertheless retain a focus, particularly around a job
title, there is unlikely to be any systematic reconsideration of these
conditions of work.

If those interested in the labour process began to take up all these
issues at both a theoretical and empirical level we would have a much
better understanding of occupational sex-typing and a much stronger
basis for breaking it down.

Acknowledgement

Thanks are due to Anne Witz for very helpful comments on an earlier
version of this paper.

References

Armstrong, P. (1982), 'If It's Only Women it Doesn't Matter So Much', in *Work Women and the Labour Market*, J. West, (ed.), London: Routledge and Kegan Paul.
Beechey, V. (1978), 'Women and Production: A critical analysis of some sociological theories of women's work' in *Feminism and Materialism*, A. Kuhn and A.M. Wolpe (eds), London: Routledge and Kegan Paul.
Beechey, V. (1983), 'What's so special about Women's employment? A Review of some recent studies of women's paid work', *Feminist Review*, **15** 23–45.
Blackburn, P. Green, K. and Liff, S. (1982), 'Science and Technology in Restructuring' *Capital and Class*, **18** 15–37.
Bruegel, I. (1979), 'Women as a reserve army of labour: A note on recent British experience', *Feminist Review*, 3, 12–23.
Cavendish, R. (1982), *Women on the Line*, London: Routledge and Kegan Paul.
Cockburn, C. (1983), *Brothers: Male Dominance and Technological Change*, London Pluto.
Cockburn, C. (1984), 'Women and Technology: 'Opportunity' is not enough', paper to the BSA annual conference, Bradford.
Connelly, P. (1978), *Last Hired, First Fired*, Toronto, Ontario: The Women's Press.
Hakim, C. (1978), 'Sexual Divisions within the Labour Force: Occupational Segregation', *Employment Gazette*, November 1978, 1264–8.
Hakim, C. (1981), 'Job Segregation: Trends in the 1970s', *Employment Gazette* December, 521–9.
Humphries, J. (1983), 'The "emancipation" of women in the 1970s and 1980s: From the latent to the floating', *Capital and Class*, **20**, 6–28.

Hunt, A. (1975), *Management Attitudes and Practices towards women at work*, London: HMSO.

Lazonic, W. (1976), 'Industrial Relations and Technical Change: The case of the self-acting mule', *Cambridge Journal of Economics*, September.

McIntosh, A. (1980), 'Women at Work: A survey of employers', *Employment Gazette*, **88**, (11), 1142-9.

Milkman, R. (1976), 'Women's work and economic crisis', *Review of Radical Political Economics*, **8**, (1).

Milkman, R. (1983), 'Female Factory Labour and Industrial Structure: Control and Conflict over "Women's Place" in Auto and Electrical Manufacturing', *Politics and Society*, **12**, (2).

Phizacklea, A. (1983), 'In the Front Line', in *One Way Ticket – Migration and Female Labour*, A. Phizacklea, (ed.), London: Routledge and Kegan Paul.

Pollert, A. (1981), *Girls, Wives, Factory Lives*, London: Macmillan.

Rubery, J. and Tarling, R. (1982), 'Women in the Recession', in *Socialist Economic Review*, London: Merlin.

5 Gendered Jobs in the Health Service: a Problem for Labour Process Analysis

Celia Davies and Jane Rosser

There is a growing body of empirical work in the labour process tradition which deals with the waged work of women. It covers manual and non-manual grades, it ranges from the nineteenth century to the present day. No collection of papers today is complete without 'something about gender'; and that something is as likely to be a theoretical critique as an empirical enquiry. Thus, it cannot be claimed that labour process theory ignores the question of gender.

But at the same time as accepting that contemporary forms of analysis are not altogether gender-blind, we can perfectly well object to the vision of the place of gender in the analysis, and in this paper we do so. The paper is in three parts: first, there is a brief examination of some of the major arguments which have been put forward about the place of gender in labour process analysis: next, there is an examination of material drawn from a current study of clerical work performed by women in the Health Service, followed by some comments on its historical development. The final discussion takes the form of a commentary on the issues raised by the empirical material in the light of our understanding of the state of the contemporary debate. The thread which links these three sections is the concept of a gendered job. What it might mean to say that a job is gendered – to claim that gender is 'written in' to a job – becomes progressively clearer as the argument proceeds.

I

Braverman's work (1974) encompassed women's waged work and the work of women in the home; this much was recognised straight away in the somewhat double-edged review of Baxandall and her colleagues (1976). Yet, perhaps because of the way Braverman had treated the sexual division of labour (see below), much of the subsequent work taking inspiration from Braverman either ignored women or did not regard their participation in the labour process as anything requiring particular comment. We can find a convenient starting point for debate however in the argument put forward by Zimbalist in the context of introducing a volume of case studies, an unusually high proportion of which deal, in one form or another, with women's waged labour.

Having made reference to what have become important and familiar themes in the critique of Braverman of an overestimation of the success of capitalist controls, an underestimation of worker resistance, and doubts about the unilineal direction of a de-skilling thesis, Zimbalist has this to say, *inter alia*, about gender:

> Various detractors have also criticised *Labor and Monopoly Capitalism* for not adequately dealing with sexism, racism, bureaucratic controls, internal labor markets, systems of pay differentials, runaway shops, etc. That is, Braverman did not present a thorough and comprehensive treatment of all the levers of capitalist control in the workplace. This, of course, is true and Braverman explicitly acknowledged these self-imposed limitations of his study. He chose rather to focus directly upon what has perhaps been the most neglected, misunderstood and mystified aspect of the labor process: the control over the design and organisation of production. Whereas few would maintain that racism, sexism, byzantine bureaucratic controls, and so on, are nature-given features of the workplace, most workers and intellectuals accept the march of technology as inevitable and immutable.
>
> (Zimbalist 1979: vvi)

The most striking feature of this passage, of course, is its confident assertion that we all apparently now understand sexism and racism for what they are, and that no one falls into the trap of seeing them as immutable or inevitable. Leaving that aside, however, the passage also claims, in effect, that capital creates places for labour indifferent to the individuals who fill them. The concepts of 'wage-labour' and 'wage-labourer', directly reflect this. It is, in Heidi Hartmann's memorable phrase, a theory of *empty places* (Hartmann 1979: 7–9). We need notice women's waged labour only in specific historical instances when its particular qualities render it attractive as a 'lever' of capitalist control. A woman's place, we might say, is in the case study, not in the theory chapter.[1]

If Zimbalist exemplifies one way in which the importance of women's waged labour can be brushed aside, an altogether different route to a similar destination comes with the argument that with the development of late monopoly capitalism, previously distinctive features of women's employment are progressively obliterated. Patriarchal controls in the workplace are recognised – the use of 'treats and favours' to engender a close personal loyalty, for example. But the claim is that these disappear, as part, some would have it, of the move from the formal to the real subordination of labour to capital. In relation to clerical work for example, it has been suggested that it becomes necessary for individual capitals to 'renounce ... the use of patriarchy in favour of more specifically capitalist means of control' (Barker and Downing 1980: 66–7). According to this argument, it is not women's work *per se* which is distinct, but the form of control over that work. Patriarchal controls, however, are less efficient, anomalous, about to disappear. They deflect our attention from the main argument. Again then, the character of waged labour as women's labour should be accorded a minor place.[2]

The two positions outlined thus far are unusual only in the sense that a rationale for according less theoretical attention to women rarely receives explicit attention and discussion. Even very recent work in Britain has proceeded with barely any mention of women[3] and the overwhelming impression a new reader receives is that the work that has been done on women's waged labour is seen as incidental rather than integral, an observation which Janet Siltanen had made of several theoretical approaches to women's work, labour process theory included (Siltanen 1981: 37). However, at least three arguments have been put forward which suggest that far from being incidental or a matter of detail, consideration of women's work poses major challenges for a labour process perspective – challenges which its proponents have seemed hesitant to take up.

First, there is the observation, borne out by a variety of specific examples, that women's second-class position as wage-labourers has been endorsed, encouraged and even initiated by male workers and by worker organisations (see Bradley, this volume). If then, as Zimbalist has it, sexism is a lever for capital, it is also a lever for labour, and can indeed be integral to a pattern of male labour resistance to capital. In so far as this calls into question the essential unity of the concept of wage-labour, and in so far as it points to a variety of interests of men, *qua* men, it is a serious challenge to existing theorising (Coyle 1982).

Second, there is the argument around skill. Braverman, as countless commentators have noted, erects the de-skilling hypothesis on the basis of the skills of the craftsman, the subsequent divorce between the work of conception and execution and the fragmentation of tasks. Braverman also, however, provides room for an approach which recognises the social construction of skill, whereby the categories in use are seen to have a base less in objective and technical criteria and more in custom, tradition and power. Phillips and Taylor (1980) have begun to develop this perspective with regard to sex and skill.

They argue:

Skill definitions are saturated with sexual bias. The work of women is often deemed inferior because it is women who do it. Women workers carry into the workplace their status as subordinate individuals, and this status comes to define the value of the work they do. Far from being an objective economic fact, skill is often an ideological category imposed on certain types of work by nature of the sex and power of the workers who perform it.

(Phillips and Taylor 1980: 79)

Phillips and Taylor are careful not to argue for a strong version of the social construction of skill thesis (i.e. one which denies any technical content to skill or any relation to training). They also suggest that there are ways in which their argument might enhance Braverman's claim of the progressive degradation of work. Others, noting for example the human relations work that women do and are expected to do, suggest that there are skills which go totally unacknowledged – something which could bear rather more inconveniently on the de-skilling thesis, and something to which we shall return later in the paper. Littler (1982: 10–11), who has usefully distinguished between weak and strong versions of the thesis, has acknowledged that the strong version of the social construction of skill thesis has severe implications for the de-skilling debate at the heart of labour process analysis and will project it, as he puts it, onto a different level. He later acknowledges that divisions between men's and women's work may mean that the de-skilling hypothesis 'needs further specification' (ibid.: 18), but he declines to provide further illumination on these points. Thus there has been a recognition that a social construction of skill perspective based on enquiries into women's work could represent a real challenge, but as yet that challenge has not been put directly.

Third, there is the vexed question of the family. Braverman's work at least had the merit of including a chapter bearing on this, some of the inadequacies of which, from a feminist point of view have been discussed recently by Beechey (1983). Central to her critique as we read it is the observation that Braverman is wedded to a moralistic and idealised view of the family; this prompts him to condemn what he sees as its essential demise under capitalism. What we should do instead is to theorise how the capitalist form of family is related to the capitalist mode of production, and not (as so many writers have been enabled to do precisely because of Braverman's approach to the family), isolate analyses of the labour process from discussion of the changing form of the family. Braverman himself perhaps sets a precedent for misunderstanding the demand to 'take on the family' in his reply to his early critics.[4] But it is probably also true to say that feminists are not agreed as to what an adequate analysis would entail. At the very least, it surely means paying attention to the specific forms of women's waged labour available as mediated through the family; Kenrick (1981) has some important observations here, and we develop this somewhat in the following sections. Ultimately however, it means insisting on a theoretical perspective which is able to countenance both production and reproduction simultaneously (cf. Picchio del Mercato 1981).

None of these three points, the first to do with men's interests *qua* men, the second to do with the social construction of skill, the third to do with the importance of the family has received any extended and explicit discussion about the difficulties it raises for labour process analysis. By far the greatest amount of the space devoted to issues of gender and the labour process has been reserved for the elaboration of arguments about the reserve army of labour, about women's place within it and specifically about the substitution of female for male labour (see, for example, Beechey 1977, Bruegel 1979, Humphries 1983). Notwithstanding that the protagonists of that debate may not see it in this way, it is all too easy for this debate to be regarded as an issue of detail, a matter indeed of 'specifying the levers', 'filling the empty places' with empirical, historical data. This, it would seem to us has been the key message of much recent work.

Finally, however, we must consider the work of Thompson (1983) who was the first to set out deliberately to review and assess the significance of work on gender as part of a general text on labour process analysis. Thompson's work has the merit of bringing into the open the constantly underlying debate about capitalism and patriarchy and the relation between the two. He finds three positions on this to be extant. First, he refers to Heidi Hartmann who has put forward and indeed elaborated in some detail an argument that patriarchy is separate from capitalism, precedes it and shapes the form which it takes; next, he draws a position from an early paper by Phillips and Taylor that capitalism and patriarchy are 'in partnership' in some way; third, he refers to Veronica Beechey's argument to do with capital's interest in women as cheap labour to set out a position that the capital accumulation process has theoretical priority in explaining the sexual division of waged labour (Thompson 1983: ch. 7)[5].

A key part of his chapter is then devoted to exploring these three by reference to historical materials around the question of the temporal order of either de-skilling or feminisation of jobs. He argues that de-skilling has largely preceded feminisation and this is a major factor in his support for the third of the positions outlined.[6]

Yet it is in this section of the chapter that Thompson makes clear that – despite his earlier acknowledgement and useful discussion of problems of Marxist analysis for understanding the sexual division of labour, despite his later treatment of the family – his position is in essence that capitalism 'takes over' patriarchal relations. Capital, in other words, finds it convenient to operate patriarchal controls in the workplace. This amounts to something very similar to a 'specifying the levers' position; it leaves the theory open to Hartmann's empty places critique and does not explore what that really entails.[7]

For us, it seems more useful to return to Braverman's initial insight concerning the way that control is written in to the design of jobs, and to use this to suggest, not empty places but *jobs already gendered* in a labour process. One example of a gendered job emerges from our empirical material, and the theme is further explored in the historical discussion which follows it.[8]

II

The material which appears in this section is drawn from a study of administrative and clerical staffs in one of the 199 District Health Authorities (DHAs) in England and Wales. Each DHA is responsible for planning, developing and managing the health services of its district within national and regional strategic guidelines. A district will usually include at least one general hospital covering a variety of acute specialties, and will provide services for the elderly, the mentally ill and mentally handicapped. It will also provide staff and back-up services for a range of health centres and clinics in its area. With the exception of hospital consultants who hold contracts with the Regional Authorities and GPs who are independent contractors, the DHA is the employer of all its staff. The total labour force of districts varies considerably; in the West Midlands, for example, the number of staff employed in a district ranges from 1,000 in the smallest to 9,000 in the largest.

Administrative and clerical staffs comprise roughly 10 per cent of the total employees of a district, and within this, those on clerical and secretarial grades far outnumber those in administrative grades. As far as men and women employees are concerned, the pattern in general is that women form the overwhelming majority of both clerical and secretarial staffs but the proportions drop dramatically in the administrative grades. In 1981, there were no women in chief administrative officer posts at district level (Dixon and Lane 1983); following the 1982 reorganisation, there were still less than half a dozen women district administrators. In our research district, the dramatic change in the proportions of posts held by women came precisely at the dividing line between administrative and clerical grades. Women were 87 per cent of those on Higher Clerical Officer grades, but only 42 per cent of those on General Administrative Assistant grade. In other districts, the sharp break can be found a little higher in the grading structure. Overall, however, the pattern is the same, fewer women as one ascends the hierarchy and an almost total dependence on women to fill the lower graded posts.

Our research district was a small one, with around 3,000 staff in all. It was situated in a rural area with those staff who were not either in the HQ unit or in the large hospital of the county town dispersed over a wide geographical area. The HQ work was divided into a familiar set of functions – general administration, planning, finance, salaries and wages, etc. Outside the HQ, both the larger groups of medical records staff and medical secretaries, and the lone members of administrative and clerical staff were found in a variety of physical settings; in purpose-built health centres, in clinics, in houses around the hospital bought up by the health authority, and in portakabins on site. In our district, as elsewhere, where staff are located depends on buildings available in the district, an infrastructure which can often be traced back to what was available well before 1948 – frequently to buildings available before 1900.

In what follows, we have drawn on a number of different sources of data, including a postal survey sent to all staffs at HCO level and above (n = 98); transcripts of interviews with a sample of 22 HCOs and GAAs and transcripts of interviews with a small group of managers (n = 11) responsible for appointing staff to these grades. The fieldwork, which was carried out in summer 1983, will not be described in further detail here, since our purpose is to use it as illustrative material only.

Our initial interest lay in the distinction between administrative and clerical work, and the nature of the tasks allocated to these grades. When questioned on this, managers at first put forward the view that there was a clear division between these two forms of work. The general administrative assistant (GAA) had to give more to the job and be more inventive, whereas the higher clerical officer (HCO)'s work was basically that of a clerk, with perhaps 'a bit of standard supervision' or maybe responsibility for a few staff or for handling money. On reflection, however, the distinction broke down, particularly when they began to consider the range of work that HCOs and GAAs actually did. It was apparent that both grades could find themselves doing the work of 'a glorified secretary' a 'senior clerk' or a 'proper administrator'.

This view was amply confirmed by interviews with staff. Some GAAs were distinctive in having responsibility for a large number of staff – the catering or domestic staff of a medium-sized hospital, for example. The work of others seemed directly comparable to that of some of the HCOs – indeed, in some cases, theirs had been HCO work until they had fought successfully for an upgrading. The HCOs varied from one extreme where the work of checking, issuing and reordering stock seemed fairly routine, through personal secretary/PA work which can only be captured in a specific example. Thus one woman reported:

I'm a General Office Manager . . . I control all the money that comes into the hospital and goes out. I am sort of cashier for anything that comes into this hospital, moneywise, cheques and what have you. I deal with all the patients' personal accounts and all their money and their pension books and their giros; I liaise with the DHSS about all this. I do all the letters for . . . solicitors, court of protection, relatives' solicitors or anything that is relative to patients' money and their current accounts. I do banking, of course. I do all the quarterly returns, monthly returns, regarding anything to do with the financial accounts . . .

I'm trying to think: quite frankly, I do it all, do you know what I mean? If anyone is away I sort of stand in. We control stats for the hospital and we control all the admissions and discharges. We keep records of everything to do with admissions and discharges . . . (I) co-ordinate the doctors. We deal with all the deaths and the relatives, see all the doctors and make sure that all the . . . forms and everything are filled out correctly. We see to the relatives. I also control all the personal property, and when I say personal property I don't mean clothes, I mean valuables such as . . . that all comes to me and rings etc. etc. What else do I do? . . . Any queries that anyone would have regarding anything, I mean, a lot of my work is taken up doing social work in a lot of ways, because I have the patients who are on the acute admissions wards who have all their little problems about not getting their giros and 'not paying me enough' and all that sort of thing and I make sure they are getting what they are entitled to. I make sure that all the pension books are sent in, downgraded, all that sort of thing.

Really there is so much of my work, I am in control of pay of course, money comes up here, anything to do with money comes to me. I pay out all the petty cash to anybody in the hospital that might spend any for any particular thing, so therefore I have to give a weekly statement to (Headquarters) when I draw my cheque. I go to the bank twice a week.

I write all the letters in my office but I am not allowed to sign them. Mr . . . and Mr . . . take my word that what I have done is correct, they never check it, they never look at the figures . . . if I am writing to anyone about anything they just sign the letters.

What we had found at this stage was a fairly close parallel to the situation described by Crompton and her colleagues for local government. Officially, as in local government, there was a criterion for the classification of work[9]; in practice a similar kind of heterogeneity a similar grey area between clerical and administrative work was present (Crompton et al. 1982 esp. p. 55ff).

But there was more to it than this, and it was clear from some of the comments of the women doing the less routine jobs at HCO level and from more than one of the managers, that there was a vested interest in keeping HCOs in that grade (See also Collinson and Knights, this volume). One manager put it this way:

From a senior manager's view, there is some merit in inertia, in the sense that

> ... some of the higher clerical jobs, certainly in hospital, are absolutely key posts. If you've got somebody in there who is doing the job exceptionally well, they don't half keep the mess out of your hair; and you perhaps become reluctant to suggest to them that there are other things in the world apart from what they're doing now. Because it does protect you enormously.

This comment has to be seen in the light of the model career in NHS administration. Ideally, managerial recruits are expected to pass through HCO jobs while still on the training scheme,[10] enter administrative posts at the completion of the scheme and thereafter spiral upwards with an average of perhaps only two years in each subsequent post. We began to picture a kind of career merry-go-round built on the stable base of the work of a knowledgeable and stable labour force, predominantly composed of women. As one of these women HCOs put it succinctly:

> You are good spadework for their job – you do all the donkey work that give them the kudos.

Because women's work was a major focus of our enquiry we asked our interviewees whether a member of the opposite sex could do their job. The men generally thought a woman could do their job with no problem. Sometimes a woman had done it previously, but even where this was not the case, few suggested that a woman would encounter difficulties. The women, however, responded quite differently. You have to be 'tactful' or 'diplomatic' the women interviewed would say; be 'a counsellor', 'smooth things over', 'not throw your weight around'.

> He could do the shorthand, the typing etc. – but he'd also have to smooth ruffled feathers.

> (A man) wouldn't have the tact! You're walking on eggshells the whole time.

> All the problems seem to end in my lap – which doesn't happen with men.

One male manager of male and female staff made the intriguing suggestion that the woman driver on his staff, who 'can go in for a chat', was more of a health visitor than a driver.

Comments such as these resonate immediately with sociological studies of secretaries and with what has been dubbed the 'office wife'[11]. Feminists and others have recently begun to analyse this, for example in terms of 'caring work' (Finch and Groves 1983), 'emotions work' (Hochschild 1979), and 'sentimental work' (Strauss et al. 1982). They are more or less emphatic in drawing parallels with work in the home, but they insist that this is a form of workplace labour which is unacknowledged and unpaid. This is an important point which needs to be placed in the context of a re-examination of the concept of skill. One woman we spoke to noted that as someone who had herself been bereaved and divorced, she was able to deal with patients' anxieties better perhaps than other people would. Crompton et al. (1982) perhaps allude to this when they note 'maturity' as a requirement for some women's jobs. When the woman in our study asked if she could go on a counselling course, however, she was turned down. There was no desire, it seemed, to formalise her caring work, to see it as part of the job rather than as a quality of the person.

There are difficulties, however, which would arise were we to focus too exclusively on women's work as caring work. First, it presents features of the work women do as if they were features of the women themselves. While it is true that men rarely seem to do caring work, not all women do it, nor do women do it all the time. Next, and as a direct result, it serves to homogenise women. Third, it directs attention away from what may be typical and gender-patterned features of the work that some women do. In sum, to direct attention to women's caring work will tend to extract the women, as women, from the labour process rather than to insert their work, as work, into it. At this point, we began to formulate the notion of gendered jobs. A gendered job was one which capitalised on the qualities and capabilities a woman had gained by virtue of having lived her life as a woman. Because there was no formal training involved and because these skills were not clearly *acquired* from experience within the workplace, these qualities and capabilities were not acknowledged as skills; they were unrewarded in financial terms, and if seen at all were seen as qualities that these women just happened to have and/or that women just happened to have more than men. Thus the women just happened to be more stable and to have acquired local knowledge; it was preferable to recruit them if they were 'mature'; and significantly, it was a bonus if they had a caring attitude although caring was not a skill to be sought, developed and acknowledged. On this model, gender is not an 'additional lever' or a convenient additional resource for control – it has become built in to the labour process itself. We develop this point below.

The final pieces of the jigsaw were not yet in place. What we had also observed was a clear distinction between HCO work of women and men at the centre or headquarters and HCO work of the women at the periphery.[12] The women workers at the periphery were the ones to whom we were turning for our examples of gendered jobs. These women worked in a hospital or health centre office; they were 'jill of all trades'; they made appointments and kept records, they ordered supplies and kept financial records. They arranged for necessary maintenance work and kept an eye on it while it was being done. They had a good knowledge of how the HQ worked, and their immediate bosses, medical and paramedical staffs, used them to mediate the mysteries of policy, procedure and practice.

The women in these jobs told us that they were the ones who held things together. We believed this. For our interviews with them were punctuated by calls and queries. Their desks were heavily loaded. The typewriter, while clearly in regular use, was often almost submerged by a large volume of files and other paperwork grouped in such ways as to suggest that they needed to keep track of many different issues simultaneously. Interviews with those on the same grade at central HQ were very different. These staff work in small open plan offices, sometimes in groups of three or four. Their desks were tidy, their demeanour was fairly distant and calm. Several – men and women – were hesitant about whether they would be of any use to our research project; they felt there was really not a lot to say about their work one way or the other.

In short, there was an enormous contrast in the routinisation, fragmentation and pace of work. It may well be that those at HQ were doing the work of the factory-like office to which Braverman refers: but those in the periphery were decidedly not. It would be tempting to describe these latter as unit administrators were it not for the confusion this would cause with those on the official administrative grades. A number of them described themselves as office managers and this gave us a further clue. What we had uncovered was one example of a gendered job – the *female office management function*. It is part, we contend, of the labour process in health care, something thus far blurred both by the conventional hierarchical descriptions (since some of these women were on HCO grade and some on GAA grade), and by the division between centre and periphery which the participants themselves proposed.

Having divided the women into those who were in female office management functions and those who were not, other features became apparent. The women differed in key respects. The women in HCO posts at the centre were young – usually under 30. They had had one perhaps two promotions, or they had come to the job late after other career directions. They did not expect to stay, anticipating a career break for child bearing. The women at the periphery, the female office managers, were almost all older. Their families were growing or grown, but they were probably still fairly tied to the area and in the midst of a span of employment in the Health Service which could be as much as 20 years. We have drawn up a brief profile of three types of women whom we met, the first at the centre, the other two in the office management functions.

Type I:
This is a young woman, and probably married. She has worked for the District for anything up to five years. She may have had a promotion. She is probably working at Headquarters. She knows and everyone knows that she will probably leave soon and have a baby. She does her job well. She sees no point in being career-minded. She really could not see what our interview was all about. The job is fairly routine, it does not stretch her but she had no complaints.

Type II:
This woman is probably between 35 and 45; her children are at school, some perhaps off her hands altogether. She might have worked for the NHS before she had her children and have been known in the District when she came back. She is not at District Headquarters. She might be in a hospital department or general office, she might be in a health centre, she might work for a group of consultants. What she is, is an office manager. She does both secretarial and administrative work. Her job has probably grown over time and she may have got an upgrading but even with it she may think her work is still undergraded. She is in command of all the detail, however, is well liked, thoroughly indispensable and enjoys every minute of her work.

Type III:
This woman is over 45, with no children now at home and long experience in her job. She has certainly been in it over ten years – and perhaps is heading for 20 or more. She could perhaps have moved up through typist and personal secretary grades and have been upgraded to HCO. She is a medical secretary or a secretary to a department with a mix of work like the type II woman or she is doing specialised clerical work and working on her own initiative. Again like the type II woman she knows all there is to know about the organisation of the work. She also knows that the place falls apart when she is not there. But she has become angry and maybe bitter. She has applied for higher graded jobs and not been considered. She has seen young people pass through and has perhaps even trained them. But she will stay on her grade until retirement.

The lesson of this is not that there is a diversity of women in employment; it is rather that jobs are gendered; women's *places* in this organisation have become forged in relation to their life-cycle stage and home commitments in a way that men's have not. The female office management function draws both on the organisational skills developed by women in household management and on their experience in the home in handling emotions, and creating an appopriate 'atmosphere' for the tasks in hand.

The level of consciousness of those involved in these gendered jobs varied. Few of the managers were aware of it; if they were, they personalised the issues. Thus they felt there were one or two older women who were bitter about being passed over for promotion, or who felt snubbed that they had not been upgraded. One manager was quoted as having said of a woman in a female office function post by that woman:

> If ... has made herself indispensable, then that's ...'s fault.

Among the women themselves, some found it enjoyable and satisfying that they had such varied and responsible work regardless of its grading. Where they were dissatisfied they most commonly attributed the problem to favouritism. Staff at Headquarters were treated better, were given 'nice little HCO jobs' – senior managers at Headquarters just did not appreciate what the work was out in the field. Others felt that the grading structure of the NHS was at fault. It was too tight or just plain chaotic.

It seems to us important, however, to seek an explanation of this low-graded yet important work of the female office function in the NHS not just in terms of the consciousness of those who participate in it, but in terms of the *historical development of a gendered labour process* in health care. Thus, it is of interest to note that while some of these posts are associated with long-existing forms of health care delivery (the general office of the small hospital dealing with geriatric care, mental illness or mental handicap), others are found in the large, high-technology, modern hospitals (the office work in the X-ray department or in the pharmacy, for example). Still others are found in association with new organisational forms which use little in the way of new facilities or techniques; these are the posts of office manager in the health centre, where the work involves co-ordinating the availability of a range of primary care services.

Unfortunately, there are few guidelines on how to conduct a labour process analysis in health care. Discussions of clerical work have begun, but the work of the health service presents other difficulties – in being human service work[13], in being reliant on the organised professions for its delivery[14], and in being a labour process outside, although clearly not unaffected by the capitalist mode of production.[15] All we can do here is to draw attention to some of the possible components of such an historical analysis.

In the voluntary hospitals before 1948, today's administrative/clerical work[16] resided mainly in the role of house governor or hospital secretary. Braverman has likened clerical work in its early stages to a craft, arguing that

> it represented a total occupation, the object of which was to keep current the records of the financial and operating condition of the enterprise, as well as its relations with the external world.
>
> (Braverman 1974: 298–9)

The hospital secretary however also acted as a co-ordinator of non-medical and sometimes of medically related matters, as a central information point and as a committee clerk. In the latter capacity he was accountable to the Board of Management. The large local authority hospitals, by contrast, had had a full-time medical superintendent responsible for medical services and business affairs, but this pattern, disliked by the medical staff, was to fall into disuse after 1948 (Acton Society Trust 1955–6). It is not immediately clear what further administrative/clerical staffs were employed in hospital work before or after 1948, but it is certainly the case that the control and the execution of work of co-ordinating care, arranging for supplies, recording, cleaning, catering, linen services was frequently in the hands of the matron and her nurses. It was only later, in the era of the health service, that the concept of non-nursing duties and what was and was not nursing proper began to be debated. This female administrative/clerical work within nursing and its fate is an important part of the history that needs to be traced.

Outside the hospital, in the community health services, there was an unacknowledged female administrative/clerical labour force also. Women volunteers were important in the division of labour in maternity and child welfare clinics, they controlled records, directed patients, and carried out a myriad of tasks concerned with the smooth running and upkeep of the service. Where volunteers did not do this, nurses and/or health visitors did. And in the GP's surgery, the administrative/clerical work was frequently also done by a woman – the GP's wife.[17] *It seems that what administrative/clerical work there was, therefore, was unacknowledged and often done by women as part of their other responsibilities.*

The major restructuring brought about by the NHS meant the taking into public ownership and the grouping of previously independent hospitals. A new structure of officials at hospital group and regional levels provided links with the Ministry of Health, from whence policy guidelines and procedures could flow. The new system attempted to rationalise provisions and to improve access to health care services. But it was no massive departure from what had previously existed. In the mid-1950s, the case still had to be made for the status of lay administration in hospitals *vis-à-vis* medicine and nursing, and the work at group level was not very clearly articulated.[18] On the other hand, the term 'hospital administrator' had come into use; in the 1940s various moves had already led to the formation of the Institute of Hospital Administrators and to the consolidation of a pattern of professional examinations and courses.

The development of the NHS must, of course, be seen in the light of developments in capitalism in Britain in the period after World War II, and the political and ideological contexts of this. Survival for the NHS was not in doubt, given its popular appeal in a period of economic growth. Nonetheless, little cash was given for capital expenditure, and although they were successfully countered, doubts arose about the apparently escalating costs of the service.[19] Demand for hospital services did not fall off, as had been predicted, and both the numbers employed and the volume of work grew steadily. Almost at once, part-time female staff became an important and new component of the labour force, and the figures on patient turnover, on length of stay and on outpatient visits all point to an intensification of work. While we cannot easily document it, administrative/clerical work must have grown considerably. In 1966, there were around 6,000 staff on administrative grades in hospitals and hospital groups in England and Wales; but there were almost 22,000 clerical staffs and another 14,000 on secretarial, typing and machine operative grades.[20]

Two principles seem to have had common currency; the first was that work that could be done by a lay person should not be done by a professional (meaning definitely a doctor and arguably a nurse). The second was that, since it was the work of the doctors that generated demands and hence costs, it was important to have a strong lay administration as a counter to medical power. Through a series of official enquiries[21] the concept of an administrative élite began to emerge and the division between 'professional' administration and 'routine' clerical work began to deepen. 'Planned movement' was the key to creating a new cadre of general administrators. First a National Administrative Trainee Scheme, then a Regional one came into being. Recruits were found in the escalating numbers of young people, men and women,[22] with A levels and degrees. It is perhaps only now that the effects of these schemes, which started in a small way, are beginning to be felt. But it is perhaps here that we can locate the start of the distinction between administrative work and the gendered jobs we have described earlier.

In the early 1960s, rising welfare expenditures coincided with the first signs of an international crisis in capitalism which was to deepen into the current recession (Gough 1979). The optimistic reaction, associated with the first Labour Government of Harold Wilson, was that the state need not reduce welfare expenditure, instead greater efficiency would solve the difficulty. Some capital expenditures were made – new hospitals and health centres date from this period, but much effort went into a reorganisation, brought into effect in 1974, designed to integrate hospital and community services and to redesign the structure between hospital and central department in three tiers of district, area and region. Functions such as planning, management services, finance and personnel were now elaborated alongside general administration. But while the work of district headquarters was enlarged and given detailed attention in this way, the administrative/clerical work at the point of service delivery remained untouched. In this sense, the thinking underlying reorganisation reinforced the professionalisation of administration and underlined still further its separation from clerical work.

As the economic crisis deepens and as the Health Service comes under threat both in terms of real budget cuts and in terms of steps towards privatisation, it is increasingly unlikely that issues of the grading and regrading of office function tasks will come onto the agenda. Yet it is not clear that there will be a new generation of women coming forward to fill gendered jobs in the way they have done previously.

The current job holders are women who were denied educational opportunity earlier in their lives, who have also had a fairly lengthy absence from the employment market for child-rearing, and who were glad to have been offered the possibility of re-entry to the labour market in however lowly a position. Younger women have had greater educational opportunities and a shorter career break. There is a question of where they will fit on their return to work, and where they will expect to fit. The gendered jobs which had gone unquestioned in an era of more clear-cut male administrative and female clerical work may thus become a problem, precisely because of the interaction of changing family forms and the labour market (cf. Kenrick 1981).

Discussion
Earlier, we defined gendered jobs as ones which capitalise on the skills women have by virtue of having lived their lives as women. We emphasised that these skills go unacknowledged and unrewarded, that where they are seen at all, they are seen as qualities which attach to a particular woman or to women as a group. By giving attention to the reports of the women themselves and of their managers we were able to be more precise. A specific form of gendered job was evident, that of the

female office management function.

This gendered job draws on at least three skills of women. First, there are organisational skills, acquired not through a formal training, but through experience in running a home, dealing with the priority-setting, scheduling, progress-chasing etc. that this involves.[23] Next, there is the comprehensive local knowledge of organisational practices and procedures which is acquired through experience and continuity of employment. This knowledge is acknowledged as vital, but at the same time is written off as 'detail' and as 'trivial'. Third, there are what are called 'womanly qualities', which as such have no cash value. These are the social skills crucial to the smooth running of the job. The presence of men, and to a lesser extent, the presence of younger women in these jobs, would be disruptive. One or two such might be deemed as individually incompetent, larger numbers might well lead to the situation where either the skills at present unrecognised would need to be formally acknowledged and indeed taught; or the job would need to be redesigned. It is not that women do the job and that it gets done in a 'woman's way'; it is not even simply that the qualities of the job and the capabilities of the job holders have become fused. It is rather both that the fusion has occurred and that the fusion itself denigrates and dismisses women's skills.

The next step will be to take the concept of gendered jobs further. Thus far we have isolated one gendered job, the one we have dubbed the female office management function. The forms taken by the gendering of jobs elsewhere in the health care division of labour is a matter for exploration.[24] We would expect, for example, that if there are gendered jobs in 'administration proper', the forms that this gendering takes – in a context where men and women are not occupationally segregated but are in direct competition for posts – will be rather different. Questions, then, of which jobs are gendered, how they are gendered, whether indeed, *all* jobs are gendered, remain open. Next, there is a further, and most important implication of our analysis, namely that men's jobs are gendered too, and hence the same analytical strategies should apply to both sexes.[25] That analytical strategy, we should perhaps underline once again, starts from the places women (or men) occupy in the division of labour and not from their common womanhood (or manhood). This is what we take Hartmann's injunction to mean, not to fill the empty places with women or men, but *to see gender in the definition of the places.*[26]

Then there is the question of patriarchal controls. We have said very little in this paper about sexism, about discriminatory treatment of women, about a 'treats and favours' approach by men to women subordinates, or about sexual harassment. This is not to deny that all these things occur; there is plenty of evidence already that they do, and a truly adequate explanation of gender in the labour process cannot ignore them. At this point we are not altogether certain how best to deal with the question of patriarchal controls and indeed, we are alert to the possibility that our research methods may have led us to underplay them.[27] We are concerned, however, not to allow the identification of such controls to be the be-all and end-all of the analysis. Starting from gendered jobs seems to us preferable, since it puts gender at once on centre-stage.

This analysis of gendered jobs in health care administration has begun to provide a demonstration of each of the three points outlined earlier as offering a challenge from gender to labour process analysis. Thus, we have indicated how the State's interest in controlling health care expenditure converged with the interests of those who wanted to develop professional administration and diverged from the interests of women doing administrative work – an alliance, perhaps, of capital and one particular strand of labour against the interest of a particular grouping of women. Our account also bears on the question of skill as socially constructed, and does so both through the difficulties presented by the terms of administrative and clerical and through the confused comments of those who operate with these terms. Finally, in analysing our case we have found it impossible to avoid talking of the changing form of the family. The women currently carrying out the particular gendered jobs we have described are available to fill those places in large measure because of how their family responsibilities have been and still are being construed. This, as we have argued, is something that is changing and will have repercussions on the division of labour in health care administration.

In the course of our research, one fairly senior NHS manager remarked that it would cause more confusion to see the HCO in the general office leave than to see the hospital administrator leave. In this paper, we have tried to take that remark seriously. We have observed that while the hospital administrator might often be a woman, the HCO is invariably so. And the HCO is often an older woman rather than a younger woman, doing a job which draws from her experience and skill. This kind of pattern is not unique to the health service, and certainly it seems that it occurs in local government too (cf. Crompton et al. 1982). The concept of a 'gendered job' as we have used it here, perhaps offers one way forward. Certainly we find ourselves in complete agreement with Phillips and Taylor (1980:81) when they say:

We do not want to find ourselves simply tacking the Woman Question onto a finished theory of the 'economy'. We want to take the issue of gender hierarchy into the heart of Marxist economic analysis itself.

Acknowledgements

The material on which this paper is based is drawn from an SSRC/DHSS sponsored study entitled *Equal Opportunities for Women in the NHS*. We would particularly like to thank Tony Elger and Sonia Liff for encouragement and constructive criticism in connection with this paper.

Notes

1. There are various other problems with the passage. For one thing, the presentation may be said seriously to misrepresent Braverman whose analysis of clerical workers and of the universal market – whatever criticisms it has attracted – nonetheless accorded women more importance than Zimbalist's etcetera clause treatment suggests. Second, the equation of sexism and racism on the one hand and pay differentials and bureaucratic controls on the other, raises more questions than it answers. Thompson (1983:181) has recently questioned whether the debate about gender divisions and ethnic divisions is comparable; and Siltanen (1981:32), although in a slightly different context, has raised objections to a reliance on some unexplicated notion of sexism. Third, and in relation to the final sentence of the passage, we can not only cast doubt on the truth of the first half of the sentence but also observe that if the second half is true, the first by no means logically follows.

2. This argument is not, however, without its contradictions, as a close reading of recent material on clerical work will show. On the one hand, it is quite possible to find instances of and persuasive arguments for deskilling or proletarianisation of this work (Glenn and Feldberg 1979; Crompton and Reid 1982); and this kind of argument has an obvious relevance to debates about the impact of new office technology. On the other hand, writers who have tackled these debates also produce important suggestions concerning the unacknowledged skills of female office workers, the continuation of aspects of the 'social office' and sources of support from managers for these features. This is clear in the work of West (1982: see especially pp. (72–3) in Crompton et al. (1982) in Barker and Downing (1980) and in the concept of 'impersonal paternalism' and in the queries about efficiency raised at the end of Glenn and Feldberg (1979). One way forward might be to tease out and explore the way in which Barker and Downing refer sometimes to the transformation of typing work, sometimes to the social office. Our own view, as will become clear below, is that there has been altogether too much attention to patriarchal controls as somehow separate from job design, and the first step is to reconceptualise this.

3. See for example Storey (1983) and Littler (1982). The exception is Thompson (1983) whose work is discussed below.

4. Thus, for example, Braverman seemed to equate 'taking on the family' with understanding the changing forms of the division of labour within it in its own right, *not* with providing a form of analysis which would constantly link this with the labour process as he conceived it (Braverman 1976: 120).

5. The three positions are not set out very clearly, and other readers may disagree with our interpretation. It is especially hard to be precise about the position Thompson associates with Phillips and Taylor since it is based on an unpublished paper in which their position would seem to differ from that in their work published later (Phillips and Taylor 1978, 1980).

6. Even on the basis of the material as presented there seem to be doubts about establishing temporal priority. Furthermore, it is not entirely clear whether the

demonstration of temporal priority would clinch the argument in the way that Thompson supposes.

7. In the end, Thompson seems to remain ambivalent about whether gender is a matter of filling in the detail of an established theoretical scheme or is somehow to be made integral to that theoretical scheme. He criticises Hartmann, arguing that capital is 'only *abstractedly* sex-blind' and 'must *immediately* confront the organisation by workers, and of society as it exists' (199–200: emphasis in the original). At the end of the chapter, however, he remarks that these debates 'have begun to open up ways of connecting the *specific developments* in this sphere to a clearer *general picture*' (209: emphasis added). The issue and their position is actually set out very clearly in Phillips and Taylor's work as follows:

> Clearly at one level the argument that the capital labour relation is not a gender relation is correct; inasmuch as the capital-labour relations is a *value relation* it is not a relation between people at all, but between abstract quantities of dead and living labour ... But: 'the capitalist labour process is the unity of the processes of valorization and the real labour process on the adequate basis of a specific form of social organisation of labour' (Brighton Labour Process Group, 1977: 6), ... As a use-value – that is, in its historic existence – labour is concrete labour, characterised as much by its femaleness as by any of its other attributes ... There is no economics which is free of gender hierarchy, no Marxist science which can direct its gaze where women are not. (Phillips and Taylor 1980: 87–88n)

8. Where does Thompson stand in relation to the three challenges to labour process analysis set out earlier? On the first point, early in the chapter he concedes separate development of patriarchy, but later, as we have just seen subordinates it to capital. (The possible unity of male capitalists and labourers is not assessed.) On our second point, concerning the social construction of skill, he says nothing. On our third point about the family, he makes a number of insightful observations about how the arguments have proceeded, and about the weaknesses of Marx and Braverman, and argues for a 'reinsertion' of the family. The form that this reinsertion must take is unclear – and in particular the way that the family affects women's availability for employment is left rather in the air.

9. Brief definitions of the work of staff at the different grades and levels are laid down by the functional Whitley Council (Whitley Councils for the Health Service. Administrative and Clerical Staffs Council, 1984).

10. A National Administrative Trainee Scheme was set up in 1958 following the Noel Hall Report (Ministry of Health 1957). The year 1960 marked the start of a Regional Trainee Scheme to run in parallel with this. Appointments were to be made on the junior administrative grade. It was still envisaged that others in the service would rise through promotions.

11. See, for example, Mills (1956) and more recent work on secretaries Benet (1972) and McNally (1979).

12. The terms 'centre' and 'periphery' as used here do not carry any theoretical content but are used loosely and as a matter of convenience.

13. For a discussion see Stevenson (1976).

14. One of the best discussions of the professions within a Marxist perspective is that of Larson (1977) especially chapter 12. But even Larson provides little leverage on how to analyse a detail labour process.

15. While Braverman sees welfare expenditures as 'an arena for political agitation' and 'a substitute for revolutionary movements' (1974: 286–7), he does not give any clues as to the nature of the labour process within the welfare sector. Furthermore, and when he comes to a discussion of productive and unproductive labour, he discusses unproductive labour within the capitalists' mode of production not outside it, and claims that the latter is in decline (ibid. 415ff).

16. We use the term 'administrative/clerical' deliberately to draw attention to the lack of detailed analyses of the labour process here and to our doubts as to whether skill differences can be simply assumed.
17. We are grateful to Mary Ann Elston for drawing attention to this in the context of her own current work.
18. These observations are drawn from an official inquiry into the administration of hospitals (Ministry of Health, Central Health Services Council (1954) and from research conducted under the auspices of the Acton Society (Action Society Trust 1955–6).
19. For details see Committee of Enquiry into the Costs of the NHS (1956), and the related research of B. Abel-Smith and R.M. Titmuss (1956).
20. These statistics are drawn from the *Digest of Health Statistics for England and Wales*, first published in 1969; later figures can be gleaned from various editions of the subsequent publication *Health and Personal Social Services Statistics*; earlier ones are harder to come by.
21. See Ministry of Health. Central Health Services Council (1954), Ministry of Health (1957), Ministry of Health (1963).
22. Not all women in NHS administration are in the gendered jobs we have described – a point emphasised later.
23. For a comparison of the job descriptions of housewife and managing director of a small firm, see Morris (1983: 22–3).
24. It is striking that those who have tried to apply a labour process perspective have taken it in reference to specific health occupations rather than to health work. For the case of nursing see, e.g. Cannings and Lazonick (1975), Bellaby and Oribabor (1980). For an attempt to theorise the division of labour in health care which includes unpaid as well as paid health workers see Stacey (1984).
25. Our research design did not allow us to explore male gendered jobs. It is perhaps worth noting that one of our (male) managers did begin to expound on the 'maleness' of managerial work, suggesting that the image of management perhaps would need to change before women would enter it in large numbers. An analysis which does see male jobs as gendered can be found in relation to the printing industry. See Cockburn (1983).
26. We have been asked where this position stands in relation to Feldberg and Glenn (1979). We find their concepts of job and gender models a valuable starting point and agree that men have been studied with a job model and women with a gender one. Our approach is intended to bypass these dichotomies by insisting that jobs have gender written into them – and gender in this sense includes assumptions about personalities and competences of men and women and of men and women at different stages in the life cycle. We would agree that there is a need to reconceptualise work and include unpaid work, but we see it as crucial to add that some of this unpaid work takes place inside the workplace and is denied the status of skill.
27. Our work involved one-off interviews in which we did not ask specific questions about patriarchal controls; not only is this the context in which a researcher is most likely to elicit a rehearsal of conventional wisdom, but it is also a context in which topics which are seen as 'trivial' or 'embarrassing' are unlikely to emerge spontaneously. It is worth noting that the research contexts in which data on patriarchal controls have emerged have involved observation and/or group discussions. For a recent discussion of the survey method and feminist research see Graham (1983).

References

Abel-Smith, B. and Titmuss, R.M. (1976), *The Cost of the NHS in England and Wales*, Cambridge: Cambridge University Press.

Acton Society Trust (1955–6) *Hospitals and the State: 1 – 6*, London: Acton Society.

Barker, J. and Downing, H. (1980), 'Word Processing and the Transformation of the Patriarchal Relations of Control in the Office', *Capital and Class*, **10**, 64–99.

Baxandall, R. et al. (1976), 'The Working Class has Two Sexes', *Monthly Review*, **28**, (3).

Beechey, V. (1977), 'Some Notes on Female Wage Labour in Capitalist Production', *Capital and Class*, **3**, 45–66.

Beechey, V. (1983), 'The Sexual Division of Labour and the Labour Process: a critical assessment of Braverman', in S. Wood (ed.) *The Degradation of Work?* London: Hutchinson.

Bellaby, P. and Oribabor, P. (1980), 'The History of the Present' – Contradiction and Struggle in Nursing' in C. Davies (ed.), *Rewriting Nursing History*, London: Croom Helm.

Benet, M.K. (1972), *Secretary: an enquiry into the female ghetto*, London: Sidgwick and Jackson.

Braverman, H. (1974), *Labor and monopoly capital*, New York: Monthly Review Press.

Braverman, H. (1976), 'Two Comments', *Monthly Review*, **28** (3).

Brighton Labour Process Group (1977), 'The Capitalist Labour Process', *Capital and Class*, **1**

Bruegel, (1979), 'Women as a reserve army of labour: a note on recent British experience', *Feminist Review*, **3**.

Cannings, K. and Lazonick, W, (1975), 'The Development of the Nursing Labor Force in the U.S.: a basic analysis', *International Journal of Health Services*, **5**.

Cockburn, C. (1983), *Brothers: Male Dominance and Technological Change*. London: Pluto Press.

Committee of Enquiry into the Cost of the NHS (1956) *Report* London: HMSO: Command 663, (Guillebaud Report).

Coyle, A. (1982), 'Sex and Skill in the Organisation of the Clothing Industry' in J. West (ed.), *Work, Women and the Labour Market*, London: Routledge and Kegan Paul.

Crompton, R. et al. (1982), 'Contemporary Clerical Work: a case study of Local Government', in J. West (ed.) *Work, Women and the Labour Market*, London: Routledge and Kegan Paul.

Crompton, R. and Reid, S. (1982), 'The Deskilling of Clerical Work' *in* S. Wood (ed.) *The Degradation of Work?* London: Hutchinson.

Dixon, M. and Lane, B. (1983), 'Women in Management in the NHS', *Health Services Manpower Review*.

Feldberg, R.L. and Glenn, E.N. (1979), 'Male and Female: job versus gender models in the sociology of work', *Social Problems* **26**.

Finch, J. and Groves, D. (eds.), (1983), *A Labour of Love: Women, Work and Caring*, London: Routledge and Kegan Paul.

Glenn, E.N. and Feldberg, R.L. (1979), 'Proletarianizing Clerical Work: Technology and Organisational Control in the Office', in A. Zimbalist (ed.), *Case Studies on the Labor Process*, New York: Monthly Review Press.

Gough, I. (1979), *The Political Economy of the Welfare State*, London: Macmillan.

Graham, H. (1983), 'Do Her Answers Fit His Questions? Women and the Survey Method', in E. Garmarnikow et al. (eds.), *The Public and the Private*, London: Heinemann.

Hartmann, H. (1979), 'The Unhappy Marriage of Marxism and Feminism: towards a more progressive Union', *Capital and Class*, **8**, 1–33.

Hochschild, A.R. (1979), 'Emotion Work, Feeling Rules and Social Structure', *American Journal of Sociology*, **85**, (3).

Humphries, J. (1983), 'The "Emancipation" of women in the 1970s and 1980s: From the Latent to the Floating', *Capital and Class*, **20**, 6–28.

Kenrick, J. (1981), 'Politics and the Construction of Women as Second-Class Workers', in F. Wilkinson (ed.), *The Dynamics of Labour Market Segmentation*, London: Academic Press.

Larson, M.S. (1977), *The Rise of Professionalism: a sociological analysis*, London: University of California Press.

Littler, C.R. (1982), *The Development of the Labour Process in Capitalist Societies*, London: Heinemann.

McNally, F. (1979), *Women for Hire: A Study of the Female Office Worker*, London: Macmillan.

Mills, C.W. (1956), *White Collar*, New York: Oxford University Press.

Ministry of Health (1957), *Report on the Grading Structure of Administrative and Clerical Staff in the Hospital*, (Noel Hall Report), London: HMSO.

Ministry of Health (1963), *Report on the Recruitment, Training and Promotion of Administrative and Clerical Staff in the Hospital Services* (Lycett Green Report), London: HMSO.

Ministry of Health, Central Health Services Council (1954), *Report on the Internal Administrtion of Hospitals* (Bradbeer Report), London: HMSO.

Morris, J. (1983), *No More Peanuts: an Evaluation of Women's Work* London: NCCL.

Phillips, A. and Taylor, B. (1978), 'Sex and Class in the Labour Process', Nuffield Conference, Windsor Great Park.

Phillips, A. and Taylor, B. (1980), 'Sex and Skill: Notes towards a Feminist Economics', *Feminist Review*, **6**.

Picchio del Mercato, A. (1981), 'Social Reproduction and the Basic Structure of Labour Markets', in F. Wilkinson (ed.) *The Dynamics of Labour Market Segmentation*, London: Academic Press.

Siltanen, J. (1981), 'A Commentary on Theories of Female Wage Labour', in Cambridge Women's Studies Group *Women in Society*, London: Virago.

Stacey, M. (1984), 'Who Are the Health Workers?', *Economic and Industrial Democracy* (2).

Stevenson, G. (1976), 'Social Relations of Production and Consumption in the Human Service Occupations', *Monthly Review*, **28** (3).

Storey, J. (1983), *Managerial Prerogative and the Question of Control*, London: Routledge and Kegan Paul.

Strauss, A. et al. (1982), 'Sentimental Work in the Technological Hospital', *Sociology of Health and Illness* **4** (3).

Thompson, P. (1983), *The Nature of Work: an introduction to debates on the labour process*, London: Macmillan.

West, J. (ed.) (1982), *Work, Women and the Labour Market*, London: Routledge and Kegan Paul.

Whitley Councils for the Health Services. Administrative and Clerical Staffs Council (1984), *Pay and Conditions of Service*, Crown Copyright.

Zimbalist, A. (ed.) (1979), *Case Studies on the Labor Process*, New York: Monthly Review Press.

6 Women and the Workplace: Gender and Control in the Labour Process

Margaret Grieco and Richard Whipp

We thus need an approach which can encompass both the conflict and the complementary association between the sexes.

(Rowbotham 1979: 970–1)

Introduction

Commentators on the organization of work and the character of the family in advanced capitalist society have stressed the apparent and pervasive subordination of women to men, most especially in the workplace and in the home. This absolute perception of relations between men and women has taken on the inflexible robes of orthodoxy. Whilst accepting that such an assumption provides a necessary and invaluable counterbalance to gender-free accounts of the social and labour processes (Sayles 1958: Gorz 1976: Price 1983), it is nonetheless increasingly at odds with an emerging paradigm of gender relations. In this paper the alternative perspective is examined and its relevance for the study of gender and the labour process is assessed in the light of our own research.

An influential view of women and work is provided by the Marxist-Feminist literature on women's subordination (Mitchell 1971; Barrett 1980). This analysis draws attention to the structural relationship between women's position in the family and women's position in the labour market: it emphasises how women's work outside the home has been ideologically determined. The argument runs, using an historical perspective, that the organized working class in the nineteenth century accepted the bourgeois ideology of women's appropriate role: 'a woman's place'. The male craft unions and a bourgeois state were successful in subordinating women workers' interests to their own. As women's work in the labour market was equated with work in the home, women were viewed not as workers but as women working (Milkman 1983). Job segregation in the workplace derived from the organization of domestic life; job segregation was an expression of the

118   *Gender and the Labour Process*

ideology of female domesticity. Women workers were confined to low-paid jobs, forced to depend on men and fulfil the role of unpaid domestic workers. The sexual division of labour in the household and within the labour market were mutually reinforcing.

Hartmann (Hartmann 1976) in a path-breaking study argued that women's work was not sex-typed purely from an ideological impulse but from patriarchy. She pointed out that male workers have material motives for maintaining job segregation by sex since it ensures lower wages for women and keeps them dependent on, and therefore subordinate to, men in the home and workplace. Here the interests of male workers are seen as complementary to the interests of capital in perpetuating a sex-segregated labour market. Men have been able to maintain this balance given their institutional strength in and outside the workplace in the nineteenth and twentieth centuries. Barrett concludes that as result of this historical process:

> a model of women's dependence has become entrenched in the relations of production of capitalism, in the division of labour in wage work and between wage labour and domestic work. [Moreover,] these divisions are systematically embedded in the structure and texture of capitalist social relations in Britain (1980: 249).

Recent studies (Alexander 1984: 139) appear to confirm the durability of this model of female subordination. A review in 1982 (SPRU 1982: 8; cf. Novarra 1980) observed how 'women still usually work in paid employment on tasks similar to those which they have traditionally performed in the home'. Apart from realising low pay and status, women's work offers poor access to training facilities and 'typically, it requires relatively little skill'.

However, the orthodox approach has been shown to contain a number of weaknesses. The theoretical concentration on ideology in explaining women's development in the family, household system and the sexual division of labour have been sharply criticised (Brenner and Rammas 1984: 47). Detailed examination of protective legislation has stressed its failure to affect the sexual division of labour (Kessler-Harris 1981), while the coverage of male craft unions is known to have been limited. Underneath the rhetoric of women's appropriate domestic role there are instances of male support for women's causes and their action (WTUL Quarterly Review 1900 July: 6). The global statements of the orthodoxy which have remained rather abstract or are located at the national level have been found wanting in explanatory power when applied to the local context. Milkman's study of female labour in the twentieth-century US auto and electrical industries shows that to understand the 'traditions' of sex-typing, the proper unit of analysis is the industry or the occupation, not the capitalist labour market as a whole (Milkman 1983: 16). She draws the distinction between the interests of collective capital and the interests of individual capitals on the level of the firm: the importance of location, management strategy and the production cycle are seen as central to the nature of female participation rates and wage work. In contrast to the orthodoxy, there is an emerging paradigm of women's work which has come from essentially empirical research and draws attention to the local sphere for women's employment (Gilligan 1982: Dublin 1979: Hareven 1982).

As with current understandings of the ability of labour to resist managerial direction (Edwards 1979: Montgomery 1979), so there is space for a more flexible approach to the contested character of the social and industrial terrain jointly occupied by men and women. Our argument is not that capital determines all, for relations between the sexes are also shaping the labour process of capital. Nor is it that one is continuously shaping the other, rather there is an interaction: an interaction influenced by local as well as national forces, by accident as well as structure. Unquestionably women are objectively subordinate in capitalist society, but it is not a simple subordination. Given female subordination, does not mean that there is no power, or no power ever, for women. Male dominance is not complete either in the home or workplace. Our research offers a corrective to the orthodox emphasis on the structural and ideological bases of total female subordination. Taking an historical perspective and a more active research approach our study asks, in the context of subordination, what form does women's work take in specific industries; how do women survive in and around work; and are there alternative forms of female power and action distinct from the traditional models of male workplace behaviour?

Accounts which emphasise male power *vis-à-vis* females have failed to pay attention to female social networks as an important dimension of social relations in the urban industrial context. Yet the evidence from a host of community studies (Young and Willmott 1957: Roberts 1971: Baker-Miller 1982) suggest that these patterns are both an historical and modern-day phenomenon. Our primary evidence points to the operation of female networks as an influence on selection to, and performance in, the workplace, both in male only and in two-gender employment situations. The economic dependence of women – their objective subordination as measured by inferior employment conditions, terms and wages – provides the explanation for the form of their collective organization and corresponding survival strategies, one of which is the female social network. This form of social organization reduces the dependence of any particular woman on a single male exchange partner. Failure by the individual male to meet his responsibilities is compensated for by transfers of assistance within the female network (Hunt 1980: Pahl 1980). By remaining within the vicinity of her family of origin, the individual working-class woman can make claims on the family pool of resources.

A number of studies have documented fundamental differences in the female/male pattern of social relations (Ross 1983: Gilligan 1982 de Lauwe 1956). Yet few have attempted to analyse why these patterns emerge. Strong personal ties are more necessary to women as a basis for claiming support in or out of crisis, given their inferior quality of existence and conditions. Women's investment in the family can either be read as a register of subordination or it can be viewed as a form of collective insurance. Our research adopts the latter approach and views this investment as part of a female strategy of control. The stress is on the ties which bind women together, thus departing from the conventional approach which only examines the ties of women to men.

Much of the orthodox literature stresses the extent to which the family is a critical institution in the suppression of women and ceases to investigate further (Richards 1974: Barrett and McIntosh 1979). This paper represents an attempt to modify this understanding, not discard it out of hand. The contention is that women do hold power within the family: this power is interstitial rather than formal but its interstitial quality should not lead to a lack of recognition (Wolf 1976). Formal power results in formal organization, interstitial power generates informal organization; it is to these patterns of informal organization that we look in attempting to identify female means of control. The traditional approach to power relations within the family has been largely ethnographic, an approach which under-theorises the significance of the numerous but scattered instances of female power which it reveals (Denis et al. 1956). Yet the family can be the institution *par excellence*, where women can combine to defend their collective interest.

The labour process debate, like conventional industrial sociology understands workplace contestation and control as bounded by the physical division between the factory and the outside world, at least regarding its treatment of labour. There is little or no consideration of the community dimension or of those linkages within the workplace which are a product of extra-industrial connections (Whipp, forthcoming). However, these ties may be formative not only of attributes within any specific workplace (Ammasari 1969) but may also determine the social composition of the workforce (Yans-McLaughlin 1971). We suggest that an approach of this kind could be usefully integrated into the labour process perspective on employment relations

(Whipp and Grieco 1984). Moreover, an understanding of the role of kin in shaping workplace experience should not be confined solely to the area of male occupational inheritance (Hobsbawm 1964: 272–315). Community based, female ties and networks can also be mobilised to produce: female job succession; female means of training and skill acquisition; and forms of female control. The study of the relationship between gender and technology must therefore admit the inter-relationship of gender, the labour process and the community.

Our data on the relationship between women and the workplace comes from four different industrial locations, spread in time from the late nineteenth century to the present day. The first study concerns the pottery industry of Staffordshire in the 1890–1930 period (Whipp 1983) which in 1902 was the sixth largest industrial employer of female labour in the UK. Women made up half of the workforce in an industry which provides a strong example of how female methods of control can operate in a world which was officially defined by males. The second data set comes from the Aberdeen fish processing trade. The family was the major training and recruitment agency within this sector where female labour was predominant. Unlike the labour in the pottery or fish processing industries the workers in our third source, the detailed reconstruction of a family history in the East End of London, were attached to no single industry but moved through a number of trades. As in the pottery industry, the information and trading networks were here the small-scale, relatively unstructured means of pooling knowledge about all aspects of work: these networks were as much the arena for female as male activity. The final source is from the steel plant in Corby where very few females were employed. These data sets (Whipp 1983; Grieco 1984) will be used to give a more open examination of gender relations at work via an empirical investigation of female subordination. Four main areas of work are explored: women, skill and technology; the destination of the wage; control; and resistance.

Women, skill and technology

The abiding concern of feminist writers on work has been to research the subordinate position of women in the labour market and their segregation into secondary jobs. This focus has diverted attention from key features of the everyday experience of certain female workers and especially in the relationship of women to skill and technology.

Technology does not only refer to plant and equipment but can include the technical knowledge and abilities of operators. Scrutiny has been given to the different types of skill and the way skill is perceived and classified. More (1980: 15–17) distinguishes between technical, objective aspects of skill (the alliance of manual skill and knowledge) and the subjective, social construction of skill, which involves the attribution of the skill label and may derive from custom or power relations (Penn 1984). Some have recognised the relevance of the social construction of skill for women workers and its prejudicial connotation. Phillips and Taylor (1980) found that skill definitions are 'saturated with sexual bias'. Women workers enter the workplace as subordinate individuals and their work is categorised according to their inferior status. Skill becomes an 'ideological category imposed on certain types of work by virtue of the sex and power of the workers who perform it' (ibid.). Two points have emerged from our own research. Although women's skills have been either unacknowledged or misrepresented this does not necessarily mean that these abilities have not existed. Second, not only do women possess technical, objective skills, they too have been active in the social construction of skill and especially in the social organization of skilled work.

It is now recognised that official statistics have minimised or obscured female participation rates in industry (Alexander et al. 1979). For example, decadal returns for the Staffordshire census, 1871–1911 show a rate of increase in the number of women pottery workers (by 12.7 per cent, 22 per cent, 10.9 per cent and 21.6 per cent respectively) whereas the standard view maintains that women workers' industrial participation rates were declining in the late nineteenth century (Collet 1911). Similarly the notion that women were found in only low-paid, marginal jobs which reflected their dependent domestic circumstances was roundly criticised by women activists in a government inquiry in 1919. As they reported there was: 'a conventional view of women's work, which still recognises for women ideals which are more or less incompatible with the facts of everyday life'. Then, as now, there was a contradiction between appearance and practice.

While few ceramic textbooks or official contemporary accounts recognised women potters as other than helpers or 'attendants' the reality was quite different. In the pottery industry women's jobs were largely, but not exclusively, lower paid than men, less skilled or involving less formal authority in the labour process. Women were present in every department and throughout the main skill divisions: they were by no means solely unskilled labour. The early stages of production saw women as assistants while in the later printing, decorating and warehouse departments, female dexterity was highly valued. Women in these stages occupied trades of high manual skill such as transferring, gilding and painting and were paid accordingly. The aggregate wage data for the industry minimises such female pay levels. Women potters also played a part in defining the worth of their trade on the shop floor. For instance, given their abilities, women transferrers were periodically in short supply. Therefore, according to a male potter, 'if a man did not treat his attendant properly she would leave him' (Royal Commission on Labour, 1893: 61–3). Yet the public language of male craft potters (notably during the trade and employment crises of the 1840s, 1880s, 1890s and in the 1920s), used to substantiate their own privileged skill position against managerial attack (see also Bradley, this volume) categorised women potters as unskilled and temporary workers and has been the only view recorded.

In the East End study the employment history of one family network involved the records of 39 members. This group of workers moved through a number of different employers including traditional; modern; small; large; local and multi-national. Both men and women from this kin group repeatedly shared place of employment and negotiated industrial proximity one to another across a range of venues. It was not an accident of geography but a matter of strategy. Movement through the skill hierarchies was not so much by formal training: instead induction and information derived from kin association was a key means for these workers of developing tacit skills (Manwaring 1982). Though they were not organised as family workgroups, as in the pottery and fishing industries, there was an important family dimension to job procurement and skill acquisition which involved both genders. The evidence from the family employment histories was that the job placement of family members was negotiated by both lines of lineage – mother's family and father's family. Put alongside other research a picture emerges where the working-class family can in fact be bilateral in its economic organisation and forms of co-operation.

There is a stronger case for the 'separation of spheres' approach to women and work in sites where heavy industry is the sole employer. Yet as the Corby research shows, even here the separation is by no means complete. Of the sample of 65 workers employed at the Corby steel works only one was a woman. One third of the sample's wives currently worked (although all had worked at some point in their married life). Certainly, most of the sample had never worked in the same enterprise as their wife. However, two thirds of the married women connected to the sample had at some point in their marriage held employment which had been a major source of income for the household: one third had occupied the role of sole breadwinner. The Corby sample is an example of the necessity to trace the pattern of family employment and the male and female roles it contains, across time.

The consequences of one-industry towns for female employment has often been remarked on. In situations of monopsony the single employer determines (it is said) the distribution of economic responsibility within the family by providing or withholding employment opportunities for women. Byington (1910; 1969) found that in one-industry towns family occupational patterns would ultimately be determined by that industry regardless of cultural preferences. Although Byington is essentially correct there is a qualification that should be made to the implication that where females are absent from the workforce they have no influence upon the social organisation of work. Evidence from Corby suggests this is far from the case. Women can control the allocation of domestic space and this has important consequences in a situation where labour is drawn from beyond the boundaries of the local labour market. As with Hareven's (1982) discussion of labour circulation in New England so in Corby, kinship was the primary basis on which labour was both recruited and accommodated. Women relatives provided the domestic space which hosted repeated labour migrations by the same individual workers. Managerial recruitment practices recognised and used these accommodation arrangements which were controlled by women (Grieco 1984).

In the pottery and fishing industries women not only played a key role in recruitment to the workplace, but they were also pivotal in recuiting individuals to specific trades and skills. The potters' union registers of 1920 are an excellent source since by this date union density was over 90 per cent. Area 23 of Burslem town lodge contained 36 working family groups (Whipp 1982): by tracing the occupation of the members the significance of the family and women to job succession becomes apparent. Male pottery workers fit the general view of male skill inheritance (Hill 1976: 175; Matsumura 1983) as 40 per cent of the sons in the sample followed the same trade as their fathers. Yet in the same sample 48 per cent of the daughters worked in the same job as their mothers. Moreover, by plotting the workers who followed their parents into the same department, the connection is even stronger – 63 per cent of the sons and 74 per cent of the daughters worked in the ame department of the production process as their father or mother respectively.

The personal testimony of pottery workers confirms that male and female potters exercised the discretion of sub-employing workers of their own choice: other members of their family or kin were natural choices. Elizabeth Ellis, who started work in 1907, related how her aunt found a job for her and trained her as a 13-year-old teapot maker, introducing her to the manual skills of 'making' as well as instructing her in the complexities of 'counts' and 'dozens' which were part of the wealth of shop floor custom. Contacts of this kind were the means by which women potters could structure the socialisation and induction of female kin to the workplace as Dublin (1979) also found for the US textile industry. Given the prevalence of labour-intensive, manual-based technology, pottery employers were happy to make use of these informal and less costly recruitment and training procedures. The women potters do not conform therefore to the model of those who argue that in the early twentieth century increased productivity and higher male wages permitted a sharper division of labour within the workplace and household. Married women potters especially, were not simply 'preferred as child care or consumer specialists' (Tilly and Scott 1978: 230-1). The local convention was that 'a woman is looked upon as lazy unless she takes her share in contributing to the family income' (Martindale 1903: 123). Moreover, women potters not only went out to work, they were active agents in the recruitment of female labour and the acquisition of skill.

Similar practices were found in the fish processing trades of Scotland. A study of ten enterprises in the Aberdeen area revealed the extent to which employers in 1977 depended on their employees for training new labour. Thompson (1983a) demonstrates the extent to which female occupational inheritance in this industry pertained in the past but assumes that training is now more formal and universal in its character. On the contrary, our evidence indicates that the older pattern persists and that female social networks still play a major role as a training agency. Table 1 gives a representation of the recruitment of female labour in the ten company sample. Figure 1 is an example of one company's workforce and its kin connectedness over time.

The use of kin as a recruitment agency may reduce management costs, but here, as in the Potteries, it could also provide workgroups with greater control over the composition and character of the labour force. The evidence from two employers is illustrative of these practices. According to the first:

> the girls train one another but they won't just train anybody. They'll train their own but ask them to train a stranger and you run up against a brick wall fast enough.

Similarly, the second employer stated:

> Although a lot of our work is casual, it's highly skilled. If you put somebody not trained on, they spoil the fish and you don't have time to teach them or even watch them when you have a rush on and you're in the middle of it all. They slow you down. . . . But if you take somebody's daughter or sister, like Helen here, you know she's had a bittie practice first even if she's only starting at it.

Table 1   Female labour and employer recruitment practices: the Aberdeen fishing sector

| Employer | Labour force size | Formal recruitment channels | | Informal recruitment channels | | Trained recruits only | Training given on job | |
		Advertising	Employment exchange	Work force recommendation only	Work force direct applications		Company	Contact
A	70	No	No	No	Yes	No	No	Yes
B	100	No	No	No	Yes	No	Yes	Yes
C	12	Yes	No	No	Yes	No	Yes	Yes
D	11	No	No	Yes	No	Yes	No	No
E	8	No	No	Yes	No	No	No	Yes
F	6	No	No	Yes	No	Yes	No	Yes
G	6	No	No	Yes	No	No	No	Yes
H	5	No	No	Yes	No	Yes	No	No
I	3	No	No	Yes	No	Yes	No	No
J	3	*Family business: categories not applicable.*						
Total	218	1	0	6	3	4	2	5

Figure 1 Workforce 1 Employment Net

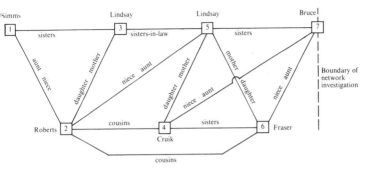

1, 2, 3, presently working in enterprise I
4, 5, 6, presently working in enterprise K
3, 2,   last job in enterprise L with 7
7.   presently working in enterprise L
I,   last job in enterprise K with 4, 5, 6

As we shall show below, these features of recruitment and training could be the opportunity for both strengthening managerial control as well as enabling resistance by female workers.

The destination of the wage

One of the central aspects of the subordinate position of women workers is their low wages (Amsden 1980: 11–40; Mitchell 1971: 144). Whilst in broad terms women's wages have been consistently lower than men's, the picture is not so straightforward. The concept of the family wage has been used (Hartmann 1976) with reference to how male workers sought women's exclusion from work and also claimed a wage sufficient to support 'their' family. To focus almost solely on male activity or even to regard male and female wages in isolation misses the way the wage is viewed by families and the influence which women have in this context.

Writers from the Webbs (1902: x) down to Blackburn (1967: 38–9) have stressed how the productivity of labour is remunerated on an individual basis. Yet as Bornat (1977) has shown in the woollen industry, to view the wage in this way misses its full significance; instead, it is necessary to trace the destination of the wage. In the potters' case the wage was not experienced in isolation. Under the sub-contract system the wage was often a group wage. Where these groups were family-based or where a large proportion of a family worked in the industry, both sets brought home a collective family wage. The distribution and consumption of income was therefore a family concern and an area where women played an active part. For example, the rule books of the male craft potters' unions in the 1890s make it a regulation that unemployment benefit would be paid according to not only the member's family's income but also his wife's. The potters are an example of Tilly and Scott's findings (1978: 113) on twentieth-century wage payment whereby: where female family members were employed across an industry or in a family workgroup, women 'were considered or apparently considered themselves members of a team, earning a family wage'.

Data on the differentials in male and female wage levels raises another question: why should women accept such differences? In order to understand the apparent acceptance of these differences in the workplace, it is necessary to focus on the destination of the male wage. Our research has found evidence of female social pressure on the individual male wage-earner who defaults on his responsibilities. The assertion is not that female control over the male wage is perfect, rather to suggest that customarily the wage does not belong unambiguously to the individual male. The work of Ellen Ross (1983: 7) on social networks earlier this century notes the positions of female influence and their related burdens. As she puts it:

> Most husbands handed over to their wives the largest part of their weekly earnings, retaining 'pocket money' for themselves ... the arrangement gave wives considerable domestic power, but it also made them solely responsible for sustaining life under very unpromising conditions.

Of particular interest in our East End research was the way in which family interest cut across gender divisions. Where women family members became aware of high-paying vacancies, rather than trying to procure them for themselves, they advised their male kin to apply or pushed them forward. Family finances were seen as benefiting overall from such advances on the part of male kin. To attempt to secure jobs of higher calibre as an individual woman was to invite failure. Women, where they share a workplace with their male kin, have an interest in identifying such opportunities and capturing them indirectly through male kin. Family is served before gender.

As in the East End, pottery males were not unambiguously the dominant party within the family wage context even though they were officially better paid. Given the high incidence of industrial disease and intermittent employment in the pottery industry, women were often the sole breadwinner during their employment career. This was the case during the severe trade disruptions of the 1890s, 1900s, 1914–18 and from 1923 onwards. Dependency was reversed; in 1908 Sam Clowes, the president of the potters' union, testified that the women potters 'are sometimes the sole support of the house'. Similar evidence has been unearthed by writers researching the relationship between women and the workplace. Brinley Thomas (1939) noted that geographical mobility was greatest in those areas where employment was afforded to males only, such as mining. In industries which employed males and females, albeit on different terms and conditions, it was less frequently the case that both sets of workers, or put differently, all members of a family, would be rendered unemployed in the same period. In cotton, male unemployment was frequently accompanied by a lesser reduction in female employment and geographical mobility amongst cotton workers was consequently considerably less. The routine employment of both genders provided the family with an important potential for survival, as one category of family member retained employment when the other was pushed out of work, leaving the family on reduced though sufficient resources for survival to remain in the locality. In situations of high and recurrent uncertainty, families develop strategies to modify the environment. In cotton, pottery and fishing the placing and maintaining of female members in work was one such strategy. Family interests cut across male collective interests: the role of breadwinner has moved more easily between men and women than has been formerly supposed.

A reading of official accounts gives the impression that the male worker enjoyed public recognition as head of the family. Our findings reflect Meacham (1977: 116) whereby the image of male authority may have persisted, yet it was the woman who was so often the effective centre of the family. Her decisions, as domestic manager, over allocation and expenditure provided a vital influence on activity in and around the labour process. A potters' union survey of 1925 shows how Harold Moore's mother would not let him take part in union action since it would upset her domestic budget. Another woman ceased paying her husband's weekly union dues (that she paid the dues is revealing) since she decided it was no longer possible to contain them within her weekly expenditure. Women's domestic roles as main breadwinner or domestic manager, within long-term, collective, family survival strategies, meant that the household context was the appropriate arena in which to seek control of the male wage. This also helps explain why women workers did not choose the workplace so readily for challenging male/female wage disparities; an area where they were heavily disadvantaged. Rather than concentrating solely on the well-known male/female wage differentials in the workplace as a direct expression of female subordination, a fuller understanding of the significance of pay could be gained by exploring the collective use to which it is put in the wider social setting of labour process and community.

Control
Labour process writers have emphasised the relative ease and almost complete success with which management has established and maintains control over women workers. Women are seen as essentially temporary workers making up an unskilled industrial reserve army of labour, ready to replace de-skilled male workers. The relationship between women's domestic and industrial behaviour is not addressed and its implications for women's availability for the labour market on their ability to move in and out of waged work is ignored (Beechey 1982). A more satisfactory explanation of how management can use women as temporary workers lies in the linking of the constant variation in production with women's household circumstances and the ideological use to which they can be put. In contrast to most labour process commentators this line of analysis reveals how management is not omnipotent in its control of female labour since it relies on women performing vital function, which women themselves can exploit.

Edwards in his study of twentieth-century workplace relations notes how women are used extensively by the Boston electronic components industry and that this labour exhibited high rates of departure and re-entry to the same workplace (Edwards 1979: 3). He does not pursue why this might be so. There is a connection between employers' use of female labour and their tolerance of absenteeism. In the fishing and pottery industries the relationship is clearly visible. The variability in product demand and consequent irregularity of production led management to rely on women to provide the necessary labour which could accommodate such uncertainty. In fishing, increases in the volume of fish processed are sudden, not steady and organizing the recruitment of totally new replacement labour to service sudden increases is clearly inefficient. Existing women workers (especially older women) were used to call in kin who were either trained or oriented to the work. In the pottery industry the local character of the workforce was important to management practices. A 1 per cent sample of industry's workforce in 1920 shows that 49.7 per cent lived within one and two miles from their workplace and 40 per cent resided within one mile. It was the work cycles of pottery manufacture which bound the domestic and industrial worlds. Moreover, women synchronised home and work routines in order to fit the long and irregular working sessions. Within the self-determined workshop practices associated with sub-contract, women learned to match variations in production runs with household requirements. As a stoneware employer admitted in 1911, in his potbank 'the employment is a free and easy one, and women do not need to be constantly at work'. The meeting place of production requirements, recruitment costs and women's self-interest is a more satisfactory starting point for the explanation of the relationship between gender and absenteeism than the traditional 'pin money' accounts of female work.

At the same time as management relies on women's flexibility as labour it has attempted to harness society's standard images of women as marginal labour in framing labour control policies. Even within industries which depend predominantly upon female labour, the marginal label is still attached. The image of women as belonging in the home is the base upon which management has manipulated female labour, for it permits the imposition of disadvantageous part-time conditions and terms. Prior to the equal opportunity legislation of the last decade there are widespread examples of British companies operating a conventional rule whereby on marriage a woman had to leave the workforce completely or was only permitted to hold part-time positions. Smith (1984) for example points out that the attention given to Cadbury as one of the creators of the secure employment contract, neglects the position of women. Female employees were required to leave the firm on marriage; a policy which was accompanied by the extensive use of part-time female labour. Rules requiring the departure of full-time female workers on marriage marginalised the status of female labour. Full-time female workers in enterprises operating these codes were necessarily younger and less experienced than their male counterparts who were not subject to the same process of cohort expulsion.

Companies which forbade females full-time employment in line with the ideological stance that women belonged in the home, often use females as a major source of labour. The benefits are considerable. Placing female labour on part-time or occasional contracts provides the employer with access to reservoirs of labour, as in the fish and pottery industries: yet it also renders female labour less visible. The casualisation of female labour allows employers who have irregular production levels to call upon extra supplies of labour at will and with less cost. For instance, part-time workers can be asked to work longer hours in peak periods. Employers' use of the image which defines the home as the proper sphere of women, when accompanied by the family's need for the female wage, ensures women as a ready source of secondary market labour. Far from removing women from the labour market such rules and codes reduce the terms upon which they compete.

What are the consequences of these poor terms and conditions for the organization of work in those households where the woman is the sole or chief breadwinner? It has already been suggested that the location of women in part-time jobs is more a consequence of pressure than preference: so even where women need, because of responsibility, and desire, because of better wages and conditions, full-time employment, they may not have the option of obtaining it. Within our contemporary material, there is a common theme whereby women try to surmount this handicap by taking a number of jobs. A typical example was of a woman who, during her husband's illness and unemployment, took an early morning job as cleaner; an afternoon job as a cook; and an evening job as an usherette. In all three jobs she was employed on a casual basis. Her employment, given its concealment from the tax net, is unlikely to appear in official statistics. Not only does management harness the social need and pressure upon this type of female worker to remain invisible, but the apparent freedom for high turnover means this type of worker does not get full membership of the labour market yet management draws the benefit from here experience.

Even where women are permanent members of a workforce, management is able to render them invisible in power terms. In the pottery industry in public discourse and especially during disputes or local protective legislation campaigns, employers portrayed the female potter as a marginal, casual worker carrying little responsibility. In private negotiations or shop floor practice women appear as skilled and experienced workers with considerable responsibility for parts of the production sequences. This finding is closely paralleled by the Lupton and Cunnison study of women garment workers where women exercised de facto supervisory roles but were not formally accorded this status (Lupton and Cunnison, 1964; see also Davies and Rosser, this volume). These instances suggest that just as female participation rates in employment have been under-recorded in official statistics, as a consequence of ideological and legal conventions, so female power represented by supervisory responsibility has been similarly missed.

A similar reduction of the visibility of female labour is encountered in home working (Allen 1983: Saifullah Khan 1979). Whilst women's wages are essential to the family budget, given the general acceptance of the construed dependence of females on males within the household, their employment remains invisible. The need for women's wages within the family, coupled with the dominant ideology that they should not work, results in their location in the poorest-paying employment sector.

The exploitation of the image of women as properly confined to the domestic sphere by employers is revealed by the ease with which they abandon it in practice during periods of change or crisis and re-establish its use thereafter (Milkman 1983: Gabin 1979). The history of the pottery industry in the nineteenth and twentieth centuries contains a catalogue of management's use of female labour to cheapen production and/or replace recalcitrant male craft workers on the shop floor while publically adhering to the ideology of the 'separation of spheres'. This highly conditional use of ideology paralleled by contradictory practice ws displayed in the 1840s and 1870s conflicts over jigger and jolly machinery and again during the 1890–1914 trade depression and the resulting increased use of casting.

Resistance

In spite of the extent of the managerial controls exercised over women workers, the networks and devices which permit these forms of direction at the same time facilitate resistance by women. It appears from our own primary material that women play a major role in the brokerage of male employment opportunity. Data drawn from a variety of industries and independently conducted by researchers in the US and the UK demonstrates that the linkage between kin membership and economic co-operation has not disappeared but persists as an important feature of survival strategies in advanced industrial societies (Tilly and Scott 1978: Wedderburn 1965; 48: Mann 1973). Put simply, manual workers help one another find employment on a social network basis (Jenkins et al. 1983). It is in this spirit that the role of women as employment brokers can be analysed.

Through their investment in the family women come to occupy the role of employment brokers – a role which enhances their ability to remain close to one another. In this objective sense, women's interests and employers' interests can be viewed as compatible. This is not to suggest that there is no exploitation but rather to identify the intersection between women's interests, given exploitation, and employers' recruitment practicies. Wives possess 'patron' characteristics which have gone unrecognised in the literature. A wife can use her influence directly on her male kin, or indirectly through her female kin on her male kin, in order to obtain employment for her husband. Mrs S Davies, of Chalres Street, Hanley, secured employment with E Johnson & Co Ltd, the pottery firm, on 13 October 1908, on the basis of her decorating skill. At the same time she negotiated a position for her ex-miner husband as an engine stoker. An interview with a manager at Doulton's in the 1970s revealed how he relied on his pottery workers, especially those who were parents, both fathers and mothers, to provide children or adult relations to fill a place. Whilst males may be defined as the workers, females are frequently the enablers or brokers.

The account of resistance in the workplace by Lupton and Cunnison (1964) sits uneasily with those analyses which point to the absolute subordination and passivity of women in the workplace. Crucial to the former account is a conception of the timing of intervention by female workers: action took place in the busy period, when the employer was most vulnerable. It was at this point that the normal division of labour was contested. Identifying resistance of this kind requires detailed study of a specific workplace.

In the same way that the garment workers of Manchester used the busiest period as the appropriate time to exert pressure, similar strategies are adopted by women in the fish processing sector, an industry which exhibits a similar pattern of female casual labour. Female fish processing labour has been traditionally migrant, 'following the herring' down the coastline of the country. Females paralleled on shore the journeys of their men at sea. A female fish worker tells of an important dispute in 1911, when female fish workers went on strike against the interests of their male kin. It was an apparently spontaneous collective act. The ties within the community which usually precluded such action against men were on this occasion overwhelmed by the ties within the community which linked one woman to another.

Apart from their control over the recruitment and training procedures it was in the 'busy periods' that female fish workers demonstrated their informal, highly localised power. It was at this time that new rates of pay were bargained over and fought for; similarly, it was then in the individual enterprise that the quality of materials were challenged and bargaining over improvements took place. Once the busy period was over, the attempt to readjust rates and conditions downwards occurred. Both employers and workers expected to bargain when production was at its height. It is not then that conditions and rates are never challenged by women workers but rather, that the results of such negotiations are temporary, though recurrent, and are seldom embodied in formal documentation. Resistance is typically workshop organized and based: it is as a consequence less visible and seldom recorded.

Similarly in the pottery industry small-scale collective action by women workers was the main expression of their discontent. The available evidence indicates a pattern of localised action by female potters and often against male interests or union policy. A group of female towers at Booth's & Co in 1911 told Mr Hollins, a union organizer, that 'the men do not seem willing to fight for us, so the best plan was to fight for ourselves'. The 1907 male sanitary workers dispute has gone down in Potteries folklore yet the equally fiercely contested strike of the women tile workers at Henry Richards at exactly the same time has received scant attention. Small-scale female action could also become widespread on occasion. For example, in November 1911 seven women aerographers' wages were reduced by the notorious Grindley Co. The entire female workforce of 160 struck successfully in support. These events were largely unrecorded at the time, just as no one has hitherto bothered to reconstruct the women potters' presence in the union collectors' ranks where they performed at an equal rate to the men.

As in the fishing industry, timing was of the essence in female action. Combining this insight with our picture of informal women's activity provides a more sound explanation of the female militancy of the Great War period. Traditional explanations for the secondary position of women in the workplace and in trade unions fail to account for why such apparently deep-rooted obstacles to female unionism could be demolished almost overnight in the Potteries. An alternative explanation contends that the informal means of female work control among the potters, which we identified, existed long before the 1914–18 period. Therefore, when economic and institutional restraints were lifted during the war, the small-scale, previously unreported variants of female action were given formal recognition and became co-ordinated on a wider scale. Women potters were continuing at the official union level what they practised routinely and informally before the war. The women potters, in their spontaneous forms of action or organic modes of organization, be it in the workshop, the home or the union, via the family or the workgroup, their experience fits the conclusion and advice that:

> Women have fared better in non-structural, non-intellectual, localised institutions', therefore 'we cannot uncover the realities of women's past if we look at them as adjuncts to or minor participants in the male power structure.
>
> (H. Smith 1976: 382–3)

A particularly interesting relationship between women, work and health is found generally in the lead-using industries. Earlier this century when abortion was illegal, female workers 'in the lead' were aware of its abortifacient properties (Knight 1977). To speak publicly of these effects and to be known to have deliberately used them was to invite criminal prosecution. Female social networks provided a safe environment for the transmission of this knowledge among women. A local doctor found in one sample of 77 women pottery workers, who used lead, eight had experienced 21 still-births; 35 admitted to having a total of 90 miscarriages. In spite of the risks women potters employed lead to bring on abortions. It was apparently a local truism that to marry a girl lead worker would ensure a marriage where family size could be easily limited. As the trade journal, the *Pottery Gazette*, decorously reported in September 1903:

> An intelligent knowledge of the so-called 'medicines' taken by the female workers will enable the (factory) inspector to attribute occasional cases of lead poisoning to the right cause'.

In contrast to the opprobrium of religious and charitable organizations, as well as magistrates who wished to 'save' the women potters, these women were appropriating part of the means of production to regulate their own reproductive capacity on their own terms.

Conclusion

A recent overview of the labour process debate (Thompson 1983b: 193–209) observed how writers almost take female powerlessness for granted. Actions outside the workplace are too often reduced to the functional requirements of capital. A reliance solely on categories derived from labour process analysis cannot therefore provide a very full account of women's work: such a perspective conveys little of the structures and processes beyond the point of production which determine the availability and use of female labour. As Yans-McLaughlin (1971) notes, cultural preferences play a part in determining patterns of work. In contrast to the dominant trend, this paper has identified community structure and workplace composition as different yet interacting aspects of a particular configuration of social relations. Female social networks and the social organization of work are intricately connected.

The relationship between the genders is both collaborative and competitive around work. Managerial strategies of control make use of and enhance the sexual divisions within society. Competition is deliberately engendered between the sexes, whilst simultaneously the collaborative relationship, via the family and social networks, is harnessed in order to retain reserve labour. Management both contributes towards the strengthening of the ideology of women's separate domestic sphere while at the same time making use of female labour. The ideology enables and determines the invisibility of woman as worker, thus preparing the ground for the extreme exploitation of female labour. Women not only have invisibility in the workplace imposed upon them but also collude in its persistence as a consequence of the relationship found within the family. Power is diverted and resistance deflected. Technological advances in office machinery and flexible manufacturing have created the possibility of extensive outworking and especially in those sectors where female employment predominates. As outwork grows as a practice the relationship between the home and the workplace is likely to become even stronger.

Although managerial control over women appears formidable it is not total or one-sided in operation. As there is collaboration and contest between men and women in the family (Stedman-Jones 1974) so in the workplace management seeks the co-operation of women, over recruitment and training for example: this enables women to exercise power within this relationship of 'antagonism and interdependence' (Bradley this volume). Those who see the family and workplace relations as critical only to the suppression of women are misguided. We argue that in the family and at work women do hold power: the power is interstitial, neither formally organized or recognized; it is exercised locally and on a small scale (Ryan 1983: 183).

It is not argued that the traditional female subordination model should be completely overturned, far from it, as our portrayal of management control indicates. More cautiously, in the light of our own evidence, and in conjunction with other research, the orthodox stress on complete female subordination and dependency in the family, home and work relationship appears as absolute and therefore inaccurate. Using historical and contemporary material it is noticeable how, irrespective of the state of technological development, the inter-relationship of community and labour process is maintained by the pivotal role of women and the family. As management attempts to use the domestic, social and ideological pressures on women over time, so does the ability of the working-class family to survive and reshape capital/labour relations persist: a process in which women play a vital part. This relationship between work, the family and the home is reproduced because it is of benefit not only to capital and men, but to women also.

References

Alexander, S. (1984), 'Women, class and sexual difference', *History Workshop* 17 Spring, 125–49.

Alexander, S. et al. (1979), 'Labouring Women', *History Workshop* 8, 174–82.

Allen, S. (1983), 'Production and reproduction: the lives of women homeworkers', *Sociological Review*, 31, 4, 649–65.

Ammasari, P. (1969), 'The Italian blue-collar worker', *International Journal of Comparative Sociology*, 10, 3–21.

Amsden, A. (ed.) (1980), *The Economics of Women and Work*, Harmondsworth: Penguin.

Baker-Miller, J. (1982), 'Ties to others' in M. Evans *The Woman Question*, London: Fontana, 95–106.

Barrett, M. (1980), *Women's Oppression Today. Problems in Marxist Feminist Analysis*, London: New Left Books.

Barrett, M. and McIntosh, M. (1979), 'Christine Delphy: Towards a materialist feminism', *Feminist Review* 1, 95–106.

Beechey, V. (1982), 'The unequal society', in Wood, S. (ed.) *The Degradation of Work*, London: Hutchinson.

Blackburn, R. (1967), 'The Unequal Society' in Blackburn, R. and Cockburn, A. (eds.), *The Incompatibles*, Harmondsworth: Penguin 15–55.

Bornat, J. (1977), 'Home and work, a new context for trade union history', *Radical America*, 12, (5), 53–69.

Brenner, J. and Ramas, M. (1984), 'Rethinking women's oppression', *New Left Review*, 144, 33–71.

Byington, M. (1910; 1969), *Homestead: the households of a mill town*, New York: Arno.

Collet, C. (1911), *Women in Industry*, London: Newcastle Economic Society.

Denis, N. et al. (1956), *Coal is Our Life*, London: Eyre and Spottiswoode.

Dublin, T. (1979), *Women at Work: the transformation of work and community in Lowell, Mass. 1826–1860*, New York: Columbia University Press.

Edwards, R. (1979), *Contested Terrain. The Transformation of the Workplace in the Twentieth Century*, London: Heinemann.

Gabin, N. (1979), 'Women workers and the U.A.W. in the post World War II period, *Labor History*, 21, 5–30.

Gilligan, C. (1982), *In a Different Voice*, Cambridge, Mass: Harvard University Press.

Gorz, A. (1976), *The Division of Labour: the Labour Process and Class Struggle in Modern Capitalism*, Brighton: Harvester.

Grieco, M. (1982), 'Family structure and industrial employment: the role of information and migration,' *Journal of Marriage and the Family*, August, 44, 3, 701–7.

Grieco, M. (1984), 'Information networks and the allocation of employment opportunity', unpublished D. Phil. thesis, Oxford University.

Hareven, T. (1982), *Family Time and Industrial Time*, Cambridge: Cambridge University Press.

Hartmann, H. (1976), 'Capitalism, patriarchy and job segregation by sex', in Blaxall, M. and Reagen, B. (eds.), *Women in the Workplace*, Chicago: Chicago University Press.

Hill, S. (1976), *The Dockers. Class and Tradition in London*, London: Heinemann.

Hobsbawm, E. (1964), *Labouring Men*, London: Weidenfeld and Nicholson.

Hunt, P. (1980), *Gender and Class Consciousness*, London: Macmillan.

Jenkin, R. et al. (1983), 'Information in the labour market: the impact of recession', *Sociology*, 7, (2), 260–7.

Kessler-Harris, A. (1981), *Women Have Always Worked*. New York: Feminist Press.

Knight, P. (1977), 'Women and abortion in Victorian and Edwardian England', *History Workshop Journal*, 4, 57–67.

de Lauwe, P. (1956), *La Vie Quotidienne des families ouvrières*, Paris: Centre de la Recherche Scientifique.

Lupton, T. and Cunnison, S. (1964), 'Workshop Behaviour' in *Closed systems and open minds: the limits of naivety in social anthropology*', London: Oliver and Boyd.

Mann, M. (1973), *Workers on the Move*, Cambridge: Cambridge University Press.

Manwaring, T. (1982), 'The Extended Internal Labour Market', IIM Berlin. Discussion paper, LMP 82.29.

Martindale, H. (1903), Evidence to *Departmental Committee on Physical Deterioration*.

Matsumura, T. (1983), *The Victorian Flint Glass Makers. The Labour Aristocracy Revisited*, Manchester: Manchester University Press.

Meacham, S. (1977), *A Life Apart*, London: Thames and Hudson.

Milkman, R. (1983), 'Female factory labor and industrial structure: control and conflict over "Women's place" in auto and electrical manufacturing', *Politics and Society*, 12, (2), 159–203.

Mitchell, J. (1971), *Women's Estate*, New York: Vintage.

Montgomery, D. (1979), *Workers' Control in America*, Cambridge: Cambridge University Press.

More, C. (1980), *Skill and the English Working Class*, London: Croom Helm.

Novarra, V. (1980), *Women's Work, Men's Work*, London: Marion Boyars.

Pahl, R. (1980), 'Employment, work and the domestic division of labour', *International Journal of Urban and Regional Research*, **4**, 1-19.

Penn, R. (1984), 'Technological change, skilled manual work and the division of labour, Mimeo., Lancaster University.

Phillips, A. and Taylor, B. (1980), 'Sex and skill: notes towards a feminist economics', *Feminist Review*, **6**, 79-88.

Price, R. (1983), 'The labour process and labour history', *Social History*, **8**, (1), 57-75.

Richards, E. (1974), 'Women in the British Economy', *History* 59, 337-57.

Roberts, R. (1971), *The Classic Slum*, Manchester: Manchester University Press.

Ross, E. (1983), 'Survival Networks', *History Workshop Journal*, **15**, 4-28.

Rowbotham, S. (1979), 'The trouble with patriarchy', *New Statesman* **98**, 970-1.

Royal Commission on Labour, (1893), 'The Employment of Women. The Staffordshire Potteries, HMSO.

Ryan, M. (1983), 'The power of women's networks', in J. Newton et al. (eds.), *Sex and Class in Women's History*, London: Routledge and Kegan Paul.

Saifullah Khan, V. (1979), 'Work and Network' in S. Wallman, (ed.), *Studies in Ethnicity, Ethnicity at Work*, London: Macmillan, 115-33.

Sayles, L. (1958), *Behaviour of Industria Work Groups*, New York: Wiley.

Smith, C. (1984), 'Work Organization Research Centre, Food Sector Study, forthcoming, Aston University.

Smith, H. (1976), 'Feminism and the methodology of women's history', in B. Carroll, (ed.), *Liberating Women's History*, Chicago: University of Illinois 368-84.

SPRU (Science Policy Research Unit), (1982), *Microelectronics and Women's Employment in Britain*, SPRU Occasional Paper no. 17.

Stedman-Jones, G. (1974), 'Working class culture and working class politics: Notes on the remaking of a working class', *Journal of Social History*, 7, 460-508.

Thomas, B. (1939), 'The influx of labour into the Midlands 1920-37', *Economica*, **5**, 410-34.

Thompson, P. (1983), *Living the Fishing*, London: Routledge and Kegan Paul.

Thompson, P. (1983), *The Nature of Work*, London: Macmillan.

Tilly, L. and Scott, J. (1978), *Women, Work and Family*, London: Holt, Rinehart and Winston.

Webb, S. and B. (1902), *Problems of Modern Industry*, London: Longman Green.

Wedderburn, D. (1965), *Redundancy and the Railwaymen*, Cambridge: Cambridge University Press.

Whipp, R. (1982), 'Some aspects of home, work and trade unionism in the British pottery industry', paper presented to Anglo-Dutch Labour History Conference, Maastricht.

Whipp, R. (1983), 'Potbank and union: a study of work and trade unionism in the pottery industry 1900-1924', unpublished Ph.D. thesis, Warwick University.

Whipp, R. and Grieco, M. (1983), 'Family and the Workplace: the social organization of work', *Warwick Economic Papers*, no. 239.

Whipp, R. and Grieco, M. (1985), 'Family and the Workplace: the social organization of work', *Management Moniter*, 3 3, 3-7.

Whipp, R. 'Labour markets and communities: an historical view', *Sociological Review*, forthcoming.

Wolf, E. (1976), 'Kinship, friendship and patron-client relations in complex societies', in M. Banton, (ed.), *The Social Anthropology of Complex Societies*, London: Tavistock.

Women's Trade Union League (1900), *Quarterly Review*, July, p. 6.

Yans-McLaughlin, V. (1971), 'Patterns of work and family organization', *Journal of Interdisciplinary History*, **2**, 299-314.

Young, M. and Willmott, P. (1957), *Family and Kinship in East London*, Harmondsworth: Penguin.

7 'Men Only': Theories and Practices of Job Segregation in Insurance

David Collinson and David Knights

Introduction

There is in the literature considerable evidence that even in the service sector of the economy, where women are concentrated overwhelmingly (Hakim 1979), jobs are segregated by sex. We provide further documentation of this here through the presentation of a case study from the insurance industry where 'male jobs' are often elevated in importance and defined as 'productive', whilst 'female jobs' are widely viewed as merely supportive and secondary: a service function within a service industry. Male jobs enjoy comparatively high material and symbolic rewards; female jobs are poorly paid, closely supervised with few opportunities for advancement. However, the intention of this paper is not simply one of adding another descriptive account of the subordinate and exploited status of women at work. Although a necessary starting point, the static picture provides little or no basis for understanding the dialectical process whereby sex discrimination in employment becomes a taken-for-granted routine through its institutionalisation in job segregation.[1] At first glance, the literature appears to have a surfeit of theoretical and empirical studies attempting to understand and explain the existence and perpetuation of the gendered segregation of jobs within the labour process. Despite this, insufficient theoretical attention has focused upon, how, why and with what consequences, capitalist and patriarchial structures of domination are drawn upon and sometimes resisted in everyday labour process routines. As a result, there is a strong tendency for accounts to be trapped within a deterministic analysis wherein the two sexes are treated as undifferentiated homogenous groups, one of which is completely dominated by the other within an overall structure of labour exploitation.

Our attempt in this chapter to overcome such a deterministic stranglehold is divided into four interrelated sections. First, we survey a selection of the relevant literature on job segregation, drawing particularly on the valuable contribution of more recent empirical studies. Second, a brief historical and contemporary background to the social construction of skill in the insurance industry is provided, which forms the basis for our case study material from one highly successful UK life insurance company. Third, by examining three key areas of management control – namely, recruitment, supervision and promotion, the empirical data displays the complex dynamics involved in the experience and reproduction of job segregation. Finally, a fourth theoretical section concludes that, in order to analyse the conditions, practices and consequences of job segregation, a theory of the structures of domination and subordination must be complemented by, and integrated with, a recognition of identity problems in contemporary society. In short, an understanding of power and domination has to be seen in the context of a pervasive preoccupation that people have with the defensive preservation of gendered and hierarchical (class) identities in their social relations. Thus if a deterministic analysis is to be avoided, it seems important to theorise how the often taken-for-granted and routine character of the reproduction of job segregation is a complex condition and consequence of the way in which consciousness and action tend to reflect and yet reinforce structural inequality and oppression. Although not elaborated in any detail until the conclusion, the avoidance of a deterministic perspective informs each of the sections including the following selective yet critical review of the literature on job segregation.

Functionalism and determinism
In the early 1970s labour process accounts of the gendered segregation of jobs consisted largely of fairly mechanical approaches in which the 'women question' was simply welded onto a radical perspective dominated by previously 'sex blind' (Hartmann 1981) Marxist categories. In particular Edwards (1975, 1979) and Reich, Gordon and Edwards (1980) developed the limitedly descriptive 'dual labour market' theory (Doeringer and Piore 1971, Barron and Norris 1976) to demonstrate how segmented labour markets were created by monopoly capitalists as a means of securing their control over labour. It was argued that the entrapment of women within the secondary sector of low-paid, unskilled and insecure jobs, aided capital by sustaining gendered divisions within the workforce. As a result of segmentation any working-class solidarity forming out of the homogenisation of labour could be prevented, thereby ensuring the continued accumulation of capital. Thus these theorists concluded that labour market segmentation is created and reproduced precisely because it is

'functional' for capital.

More recently, however, such deterministic analyses which are symptomatic of an overly narrow economistic perspective, have been criticised by contributors to the labour process debate (Aronowitz 1978; Beechey 1982; Elger 1982; Littler and Salaman 1982). For, in treating managerial power as totally omniscient and the labour force as passive and submissive, the dialectical dynamic of social relations is lost and analysis often drifts towards conspiracy (Thompson 1983: 202). Here the contradictions of control and resistance are ignored giving way to a Marxist version of structural functionalism where actions are explained in terms of their consequences in contributing to fulfilling the needs of the capitalist system (Giddens 1979). This assumption, albeit sometimes inadvertent, that capitalism is a 'living entity' with its own purposes, reasons and 'needs' is evident even in work concerned directly with the position of women. Such writers (e.g. Zaretstky 1976, Eisenstein 1979, Marshall, 1982) simply conflate gender analyses with a 'vulgar' Marxist functionalism. In addition to the intellectual objection to these teleological explanations, the reification of capitalist 'needs' assumes the subordination of 'domestic and gender relationships to class relationships' as well as the impossibility of emancipatory change. (Gamarnikow et al. 1983: 10).

However, various writers (Beechey 1977; Kuhn 1978; Amsden 1980; Humphries 1980; Barrett 1980) have sought to expose the 'chronic problem' (Connell 1983: 36) of explaining gender and class reproduction in functionalist terms. Supporting their arguments, we suggest that it is only by assuming a 'determinate conceptualisation of the subject', (Kuhn op. cit.: 45) that materialistic accounts of waged and/or 'privatised' domestic labour can render plausible their Marxist functionalist circularity (Molyneux 1979). Only then, for example, is it possible to argue that women's domestic oppression is 'functional' for capital because it holds down the price of labour (Benston 1969; Harrison 1973; Wajcman 1983), whilst ensuring the continued reproduction (Dalla Costa and James 1972; Seccombe 1974; Gardiner 1976) of an easily disposable (Marshall 1982) and acquiescent (Campioni 1976) workforce. Such analyses are theoretically con-piratorial because, although they recognise the significant interrelation between work (production) and domestic relations (social reproduction), they ascribe too much intentionality to those (i.e. capitalists) who stand to benefit from women's unpaid labour. One specific argument against both functionalist and deterministic analyses, which we will seek to elaborate throughout this chapter, concerns their refusal to treat the active human subject as problematic (Coward and Ellis 1977: 94). Attention to this limitation within the Marxian paradigm has been drawn by Hollway (1984), for example, who demonstrates how subjects become positioned within 'gendered differentiated discourses' which are themselves products of dominant social practices or institutions (eg. the family) whose history may have a relative degree of autonomy from the 'totality'. (Kuhn, op. cit.). However, within Marxist functionalism, the social reproduction of capitalist domination (the 'totality') and its relationship to gender inequality lacks historical specificity and thereby is assumed rather than explained (Middleton 1983: 27).

Confronting the theoretical slippage into a Marxist determinism, where sexual oppression is subsumed within an overall analysis of the 'totality' of economic exploitation, Beechey (1977) and Barrett (1980) have questioned its failure to theorise how sexual divisions distort supply-demand relations in the labour market. Others (Rubery 1980; Beechey 1978; Phillips and Taylor 1980; Coyle 1982; Cockburn 1983) have demonstrated how male-dominated trade unions seek to resist management in ways that exclude women. These theorists explain the reproduction of job segregation, in part, as a consequence of male workers' defensive strategies to secure jobs and high wages by protecting their skilled status from the threat of new technology and a 'reserve army' of cheap and flexible female labour (Armstrong 1982). Furthermore, the feminist critique of 'vulgar' Marxist determinism has been strengthened by evidence both of internal sexism within union relations (Pollert 1981; Westwood 1984) and of the continued subordination of women in apparently 'socialist' societies such as Cuba (Thompson 1983) and Eastern Europe (Molyneux 1981). Partly as a result of such evidence, others (e.g. Millett 1971; Firestone 1971; Delphy 1977; Hartmann 1979) have sought to explain the historical oppression of women by reference to a separate and autonomous conception of patriarchy (Barrett 1980). One problem with these approaches is that, in seeking to account for male alliances against women that predate capitalism and transcend class boundaries, they treat the two sexes as single distinct homogeneous groups (Coward 1983) and tend thereby to ignore the exclusionary practices of some males against other males (Thompson, 1983: 202). This results in the replacement of one form of historical determinism (class) with another (patriarchy).

Our concern here is not with establishing priority for class or gender analysis[2] but rather to disclose how exploitation and oppression are simultaneously 'interwoven' (West 1982) and interpenetrating' (Thompson 1983: 203) in the reproduction of everyday hierarchical relations. However, this reproduction has to be examined as a complex medium as well as an outcome of social relations of control, resistance and subordination that embody various contradictions[3]. Abandoning the structuralist straitjacket of a self-fulfilling functionalist analysis, in this chapter we attempt to capture the 'composite dynamic' of both capitalism and patriarchy by the following recommendation: 'To rethink the "structures" themselves in terms of the practices that compose them'. (Connell, 1983: 64) To expose these practices it is necessary, 'to see the role of consciousness in material structure and processes, and vice versa.' (Pollert 1983:98) Indeed, this concern has been mirrored by recent accounts of the gendered segregation of the labour process[4] which have begun to describe the practices of reproduction by drawing upon detailed historical and empirical research (see papers in this volume). In contrast to the abstract formalism of earlier Marxist contributions to the labour process and the preoccupation of empirical research with the male dominated shop floor in manufacturing, more recent studies have concentrated upon the problems of gender at work and demonstrated the significance of female as well as male resistance (Barker and Downing 1980; Pollert 1981, 1983; Cavendish 1982; Wajcman 1983; Westwood 1984; Whipp and Grieco, this volume). They have started to focus attention upon the complex and dynamic ways in which women have interpreted and 'coped with' their subordinate position. Moreover, they have provided a theoretical and methodological critique of earlier accounts that seek to explain male domination in terms of systematic economic exploitation. As Pollert has argued:

> There have been analyses of women workers in terms of the 'reserve army of labour', the 'dual labour market' and 'domestic labour' but the women themselves have been left out. They cannot be treated as the abstractions of economists – least of all marxist ones (1981: 236–7).

And yet, as Beechey (1984: 32) has observed, some of these recent empirical accounts also retain a 'curiously deterministic feel'. Partly, we suggest, perhaps because of too close an identification with the victims of oppression, a number of these researchers have continued to assume that women's consciousness, in the final analysis, is 'entirely determined by external structures' (Beechey 1984: 34). Even here then, empirical studies of the labour process that recognise the importance of gender analysis have often resorted to deterministic accounts in which the historical subject in meaning, action and relations is simply described as a product of the structured constraints of patriarchal and capitalist domination. The limitation of these studies, then, is their failure to provide a theoretical understanding of the conditions and consequences of patriarchal and capitalist domination as it is routinely reproduced in the social relations between, and the strategies adopted by, those in positions of both institutional power and subordination.

Contradiction and identity

Following earlier studies of male manual workers (Nichols and Armstrong 1973; Nichols and Beynon 1977; Willis 1977), certain contemporary accounts of the labour process have begun to describe the material and ideological contradictions that confront, yet are reproduced by, women in the context of their everyday working lives. However, although authors such as Barker and Downing (1980); Pollert (1981, 1983); and Wajcman (1983) provide rich ethnographic data describing the contradictory often individualistic, ways in which working-class females generate the confidence to resist external control, little theoretical explanation is offered as to how these oppositional cultures tend to reproduce the conditions of women's continued subordination. Whilst resistance is recognised, its grounds and unintended consequences are rarely theorised. Appropriately though, these authors reject the determinism of the 'dominant ideology thesis' (Abercrombie and Turner 1978) in favour of a conception of 'dual or oppositional consciousness' (Mann 1970; 1973), of 'unreflective consciousness' (Prandy 1979), or some notion of 'fragmented commonsense' (Gramsci 1971) all of which are used to explain why the direct personal experiences of power and subordination fail to articulate with a broader ranging political understanding of class and gender deprivation (Pollert 1981: 87, 157; Pollert 1983: 113; Wajcman 1983: 175–81). Still in our view, these explanations are incomplete and, by virtue of this, vulnerable to the same critique of determinism from which they seek an escape. It is true that individual consciousness, even when collectively expressed, imprisons resistance, within what Pollert (op. cit.: 151) describes as 'shop-floor *style*'. But if theory is to break out of the deterministic trap it must acknowledge without reproducing the individualism which is the condition and consequence of typical forms of shop floor resistance. To do this, accounts cannot just take the relations of power for granted since this involves adopting precisely the same common-sense attitude that it attributes to men and women workers in order to explain discrepancies between their action and consciousness. This common sense may reflect highly divergent political ideologies but it fails to question the everyday concern to secure the self through gaining social confirmation of personal identity. It is this preoccupation with individual security, we would argue, which militates against fully collective strategies of resistance and thereby sustains the contradiction of 'dual', 'unreflective' or 'fragmented' common sense reflected in the double discrepancy within and between word and deed or consciousness and action (Knights and Roberts 1983; Knights and Willmott 1985).

In contrast to those studies which seek to explain women's failure to challenge their subordination effectively in terms of contradictions at the level of consciousness, Cockburn (1983) and Westwood (1984) focus more directly upon the identity problematic. Both acknowledge without fully theorising the contradictions embedded in the construction of 'masculinity' and 'femininity'[5] (respectively), as gendered identities which inspire, yet paradoxically limit, shop floor resistance. Cockburn in particular, recognises the self-defeating 'fragility in men's reliance on work as a prop for their masculine identity' (ibid.: 135) and the way that union opposition to management is often built upon reproducing internal working-class divisions. And yet, in the final analysis, she still retains a passive theory of consciousness and action where contradiction is theorised as the outcome of the structural clash of the dominant ideologies of bourgeois (capitalist) and male (patriarchal) hegemony (ibid.: 205, 213). By contrast, as we have intimated, a theory of social reproduction and contradiction cannot limit itself to questioning the preference for one version of self (gender) over another (class) (ibid.: 223). Rather, it must problematise the social and psychological constitution of the historical subject and especially the construction and maintenance of identity in the context of conditions of control, resistance and subordination. This chapter will suggest that in order properly to understand the social reproduction of domination and subordination we need to theorise the processes whereby gender and hierarchical identity inequalities are both the medium and outcome of material and/or symbolic insecurity. In illustrating this thesis empirically, we seek to analyse the subjective intentions as well as the 'objective' or structural conditions and consequences of the actions of powerful and subordinate individuals or groups. By so doing, we hope to be able to demonstrate that, although control as well as resistance can have self-defeating consequences, the overall outcome of these interpenetrating strategies is the institutionalised reproduction of gender-based job segregation.

But first a brief historical account of the changing definitions of skill in office work will be provided as a background to the case study.

Job segregation and the social construction of skill in the life insurance industry

Life insurance is a commodity that is sold rather than bought. Moreover, since the underwriting of a life policy is an administrative act that can only take place once a sale has been made, conventional manufacturing divisions are turned on their head in insurance. Here, production and sales become one and the same activity. Not surprisingly, therefore, sales is considered one of, if not, the most important aspect(s) of the business. Partly as a result of this, life insurance has come to be characterised by a rigid job segregation where men are employed as inspectors (i.e. salespeople) working externally in 'the field' whilst women occupy most of the downgraded clerical positions restricted to internal office work. With few exceptions,[6] women work as a back-up clerical service for an almost totally male salesforce who seek to promote their company's policies to intermediaries. These intermediaries, who then sell directly to the public, are called agents and consist of insurance brokers, accountants, solicitors, building society and bank managers: all predominantly male organisations or professions.

Historically, it was only at the turn of the century that clerical work in insurance evolved from a well-paid and prestigious occupation for a small group of middle-class males into a devalued and subordinate position occupied predominantly by females (Lockwood 1958; Supple 1970). Prior to this transition in the subordinate ranks, the insurance world had been the exclusive domain of men. But, with the 'feminisation' (Davies 1974; Kanter 1977) of clerical work in general, women began to enter the office. It has been well documented in the literature how the demand for females was partly stimulated by the invention of the typewriter in 1875 as well as by the increased employer utilisation of secretarial shorthand skills (Supple 1970; Silverstone 1976; Downing 1980; Morgall 1981). As a result, the percentage of females in the clerical ranks spiralled from 0.1 per cent in 1851 to 72 per cent in 1971 with a corresponding dramatic rise in the number of available positions (Vinnicombe 1980: 6). Despite male resistance, the recruitment of women was facilitated by a 'massive ideological shift' (Thompson 1983: 203) in which females came to be seen as 'naturally' more obedient, productive and in possession of 'greater' skills of dexterity (Silverstone op. cit.; Davies 1974: 259). Some writers (e.g. Thompson, op. cit.: 204), following other studies that emphasise de-skilling as the impetus for job segregation (Coyle 1982), have explained this process of feminisation and its accompanying ideology as a direct consequence of capital's concern to introduce new technology and cheapen the price of labour. Alternatively, Phillips and Taylor (1980) argue that the degraded status of clerical work was not so much a product of actual task de-skilling and/or the replacement of men by women, but of 'the inferior status of the women who perform' this largely new work. They assert that socially constructed definitions of skilled status are always 'sex saturated'. But again, we argue here that a concern to establish the historical priority of capitalist appropriation and/or patriarichal domination is less important than exploring the dynamic processes of the social reproduction of power. Nevertheless it is plausible to argue that the segregation of clerical work was facilitated by a combination of these factors. In other words, the social and historical subordination of women, the introduction of new technology with its accompanying gendered ideology as well as the cheapness and flexibility of female labour power all contributed to the development of job segregation in the office. The twentieth-century influx of women into insurance coincided with the growth of branch networks as companies expanded to take advantage of the national potential for the marketing of insurance through sales promotion in the regions (Supple, 1970). It is these, predominantly male sales personnel who have usurped the status, salary and career prospects once held by the nineteenth-century male office insurance clerk. As the following case study suggests, insurance branch managers are invariably promoted after a successful career as a sales inspector. And so, in the context of job segregation it will never again be said of the Royal Exchange or indeed of any other insurance company that:

> The distinction between managerial work and clerical responsibilities was not always a sharp one; managers came from the same grades, and the same backgrounds, as their clerks.
>
> (Supple 1970: 375.6)

Instead, women have been tied to the office hierarchy having experienced great resistance to their becoming inspectors. As Poval et al. (1982) and Podmore and Spencer (this volume) also report, the high prestige middle-class world of the professions and of finance in particular, remains a bastion of male dominance from which females are either excluded or channelled into subordinated 'women's work'.

Despite the work involving predominantly mental rather than manual skills, a certain 'masculine mystique' abounds in the selling of insurance that is more usually associated with the heavy physical world of shop floor production (Willis 1977). Conventionally, the task is described in terms of an heroic drama in which 'intrepid' and autonomous males stride out into the financial world and against the odds return with new business. Since selling is production in insurance, the male sales inspectors have little difficulty in promoting an aura of grandeur about their presence and an almost mystical perception of their skills especially by contrast with the internal office staff of women clerks whose work is assumed to be dependent, supportive and secondary. These workplace gender relations thereby come to mirror the image of the conventional domestic division of labour where the husband adopts the role of breadwinner while the wife remains imprisoned within the home (see also Sturdy 1985).

In seeking to project a 'professional image' and to develop a career, ambitious male inspectors draw on work as a significant resource from which to confirm a differentiated gendered identity. The professional salesman's concern to manage a confident air of competence is linked to a particularly masculine preoccupation (Tolson 1977) with being dominant and assertive, whilst constructing an appearance of self-control and resilience to 'take the knocks' in the 'aggressive financial marketplace'. Here gender and hierarchical identity interact with the social construction of inspector's skills in a way which reflects and reinforces the segregation of jobs. For an ideology is sustained that defines the gender-imbued attributes of authority, – ambition, competitiveness, aggressive self-assertiveness and tenacity of purpose – as essential qualifications to perform the role of sales inspector. Paradoxically, in practice, much of the inspector's work consists of developing long-term 'business relationships' with agents thereby encouraging them to sell the company product. As the senior inspector in our case study commented in explaining his success,

> I've got my accountants well trained. They do their business with me and they do the selling.

Far from aggression, the nurturing of such mutually instrumental relations requires a degree of interpersonal skill that is facilitated by the gendered identification of exclusively male relationships. Thus gender plays a significant part in contributing to the development of trust and 'rapport' in inspectors' business relationships.

And yet these predominantly masculine relations with professional intermediaries are crucially dependent upon the clerical back-up of the female office staff. This is because efficient long-term client support is essential to companies with well-established products, since a good after-sales service constitutes a key selling feature. It is therefore paradoxical that the strategic importance of office work is routinely devalued in a way which reflects and reinforces a failure formally and institutionally to acknowledge the interdependence between sales and office staff. In terms of income, prestige, areas of personal autonomy and discretion, expenses, perks, etc., the salesforce enjoy significant advantages over the clerical staff.

The contradictions of this institutionalised devaluation are compounded by the women's deployment of 'tacit skills' (Manwaring and Wood 1985) and personalised knowledge in their 'telephone relations' with clients. For example, clients often have idiosyncratic requirements with which the clerical worker responsible for that particular account will be familiar. The result is that each clerical assistant develops a 'Stock of Working knowledge' which makes them uniquely able to 'service' effectively individual clients. Customer relations thereby come to be imbued with a particular 'mode of femininity' (Downing 1980) which, although essential to the efficient completion of administrative work, is not formally acknowledged, for instance in job descriptions. The significance of this 'support' role is further emphasised when women also act as caring 'ego-masseurs' or 'office wives' (ibid.) for sales inspectors who sometimes return to the office dejected after unsuccessful appointments. These informal responsibilities are taken for granted and are an example of how 'gendered jobs' (see Davies and Rosser, this volume) are both the medium and outcome of the structured segregation of work. As our case study at Insco will demonstrate, management recognise some of the cost-saving benefits of employing women in gendered jobs (see pp. 161–2).   Although not necessarily intended, however, these gendered jobs facilitate the reproduction of hierarchical and sexual divisions within the labour process.

Management control

In the life insurance business the branch manager's capacity to control *his* employees is contingent upon incentive/supervisory, promotion and recruitment systems. As an ex-salesperson *himself*[7] he has internalised the middle-class male values associated with selling and consequently tends consciously and unconsciously to reproduce job segregation and therefore discrimination against women. The average salesperson earns a basic salary of around £9,000. Whilst young inspectors will begin on £6,114 the maximum basic salary for a senior agency inspector is £12,564. This can be increased dramatically by overriding commission paid until recently at the rate of 4 per cent of new premium income above the target of £99,000 of annual business. In addition to a total income of up to £20,000, the following minimum benefits are available in the salesperson's 'package':

1. company car (1300cc)
2. running expenses £2,529
3. entertainment expenses £564 p.a.
4. non-contributory superannuation fund
5. private patients' plan ('concessionary rates for *wife* and children)
6. concessionary mortgage rates
7. permanent health insurance.

An HAY/MSL appraisal system is in operation but has the confidence of neither the branch manager nor the employees, largely because it reduces the autonomy of the former and has resulted in blockages in upward mobility for the latter. Still, the inspectors enjoy a great deal of personal autonomy in their daily 'fieldwork', which is assessed principally in terms of sales results. In contrast, the female clerical staff are closely supervised by an office manager whose permission they require simply in order to leave the office. Whilst the branch manager is concerned with the recruitment, support and necessary but limited supervision of the salesforce, he leaves the office manager to appoint, organise and control 'the girls in the office'.

This sex-segregated labour force is created by masculine-imbued images of selling as principally a man's career. One danger of such segregation however, is that what would ordinarily be seen as a problem of controlling subordinates is readily interpreted as the difficulties that women present in running a successful enterprise. The sales*men* are no problem for the controls are built into the very structures of the job leading to a form of 'self-management'. In positions of much greater subordination and with fewer incentives to improve their productivity, the women office workers are seen to require much more supervision and control. Suffering the consequences of such control, they express discontent and dissatisfaction in defensive ways that are then attributed by managers not to the women's experience of subordination and blocked mobility but to their gender. This can then be used to further disqualify them from jobs in sales since discontented or 'moody' behaviour is seen as inappropriate to the task of promoting the company's products through 'professional' intermediaries. Based on this kind of distorted knowledge, when a female clerk perceives herself capable of a sales position as in our third case history, the branch manager appears to define such a development as a risk best avoided. With no experience of women performing a sales task already predefined as necessitating exclusively 'male skills' and a distorted perception of women as emotionally unstable, it is not surprising that the promotion of female clerks into selling is considered as a high-risk strategy.

We now turn to a more detailed consideration of the empirical evidence on recruitment, supervision and promotion at Insco. In particular, our concern is to demonstrate how management control, the elevation of the sales inspector's tasks and skills, and the defensiveness of female clerical staff are not only interrelated factors, but mutually reinforcing conditions and partly consequences of the institutionalised reproduction of job segregation.

'Men only'

Nationally, Insco consists of 33 branches divided into three regions. Research took the form of participant observation and depth inter-viewing in one of the largest branches and at central headquarters. All management and clerical staff and a sample of the inspectors were interviewed at the branch (see below), and personnel in head office. The UK personnel profile is as follows:

175 inspectors	(approximately 10 women)
23 trainees	(4 women)
19 office managers	(2 women)
142 clerical staff	(all women)
2 head offices (employing together 850 people).	

In terms of equal opportunity the head office interpretation of these figures is one of 'progressive optimism'. As the (female) assistant national personnel manager stated:

> I can honestly say that at Insco, if they (women) have the right drive and ambition, there really shouldn't be anything to stop them. The fact that we haven't got that many females as heads of departments, it's probably a bit early. But I'd be the first to say if I thought there was any sort of discrimination... of course we have individuals who are prejudiced against colour or women, but we can't do anything about that.

Her final aside indicates the level of autonomy enjoyed by branch managers who wish to discriminate. Moreover, it is perhaps not just coincidence that most of the women who are in sales, work in branches in the south of England.[8] Evidence that regionalised job segregation is ignored by head office personnel is provided by the (male) manager responsible for the national recruitment of trainee salespeople. Indeed his paternalistic concern to 'protect' females is a pervasive male orientation throughout Insco, which has the consequence of reinforcing job segregation:

> I think looking round, there are quite patently one or two of the bigger branches without mentioning any names... where I think the manager isn't quite so keen on training female inspectors. But I wouldn't be looking to press because if the manager's not committed I don't feel it's the right environment for a young lady to succeed.

Here, the manager could be describing our case study since it not only constitutes the largest branch outside London, but clearly displays the way in which jobs are segregated by sex. In December 1983 the branch consisted of:

1 male branch manager
1 male office manager
10 male salespeople (inspectors)
1 male trainee inspector
6 female clerical staff
1 female clerical trainee.

In any individual branch that enjoys a great deal of daily autonomy from head office its manager occupies a central position of considerable power and influence. Recruitment, supervision and promotion are key areas in which this control is reflected and reinforced. We will now consider empirical evidence from each of these in turn.

Recruitment
The company has a nation-wide policy of 'growing their own' salespeople (18–24 year-olds) by appointing after A levels or, increasingly, with a degree. In contrast, female clerical staff are recruited at a younger age (16–18) with O levels only.

Eric Brown, the branch manager, treats the selection of trainee inspectors very seriously since he regards 'career' recruitment decisions as a crucially important element that, in his past 15 years at Insco, has contributed significantly to the remarkable commercial success of the branch. Becoming manager at the age of 35, he inherited a branch with a very low volume of business and has transformed it to a point where it is now the 'most successful in the company'.

Insulated from the recession, the branch's volume of work in 1983 was up by 50 per cent and, partly as a consequence of this, Eric decided with some reluctance that it was an appropriate time to recruit a trainee sales inspector. Past experiences with trainees had convinced him that remaining below his 'fixed establishment' was often preferable to hasty replacement appointments despite the pressure from head office to maintain a steady supply of newly trained inspectors. This defensive orientation to recruitment reflects Eric's responsibility for the commercial success of the branch, but it extends further than this, since a mistake in recruitment is quite difficult and extremely costly to correct.[9] This provides the rationale for his cautious attitude towards recruitment, part of which, as we shall see, involves excluding women from sales inspectors' jobs. As with most personnel involved with sales, Eric's identity is very much linked to the success of the office and, in the sphere of recruitment, this involves 'picking winners', as he puts it. He wants people who will be successful members of his 'team' and, given his prejudice, this is a condition with which women have difficulty in complying:

I'm looking for people who will work with me. So I look for someone who I think I can mould to my ways, but they must already have the necessary spark and drive.

Discussing his recent experience of seeking to recruit a trainee inspector, Eric provided plenty of evidence of the importance of recruitment and of his determination to discriminate on the grounds of sex. Often recruitment is pursued informally through 'word of mouth' as two of Eric's most recent trainees had been.[10] However, for the new appointment, Eric had advertised in the local job centre only to be terribly disappointed by the response and all the more determined to appoint only those he is convinced will stay a long time and, thereby, sustain his low rate of staff turnover. As he described the process:

> A very depressing experience. It was very soul-destroying because out of the 20 there were may be two that I would have employed, not necessarily as an inspector, but in any job in the company. If someone else had not appeared I don't know what I'd have done. The thought of going back to the job centre was terrible. I was really desperate. We've tried the paper in the past and you get a lot of cranks writing in but going to agencies for staff can also be a nightmare. So all this makes keeping the staff you've got very important rather than go through that nightmare.

He was disappointed that a requirement of two A levels, which he felt was not even necessary for the job, had not 'blocked out a lot: they seem to hand qualifications out as a matter of course these days'.

Eric then explained why, despite his 'desperation', he would not be advertising in the *Manchester Evening News*:

> If we did we'd have to think carefully about how to define the job and how to frame the advert ... then there's also this rubbish about sex you've got to watch out for.

> How do you mean?

> Well, say there's 20,000 inspectors in the country, 99 per cent are males, 1 per cent are females of which $\frac{1}{2}$ per cent are failures, $\frac{1}{2}$ per cent are successful. Females tend not to last very long and we want peple to stay for 40 years. So weeding out the females is a bit of a problem, especially with the job centre. You can't say to them you don't want girls.

Eric had been obliged to agree to interview four females but, fortunately for him, his 'weeding problem' was largely resolved because:

> As it turned out three people they sent did not turn up for the interview and they were all girls [*laughs*] ... the one girl who did arrive was clearly unsuitable.

About this particular candidate, Eric conceded that she had two of the required characteristics in that she was 'presentable' and 'well spoken' having spent a year at Liverpool University.

> But the trouble was that she talked too much. She obviously wasn't prepared to work.
>
> Did her 'dropping out' make you think she was not a good worker?
>
> No, actually I thought someone in this situation would be ideal, if it was a male.

Requiring someone who 'has a bit of sense', which Eric defined as 'more important than intellect', this candidate's relative success in, and then ultimate rejection of, education would indicate her appropriateness for the job. Yet she was 'clearly unsuitable' for Eric, because of her sex. In the context of sales, where the relative absence of women provides little evidence to counter male prejudices, Eric was reluctant to 'risk' the employment of a female since, in his view, it might threaten the continued commercial success of Insco and could create unnecessary problems easily avoided by recruiting only men. For Eric, female salespeople would threaten the branch's viability and especially the low labour turnover rate. He subscribed to the generalised myth that women leave as soon as they get married or to have babies,[11] but an additional rationalisation for avoiding recruiting women into sales, and one we have heard repeated in a number of insurance companies, is the 'fact' that they would have difficulty coping with rejection and, in particular, the sexism of the intermediaries who are their clients:

> Women aren't taken seriously in the insurance world. It can be a soul destroying job. Inspectors have to advise our professional clients who recommend insurance and pensions to their clients and we want them to recommend us. Yes, it can be a soul-destroying job, and women are either not hard-bitten enough to ride off insults or those that can are pretty unpleasant people.

Here Eric suggests that to be a 'successful' salesperson, certain inner strengths and personal resources are not only a prerequisite but also tend to be found only in men. The branch manager's willingness to concede to, and draw upon, (an exaggerated degree of) clients' aggressive male prejudice is merely an extension of Eric's own personal prejudice and defensive concern to sustain company growth with what he considers the minimum of risk. Eric had arranged with the job centre that they would first phone him with the details of anybody interested in the job, before he would agree to see them. As he elaborated:

> The job centre would ring me up saying 'I have Mr Jones here. I think he
> suits your requirements perfectly. Could he come and see you?' Then I'd say,
> '*The man*' I'm looking for has to have management potential. do you think
> *he* has?' They would always say yes, but when they arrived *he* clearly wasn't.
> You get some ghastly stuff coming through that door. By no stretch of the
> imagination would I ever employ any of them. I've got my reputation to
> keep up.

This statement is merely one of many displaying Eric's taken-for-
granted assumptions that the future job holder will be male. Of the
candidates interviewed, Eric was willing to 'look at' only one person
again. As the son of a schoolmaster, Eric considered this candidate to
be 'well-groomed', which he believed was also an important
consideration when judging people on their future abilities to sell
insurance. That many candidates were rejected precisely because they
were 'very badly spoken' both reflects and reinforces the middle-class,
as well as masculine, character of the financial world generally, and the
insurance industry in particular.

In all 15 insurance companies we have so far researched, selling is
seen to require not only the ability to communicate and persuade but
also to be resilient and aggressive in a highly competitive marketplace.
Now there is no doubting the competitive nature of the business but, as
a market leader in personal pensions, Insco has a solid product to sell.
What intermediaries value therefore, once they have accepted the
quality of the product, is a 'good' back-up service and this is provided
paradoxically, primarily by the women in the office. The exaggeration
of resilience and aggression as a condition of employment simply
reflects Eric's prejudice and legitimises, in his own eyes at least, the
belief that he must employ only men as inspectors. Eric argued that
inspectors ought to exhibit certain characteristics that he regards as
exclusively male, such as; independence, drive, ambition, and
competitiveness'.[12]

> I'm looking for whether they've got drive, initiative and are basically a
> self-starter. So *he* must want to get on, and get on by *his* own efforts.

The inevitably large degree of personal autonomy enjoyed by
inspectors requires that managerial control be more subtle and opaque
than that experienced by the inside clerical staff. Consequently the
work of inspectors is organised and accomplished through the material
and symbolic incentive systems of 'targets' and upgrading within the
same job. Thus the company's social organisation of work reflects and
reinforces the competitive character of the product market since
individual salespeople become rivals in the race for artificially induced
scarce financial and symbolic rewards. Whilst this structured

competition could generate internal conflict, Eric argues that the people he selects are able to complete their work in a dignified, 'professional' manner:

> Interviewing is a lot to do with personal hunch whether you think *he* is a good worker, whether you like *him*, whether *he* has integrity. Someone with integrity is a very useful *man* for us. The inspectors here help one another even though they are competing against each other.

This capacity to compete with 'integrity' however seems to be the exclusive domain of the male species, according to Eric. In contrast, the female clerical staff, whose work is not tied to bonus targets, seem to him to be in a recurring state of conflict. This tension creates problems for Eric, not least in a much higher labour turnover rate and therefore in a pressure to recruit. He explains these 'problems' not as a consequence of the highly subordinated and controlled character of clerical work, but as directly related to the employee's sex:

> It is the opposite amongst the girls. You'll never get harmony there. I've been told on the grapevine that two of the girls are not getting on at the moment but when there's conflict they often don't show it. We're always losing clerical staff. The girls tend to float around if you're not careful.

Despite this instability, Eric takes some praise for the two senior clerks remaining with Insco for six and four years respectively. Having managed this present staff problem by shuffling around the 'warring elements' Eric felt justified in claiming:

> We often chop and change jobs around to suit our staff. I don't know any other employers who are so sensitive to their staff.

Supervision

The hierarchical structure of the clerical department is as follows:

	Salary	*Grades* (A–G)
Branch manager		G)
Office manager	8,500	E) Male
Senior pensions clerk	5,895	C
Pensions clerk	5,122	B
Two clerks	4,578	A
Two clerical assistants		6 month contract
One trainee	2,900–3500	

The clerical staff enjoy some benefits including flexi-time, superannuation scheme, private pensions' plan, luncheon vouchers, free and automatic membership of the company-sponsored staff association and a concessionary mortgage package (for grades C and B only). Allan, the office manager, not only recruits all the female clerical staff, but is responsible for their supervision on a daily basis. In explaining why his recruitment is restricted to 16–17 year-old female school-leavers, Allan disclosed the economic vested interests embedded in the reproduction of gendered job segregation:

> Men could do the job, but the starting salary is too low. You'd never get a bloke to do it.

This practice clearly had implications for the women's orientation to, and position in, work as the 'life cycle' analysis of Beynon and Blackburn (cited in Wajcman 1983) suggests. Of the seven women, the oldest was 23 and just one, Carole the pensions clerk, was married. Yet, it was taken for granted that the others would soon be married, have children and then leave. Moreover, the resulting atmosphere of masculine paternalism in the office was further entrenched by the orientation of the inspectors themselves, the vast majority of whom were over 35.

Whilst Eric Brown remains socially and physically distant from the clerical staff,[13] Allan works alongside them in the open plan office. This physical arrangement, as de Kadt (1979: 245) has argued, facilitates 'constant surveillance' which adequately describes Allan's style of supervision. Like Eric Brown, he views his hierarchical position very much as a reflection of his own personal status and dignity. Using a mixture of patronising humour, sarcasm and indifference, Allan seeks to maintain his symbolic distance of authority and thereby to 'motivate' the clerical staff to work independently. He proudly boasts about his

> reputation for getting people's backs up who work for me. I will help them if I consider they need it, but sometimes I give them the impression that I can't be bothered. I prefer them to learn by looking for themselves. So I'm fairly abrupt and indifferent. I'm not worried if they like me but I do want their respect . . . I don't like them to take advantage . . . they often say 'Oh, we can't understand you, Allan, we try to be nice to you but you're not nice back.' I think there's only one I've not made cry . . . I don't think I have to do the job. My job is to keep them as busy as possible. I'd rather me be bored than them, otherwise if you do bring work for them again, it just leads to them moaning and groaning. You can't keep all six happy at the same time. With some you can tell their monthly changes, even the other girls say so. Sometimes when they're having a good chunner about the inspectors I have to impress on the girls that if it was not for the men, there'd be no jobs for them, if the blokes don't go out and sell insurance.

Clearly, the mundane nature of clerical work is compounded by Allan's coercive and aggressive approach to maintaining his control. Unable even to leave the office without Allan's permission, the women are limited to these segregated, subordinate posts.

Conventionally, clerks were each responsible for processing the work of two inspectors. But in 1983 teams were introduced to increase the scope and variety of clerical work as well as to separate the 'warring elements'. These changes were counter-productive, however. First, they generated resentment against the senior clerks who, having been made 'team leaders' were seen to be acting as if they had been promoted. Second, it was felt that some people were not doing their share of the work. As Liz, one of the clerks, complained:

> Before we were all girls together. Now we're split up. Nobody used to check my work. Now I have to give it to Lyn to check. The idea behind it was to save time but it's not. Allan thinks it's marvellous because it's his bloody idea. Carole thinks it's marvellous because she's a team leader. She does not do any work. But I feel on a level par with her, she's only worked here one month longer than me. So there are quite a few arguments about 'I've done so much work, and she's done none.'

These recurring problems resulted in the staff being split again into three teams of two. Their sense of dissatisfaction and the preoccupation with comparing self to 'other' was exacerbated by the close supervision and arbitrary control of the office manager. This seemed to generate one of three responses: the women either looked elsewhere for a better job, carried on with resigned indifference, or hoped to progress up the clerical hierarchy. These defensive responses represented individual attempts to resolve problems of management coercion and the devaluation of clerical work that could only be resisted effectively by collective action. Yet the preoccupation with personal material and symbolic security seemed to preclude the possibility of developing the critical confidence and mutual trust on which collective action would depend. For instance, partly because of Allan's style of supervision, Sue was thinking of leaving.

> He is not an ideal personnel manager because he's bored. He tends to cause a lot of problems, telling stories about one girl to another. Personnel is supposed to relieve tension, not cause it! So you're not prepared to put yourself out if you're feeling disagreeable towards Allan. He is so inconsistent. He can be really nice and then turn around and just be the opposite.

Complaints about Allan's arbitrary and unnecessary exercise of power were echoed by all the women. For example, Carole understood the incidence of internal conflict amongst the staff as a direct consequence of their subordination to his 'gender specific forms of control' (Downing 1980: 280):

> I'm afraid I don't like Allan 'cos I don't think he does anything and it annoys me when he sits there and won't help you. He likes to assert his power as office manager. He's started checking our post and putting a big cross through work that was right in the first place! In the office, he's such a swine! He says he's not there to watch us but he is. He can be very awkward about things like flexi-time and holidays . . . On the whole we get on very well with each other. But when Allan's here, we don't. He sees himself as an object to have our anger diverted at so it deflects away from everybody else, but it doesn't quite work like that and we all pick at each other. Allan says it's because we're an office of girls,[14] but I don't think it is.

When we suggested that

> In the Company, he seems to be generally well-respected as an office manager?

Carole responded:

> Yes, but not by us.

Allan's direct control generates more resentment in the office than Eric Brown's well-known refusal to recruit women as inspectors, which tends to be routinely taken for granted and unchallenged.

The conflict that does exist between the women is also related to their dependence upon the resignation or upward advance of the person next in line in the career ladder. These problems of 'waiting for somebody to leave' are exacerbated when the opportunities for promotion are severely limited. Up until her recent marriage, Carole had considered leaving but, now reluctant to face such an upheaval, is resigned to her position:

> I think I'm stuck. I can't move until Lyn moves and I can't see Lyn moving. Now I'm married I get the feeling I won't get anywhere, because they're expecting me to have children at any minute. Apparently, this is a woman's role! All the others in the office are expecting me to leave too.

Likewise, Liz has accommodated herself to the situation, because 'security is what I value, in this day and age it's a must.' Having been assured that no one is to be made redundant, she is reluctant to take risks – 'I don't want to give up this comfort. This is a cushy number.'

Viewing the possibility of becoming an inspector as a threat to her job security, Liz, like the managers, had internalised the assumptions informing the segregation of jobs. To transfer into the field would undermine her conception of being a woman:

> My personal view is that what you have to do as an inspector, involves a lot of hard work and earache, which is not something for a woman. Women are always going to get married and have kids anyway. I'd not like to go outside mainly because you have to move. That's standard company practice.[15] I don't think anyone is interested in being an inspector. They all know how difficult the job is.[16] Once you're out there the only escape is to other companies, and the other thing is that my leisure time would be working time if I became an inspector.

The cost of Liz's preoccupation with security is reflected in her indifference and general air of despondency at work. As Lyn, a team leader, described her:

> Liz doesn't give the impression of being enthusisastic. She doesn't seem keen really. She does all the work but its her attitude, just the impression she gives, I don't know why.

In a very similar way, the other team leader, Carole criticised Karen with whom she works:

> Karen hasn't got much of a clue, and she doesn't seem to want to know either. So basically it's me with a typist. It's not easy to teach somebody who's not interested.

Karen has since expressed her indifference more directly by resigning and going to work elsewhere. In the context of highly subordinated, poorly paid positions which provide few opportunities to 'advance', indifference, as a defensive mode of managing to retain a measure of dignity in the face of its erosion, is all-pervasive within contemporary work situations (Sennett and Cobb 1977; Knights and Roberts 1983; Knights and Collinson 1985). Yet Eric Brown explains the women's orientation in terms of gender, with no reference to the nature of the job or the structure of control. For him, it is their lack of ambition, as females, which he sees, not as a consequence, but as a necessary precondition for doing clerical work:

> Actually there's girls out there who are more intelligent than anyone else in the branch . . . but they've no drive . . . which suits us fine. We rely on people's inertia since our salaries are not very attractive. So we try to keep people coming in at the bottom so that we can train them to our ways, get them used to the company.

Indeed this self-confirming justification was even more strongly asserted by the national personnel officer at head office.

> They're normally not career-minded people, 'O' level entrants with limited
> potential. They're there basically to do the 'number crunching' and 'pen
> pushing'. If they had been career-minded they would have left that grade
> long since. I'm talking about grades A, B or even C. The door is always open
> to move into the career structure, but we've found by and large, they're girls,
> who are not particularly ambitious, looking forward to getting married,
> leaving and having a family and that's about the measure of it.

This tendency to legitimise oppressive structures on voluntaristic
grounds or what might be termed 'gendered psychologism' is expressed
quite frequently and often internalised by those who experience its
consequences. However, not only does the clerical structure
presuppose an absence of female ambition and long-term commitment,
a great deal of managerial resistance may be mounted against any
attempt to overcome this segregation, as can be seen from the following
examination of a promotion.

Promotion
The blocked mobility in the office is recognised by Allan to create
motivational problems for him. Indieed he was quite delighted when
Karen handed in her notice:

> The problem with this office is that too few leave. You need a fair amount of
> turnover to keep everybody happy. Take Lyn, it's taken her six years to
> reach senior pensions clerk but she can't move now unless I get run over by a
> bus.

Allan is directly faced with the consequences of employee indifference
and dissatisfaction which tends to accompany extreme subordination
and blocked mobility. This is one reason why he would prefer more
staff turnover and movement up the hierarchical career ladder. Clearly,
the possibility of personal advancement is threatened if, through job
segregation, those in higher positions are unable to 'progress'.
Although recognising Lyn's experience as an exemplification of the
company's blocked mobility, Allan failed to include sex discrimination
as a major obstacle for her upward advance into the ranks of the
inspectors. Yet, her experience confirmed to everyone in the office that
at Insco, women were not wanted as inspectors. Since joining in 1977,
23-year-old Lyn had been considering a transfer into the
predominantly male world of sales. Repeatedly discontented with the
mundane nature of her clerical jobs, Lyn had threatened to leave prior
to her promotion to senior pensions clerk in March 1982. Four years
ago she secured another job, but was dissuaded from accepting it by

Eric. When she informed him of her intentions, Eric was quite shocked, not least because it contradicted his view of the clerical staff's inertia. As Lyn expressed it:

> He nearly had a stroke. He was stunned. He had no idea that I was fed up. He said, 'Now come on, what's the problem?' and eventually I agreed to stay, on the basis that I got a decent salary rise and they send me on a course to head office. I came back thinking the company was wonderful. So as I say he had tried to keep me before, which I felt good about really ... he'd never tried this with anyone before so I felt appreciated. They don't make a habit of patting you on the back and telling you how good you are, here.

As the fifth anniversary of Lyn's appointment drew closer (1 November 1982), she stated categorically to Allan that unless she became an inspector in the near future, she would definitely be leaving this time. Informed of this ultimatum, Eric, in the guise of a 'celebration' of her first five years employment, invited Lyn out for a meal. During the evening the subject of her frustrated ambition was discussed. Once Lyn's determination to be promoted was confirmed, Eric began to raise various problems, hurdles and objections to her taking on an inspector's job, all of which directly or indirectly related to her sex. The first doubt raised by Eric related to her 'credibility' in the field:

> He hinted that I was too young. He said that really for brokers to take me seriously I'd have to be 25 or so. He said 'It's nothing personal but established brokers are sick of seeing youngsters with three months' experience. They can tell after a few questions if you know what you're talking about. In most cases they won't even see young people. I think you'll find it very difficult unless you're 24 or 25.'

At this point, however, Lyn was able to penetrate the sexually prejudiced contradictions. Eric had only just appointed a much younger, male trainee, so when she was asked:

> Is that the same for blokes?

she replied:

> Well, no, of course it isn't! Being female you see, I'd have to be that bit older. What got me was why should a flaming young 23-year-old fella know more than I do at the same age? I was a bit peeved about that.

So, at one level, she was aware of the male prejudice that was confronting her:

> Mr Brown seems to think that all women come to work after leaving school

then get married, have kids, then leave and that's it. I think he's beginning to realise he's got problems with me. I just won't fall in line with what his standard view of women is!

Yet at another level, as the meal progressed, she became increasingly equivocal about her ambitions. Despite extensive knowledge of insurance selling she would first have to become a trainee, or a 'glorified messenger boy', as she put it. Having completed her training in Manchester and in head office, Lyn believed that she would then *have* to go to another branch since company policy prohibited trainees from returning to the same branch.

I could be sent anywhere. It just depends where there's a vacancy and he kept harping on about whether I was prepared to move.

Although this mobility requirement was not originally a problem for Lyn, the conversation with Eric sowed the seeds of doubt in her mind. At that time she was living at home with her parents where she confessed to being 'spoilt to death' paying only £15 per week. To move would be to face the prospect of a steady flow of bills and the responsibility of a mortgage.[17] On becoming an inspector and facing these aforementioned 'pressures', the need to reach high target incentive levels constituted a further factor in the erosion of her confidence. Again this doubt was inculcated by the branch manager:

Mr Brown said, 'What would you think to having a target hanging over your head?' and I must admit it scared the 'whatsit' out of me. When you think about it, your job comes down to the fact that you've got to get so much business. The market is getting more and more difficult. Then there's three million unemployed out there. I don't think Insco is going to kick me out just like that, but it is something to think of, that every year you've got to get that target. Something you've got to seriously consider which I hadn't done until he mentioned it. Having a target does worry me. Whereas now, I know at the end of each day I've just got to get so much work done and everything's fine. To think every year I'd have a higher target to reach. The blokes make it look so easy. It was only when Mike[18] came that we began to realise how difficult it was. After six months he was nowhere near target.

Increasingly, Lyn became confused and doubtful about her own capabilities. The apparently 'aggressive', hostile and dangerous public world of selling seemed merely to re-confirm her sense of security in the office. She began to internalise Eric's doubt, whose experience and understanding of product market conditions she respected.

You'd have to have a certain type of woman to go out and face some of the brokers who are absolutely quite obnoxious to the fellas. Their attitude wouldn't change with women. I could just imagine, if you're not the right type of person a woman could go into a brokers and end up in tears and that would be it. You couldn't go back. So from the company's point of view, it may be that they favour fellas anyway. You've got to have a heart of iron really. You've got to let it run off you like water off a duck's back. Yes, I think men are better at that.

However, Eric did not merely object to Lyn's promotion because of the masculine characteristics he considered necessary for the selling of insurance but also on the grounds of 'female instability' and Lyn's personality 'deficiencies'. Significantly Lyn agreed with both of these objections:

It's all right saying equal opportunities but I don't think you will ever get employers to look at women in the same light at all. They will have to take into consideration that women do have this tendency to get married, get pregnant and have kids. So why should they go through all this trouble of promoting her and getting her set up? In my case it isn't true but this is generally what happens – you can't fault them on that. When you get the one who wants a career rather than just a job they don't get recognised because everyone puts them in the same category.

Under the umbrella of paternalistic protection that Lyn, in her deference, found difficult to question, Eric sowed further seeds of doubt about her ability to do the inspector's job by highlighting a certain personality trait:

I'm very temperamental, you see. This is another thing Mr Brown drew to my attention. I can get very annoyed very easily and I also get strong moods. He said 'There's no way you could go out to a broker with some of the moods you have.'[19]

Lyn's growing fears of the market and the possibility of experiencing 'a hard time when brokers kick you out or won't see you' resulted in her accepting Eric's view that:

If I was older [emphasis] I'd be more calm. By the time I'm 25 he reckons I'll be fine. But he doesn't think that at the moment it would be right for me to start ... At first I was a bit annoyed then I began to realise he was only thinking of me.

Yet this was only after she had secured his reluctant acquiescence to her promotion because 'He knew I would leave if he said no'. Although becoming an inspector had been her goal for several years, Eric's protective warnings and reservations persuaded Lyn to refuse the chance just when it was offered. Further discouragement took the form of being told that having left, it would be extremely difficult for her to return, since changes would have to be made in the organisation of the clerical staff. Rather than sacrifice/risk her position as the senior clerk she chose the continued 'security' of the office.

She has since started to consider the possibility of becoming an office manager, thereby conforming to the company's segregation of jobs, and also to her own idea of appropriate female employment. Like Liz, Lyn's decisions are informed by and thereby reinforce a primarily gendered conception of self:

> From a woman's point of view, she might prefer . . . if she wants a career, . . .
> my idea of a career would be like . . . getting high up inside. That would be
> my idea, a woman's idea of going higher up within the company on the
> inside. Ideally, that is what I'd like to do, I think.

Yet even if Allan were to leave, Lyn is almost certain that, despite being his 'natural' successor, as a woman she would have little chance of being appointed because of Eric's prejudices.

The 'knock-on' effect in terms of career development for the remaining clerical staff resulted in widespread disappointment when, at the last moment, Lyn decided against becoming an inspector. This was compounded by the news sometime later that her indecision had resulted in it being 'very unlikely' that others from the clerical staff would be considered for an inspector traineeship. Lyn, like Liz, had been persuaded of the benefits and security of office work. She remains unsure about whether Eric's doubts merely expressed his unjustifiable prejudice, were based on an instrumental attempt to retain his most experienced clerk, or reflected his paternalism in seeking to protect her from the sexism of clients. Whatever the reason, the effect of this subtle form of gendered control was to heighten Lyn's material and symbolic insecurities which thereby generated her defensive preoccupation with protecting and valuing the security and stability of life in the office. As a result, Lyn acted in a way which reproduced the contradictions of job segregation and contributed to the conditions of her own subordination.

Whilst still committed to being an inspector when she reaches 25, she has however become self-critical about her indecisiveness and attachment to the security of work and home.

In answer to our question:

> Of all the reasons you've given for not becoming an inspector which is the
> most important?

she responded:

I think it's me that's the problem. I know if it carries on like this Allan is going to remain office manager. I know there'll come a time when I get fed up again . . . There's just this financial problem of the mortgage . . . but if I really wanted to, it wouldn't stop me . . . It's not the inspector's job in here that bothers me. I know the training is good and I'm confident in myself. So it boils down to the move and the finances. It's a pretty big step and I'm spoilt at home.

So, despite receiving a great deal of encouragement from brokers and some inspectors, Lyn declined the opportunity to become an inspector. Eric Brown's retrospective account of these events demonstrates the paternalism and inter-related male prejudice embedded in his great reluctance to 'risk' employing a female inspector,

I have in fact talked her out of leaving two or three times. She backed away from it (i.e., being an inspector) a few months ago which I didn't try and talk her out of because I didn't think it was the right time. I still think she's got some growing-up to do. She is rather vulnerable, to send her out on the road. She needs the maturity to be able to call on people and take the rebuffs and the advances. You need total commitment to start off with, but if she carries on to mature we'll make her an inspector if she sticks it out.

Having contributed substantially to Lyn's doubts and uncertainties, Eric then used these as evidence of her unsuitability.   After Lyn refused, Eric offered the traineeship to Allan, who was an ideal candidate, not least because of his sex.[20] Since Allan also refused the offer, Carole, the pensions clerk, asked about the possibility of her applying. After considering this carefully Eric asked her if she was serious, at which point Carole said:

Well, if you thought I was going to be hopeless I wouldn't bother, but if you thought I was going to be good I might try it. I didn't fancy trying it and failing.

Here again we see how personal insecurity, self-depreciation (Pollert 1983: 103) and a deferential respect for the views of male-dominated authority is a condition as well as a consequence of job segregation mediated through paternalistic management control. If Carole or Lyn had been less dependent on the support and confirmation of the branch manager they, as individuals, could have undermined the 'masculine' myths on which job segregation is constructed. Again Eric raised the 'problems of having to be mobile', of working with sexist clients, etc. Yet Carole's willingness to concede the validity of these arguments is a consequence of the deferential respect which she confers upon Eric Brown, who is unanimously seen as a charismatic, authoritative 'leader' by all the women. In her willingness to internalise Eric's view of the problems of sales work for women, Carole excluded herself from applying:

> Mr Brown is right. If you're a woman going out selling insurance you've got to be that much better than your male counterpart just to try to prove yourself. If a man comes round it's all right, but if a woman does, you think 'Does she know what she's talking about?' I've done it myself.

Expressing at best, a defensive ambivalence and uncertainty about their capabilities, at worst a willing acquiescence to their subordination, the clerical staff thereby contributed to the reproduction of job segregation, and as an unintended consequence, to male prejudice. With Carole and Lyn both unwilling to risk their present security, it was inevitable that a male would be appointed for the traineeship beginning on 1 January 1983. Likewise for the more recent post, a male with past insurance experience was offered the job. However, he refused and interviews again took place in December 1983 at which point, with no internal application received, another male (graduate) candidate from the job centre was appointed.

Summary and conclusion: theorising the reproduction of job segregation

This case study has displayed how management control in the context of recruitment, supervision and promotion reflects but also reproduces the gendered segregation of insurance work. However it has also demonstrated how the practices that constitute this reproduction are in no sense unilinear, coherent or without contradiction. Convinced that the success of his branch is a product of a careful strategy of recruitment, Eric Brown is unprepared to take 'risks' by employing women sales 'reps' and uses his paternalistic control to exclude them even at the cost of causing discontent and indifference amongst the office staff. By delegating responsibility for the office to Allan, Eric is insulated from the full impact of job segregation on employee relations. Yet he still concludes from his limited and prejudicial understanding of the internal conflicts and 'inertia' of the office staff that women are unsuitable for sales. Treating the office staff's behaviour as a product of their sex, not their subordination, the branch manager draws upon the outcomes of job segregation in accounting for his reproduction of its conditions.

The contradictions of control are clearly displayed in office relations where Allan's highly coercive approach generates a level of anxiety or frustrated resentment which is expressed in internal conflict, poor standards of work,[21] indifference, disenchantment or even resignation. And yet, in seeking such individualistic rather than collective solutions to their problems, the women inadvertently reproduce the conditions of their own subordination by failing to challenge the institutionalised devaluation of clerical work. As a defensive response to control, their concern with personal material and symbolic security expressed either in resignation, deference, indifference or the search for future promotion within the clerical ranks merely reproduces the contradictions of job segregation. Quite clearly, the promotion of a minority of 'token' women to inspectors does begin to reverse the institutionalisation of gendered job segregation.[22] However, it fails to challenge but unintentionally reinforces the subordinated and degraded status of clerical work. The only way in which an effective resistance to the unwarranted comparatively low status of gendered clerical work in insurance could be accomplished would be through collective action. Herein lie our misgivings with recent empirical contributions to the debate on gendered segregation within the labour process. For these studies take insufficient account of the way in which all organisational members, including managers, reinforce the contradictions of control and resistance precisely because of their preoccupation with maintaining material and symbolic security for themselves in a precarious class-ridden and sex-segregated competitive world. As we have seen at Insco, this is expressed both in Eric Brown's great reluctance to 'risk' the employment of female inspectors and in the women's lack of confidence to demand promotion. Preferring not to sacrifice the apparent 'safety' of the office and the 'security' of their subordinate status, the women neither pursue the material and symbolic opportunities of the field nor organise a collective challenge to the unequal gendered distribution of power, income and status. But rarely in the literature are the institutional and social conditions and consequences of the preoccupation with personal security and its translation into stabilising social identity theorised. Indeed, there remains a 'theoretical blackhole' between the analysis of historically derived capitalist and partriarchal structures and their conditions and consequences at the level of individual action. However, as Kuhn (1978: 45) has argued, this concern with 'the subject' and with social processes does not constitute a demand for voluntarism, nor we argue, for either 'blaming the victim' or denying the significance and resilience of capitalism and patriarchy as systems of domination and exploitation. Rather, it provides an escape from structural determinism in order to analyse and more closely represent the dynamic processes wherein domination, subordination and resistance are reproduced in social relations that embody fundamental contradictions.

In order to pursue this kind of analysis, however, it is necessary to invoke an existential as well as a structural theory of the conditions and consequences of individual insecurity in contemporary society (cf. Knights and Willmott 1985). For whilst the competitive struggle for material and symbolic status encouraged by capitalist and patriarchal structures serve to reproduce class and gender-based systems of domination, its conditions of plausibility, if not possibility, are rooted in the existential and psychic anxieties and insecurities which are the legacy of human self-consciousness (Freud), our ontological nature (Laing), a fear of freedom (Fromm), and the subject mirror-image split (Lacan).[23] This psychic, ontological or existential condition does render us particularly vulnerable to the illusion that anxiety and insecurity can be overcome through conformity to some 'objective' image of success, worthiness, status or power. Hence the preoccupation with gendered and/or hierarchical identity which is the institutional-ised form of that objective image. But this attempt to remove the necessary ambiguity of self in the 'lived through flow of experience' (Merleau-Ponty 1962) by subordinating the active subjective ego to the task of sustaining a coherent, objectively validated image or institutionally valued identity is full of contradictions.

First and foremost, the dual nature of self, wherein it is simultaneously an active *subject* as well as an *object* of both our own and others' evaluations, renders the 'idea of a coherent subject (is) a fantasy ... (for) ... not only is identity a construct but it is also continuously and precariously reconstructed' (Coward 1983: 265). It is the particularly acute nature of this precariousness with regard to gender identity that constitutes the conditions and consequences of sexist social relations. Second, because the socially constructed character of self makes us dependent upon external judgements and evaluations, there is a tendency at best to use others instrumentally and at worst to control them in pursuit of a 'secure' identity. Combined with the structural pressures to compete for power, privilege and status, this tendency within contemporary capitalism not only reinforces the precariousness of identity but also can result in social relations becoming completely amoral as instrumental interests, albeit often reciprocal, dominate human conduct. Third, the preoccupation with identity involves us in a level of instrumentality towards ourselves wherein the power of the subject is diverted into protecting the objective image of self thus diminishing any collective, creative potential to transform the structure of social relations in a direction that would undermine capitalist and patriarchal domination. Finally, since we are unable ultimately to predict, let alone control, others' judgements and evaluations of self, the preoccupation with identity not only reflects but actually reinforces the insecurity it seeks to overcome.

Despite the self-defeating nature of the concern to secure identity, few studies within the labour process literature have sought to theorise its contradictions. Rather, they tend to take for granted the routines that reflect and reinforce the preoccupation with identity whilst criticising the institutions and structures which admittedly condition, but are also a consequence of, strategies designed to secure the self. As a result, they fail to examine how the illusion of security promised by gender and/or hierarchical identity contributes to the reproduction of relations of domination and subordination. It is this failure, we suggest, that pushes analysis onto the slippery slope of determinism. For although the structural pressures to support prevailing class (property) relations through conforming to the institutional goals and demands of patriarchal capitalism cannot be denied, their plausibility is continually reinforced by the promise of security that 'success' in achieving social positions of dominance offers. That the promise often turns out to be something of an illusion serves only to ensure the competitive spirit as if, like a phoenix rising from the ashes, failure arouses even greater determination to 'succeed'. Alternatively, subordination leads to a defensive indifference wherein identity is protected by distancing self mentally from the conditions of domination so as to discount the power of others to undermine personal significance.

The absence of this social psychology from labour process theory means that it is unable to recognise how individuals, such as the men and women in our study, seek security either through controlling, and/or subordinating themselves to, others. Neither is account taken of the unintended consequences of processes of domination and subordination that follow partly because individuals cannot even render themselves, let alone others, completely objects of instrumental means. Moreover, just as the failure to theorise identity gives an incomplete analysis of the structures and strategies of power, so also it is oblivious of how the dominated can perceive their subordination as a form of security which leaves them indifferent or unconcerned to challenge the practices of domination and control. But again, as the experience of the women at Insco suggests, the 'security' promised by their indifference or compliance is precarious since it reinforces their position as passive victims of an oppressive and exploitative management. Their job insecurity is further compounded by the possible introduction of new technology which, according to personnel at Insco's head office, is likely to further de-grade and de-skill clerical tasks that in the future will be performed predominantly by temporary staff. In as much as the clerical workers have only managed their material and symbolic deprivation individually, and largely defensively, the further erosion of power, status and dignity through new technology meets with little if no resistance in this and other insurance offices where we have conducted research (see also Storey 1986).

In sum, this paper has sought to theorise the reproduction of the gendered segregation of jobs by drawing attention not only to the capitalist and patriarchal structures of power but also to the identity-securing strategies of the participants involved in domination, subordination and resistance. In examining these strategies, we have at the same time focused upon how their consequences often escape subjective intention although, in the case study presented, reproducing an institutionalisation of gendered job segregation. We have tried to avoid merely attributing blame, conspiratorial motive or sex prejudice to individuals wherever possible for that runs the danger of psychological reductionist explanations of gendered job segregation. No doubt prejudice informs sex discriminatory practices just as their consequences often confirm the (ir)rationality that underlies such prejudice. But the institutionalisation of gendered job segregation is a much more complex medium and outcome of the interplay of identity pursuits and their interpenetration with capitalist and patriarchal structures of domination. More precisely, these structures are themselves the conditions and consequence of both sexes aggressively and/or defensively seeking to advance or protect particular identities as a means of managing existential, material and social insecurity. The political will to transform the structures of capitalist and patriarchal domination is quite vigorous and intense within the feminist movement at the present time. However, to the extent that root insecurity is perceived and managed privately and individually, rather than treated as a social problem which is shared regardless of sex, the cathexis or power embodied in current resistance to institutionalised gendered subordination may well be diverted so as to reproduce the structures it seeks to undermine.

Acknowledgements
We thank Laura Bennett and others at the UMIST/ASTON labour conference for critical comments made on an earlier draft of this paper.

Notes
1.   Hakim (1979:1) suggests that 'occupational segregation on the basis of sex exists when men and women do different kinds of work, so that one can speak of two separate labour forces, one male and one female, which are not in competition with each other for the same jobs'. Our use of the term 'job segregation' is intended to

      imply the additional characteristic of unequal material and symbolic status between the jobs so segregated.

2.   Indeed as Connell (1983:34) has argued such questions of origin are impossible to answer:

> Both gender and class divisions can be traced through a complete evolution and interaction since (the Palaeolithic). It is this evolution and interaction that is the object of real historical knowledge. What concerns us is the dynamic, not its largely unknowable point of departure. Only myth, not history, makes determinations out of origins.

3.   This is not the place to discuss these contradictions but the equal opportunity advocates do have a point when they argue that sex discrimination results in half the 'talent' in the country being excluded or given restricted access to the labour market, thus limiting the potential efficiency of industry and commerce (Hakim ibid.).

4.   It seems somewhat strange that most of these studies are located in manufacturing industry when only 20 per cent of working women are employed in this sector compared with 75 per cent in services (Wajcman 1983:6).

5.   Indeed Barker and Downing (1980) also describe the 'feminine' modes of resistance of clerical workers that reflect and so reinforce the ideology of the 'office wife'.

6.   Their employment in sales is evident in certain recently established companies selling direct to the public. But even here the strong preference is for divorced women who it is felt will have the necessary maturity and ambition that is apparently lacking in married and young single women (see Collinson and Knights 1985).

7.   This was true of the case study from which this overview is partially derived but it is also typical of sales departments in general (see Knights 1973).

8.   There is some evidence to suggest that discrimination is perhaps less pervasive in the south of England than further north. For example, this manager disclosed that a female senior inspector in Southampton had recently 'narrowly' failed to secure a branch manager's post in London. Admittedly, however, his account of the appointment decision still generates cause for concern:

> It was a close run thing...One's got a bit of reluctance appointing a woman because you feel they're going to get married and have a family. I try not to put too much importance on that and judge them on their merits and she was very close.

9.   Eric admits to losing only two inspectors in 15 years, whilst nationally labour turnover for inspectors is running at 12 per cent per annum.

10   One was the son of a client, the other the son of another branch manager of Company A.

11   The comparatively higher rate of staff turnover amongst the women clerks was attributed to sex not poor rates of pay, subordination and a coercive system of management control (see p. 157 for details).

12   Paradoxically, if his recruits really exhibited these personal characteristics he would have difficulty holding on to his low staff turnover since promotion opportunities for inspectors are extremely limited. All 175 inspectors are in competition with one another for the occasional branch manager vacancy. Rarely are they ever promoted to head office.

13   Eric's hierarchical distance is compounded by a reputed 'uneasiness with women' which expresses itself in a highly paternalistic way of relating to them. As Allan elaborated, 'The girls are terrified of him. His manner is very shy. He does not talk to them much, yet he can't understand why he frightens them. He'd rather deal with the men. But he'd do anything for them, he's like a big dad if they're having problems.'

14   He confirmed this view on several occasions when arguing that generally men in groups tend to 'get on better' than do women. Indeed an awareness of gender difference permeates office interaction. For example, at Christmas the inspectors

take the clerical staff for a meal. Thompson (1983:197) has argued that this was one way of 'connecting to the dominant themes of consumerism, family and sexual attraction in women's lives'. Such a view is implicit in the following observations by Allan:

> They (the women) really like that because they can get dressed up for it. Its better than buying a bunch of flowers.

This awareness of gender is often expressed quite explicitly in two-way sexual innuendo as well as more covertly when inspectors and/or Allan privately disclose their attraction for one of the clerical staff. Allan in fact argues that he retains his highly coercive form of supervision in order to rebuff the women's 'femine' modes of manipulation:

> If I was nice with them they'd twist me round their little finger with the guiles they use, putting their arm round my shoulder. It can drive you mad sometimes, so I have to avoid this: its the only way I can manage.

However when he fails to get his way, for example when the women decided to cancel a company arrangement with a local café in favour of luncheon vouchers, although this would cost them an extra £60 in increased tax, Allan's awareness of gender difference is transformed into prejudice:

> They're bloody stupid. Women aren't rational. They let their heart rule their head.

15. Whilst several of the women were under the impression that a requirement to be mobile was a formalised aspect of company practice, this was not strictly true. Although this was repeatedly emphasised by Eric Brown as we shall see in the next example of a woman seeking promotion, personnel at head office assured us that it was not correct for trainees in general. Of course, since so few women had risen through the ranks, there was little precedent available on which to judge. But if this policy were enforced it could constitute a form of indirect discrimination since it is more difficult for married women to comply with a geographical mobility rule.

16. And yet Liz's *image* of inspecting is contradicted by her experience of its practice.

> I've been out on calls with Mike (an inspector) and thought 'I could do that, meeting the customer'. They tend to be a bit thick. They'll believe anything you say.

17. Given that mortgages for insurance staff are provided at a discounted interest rate, management might have pointed out to her that such a venture would probably be in her long-term interests rather than an obstacle to taking the promotion. The anxiety about a mortgage further reflects strongly internalised cultural sex-based perceptions of responsibility. In contrast to Lyn, Carole's married status has worked to exclude her from receiving a discounted interest rate because of Eric's prejudice. That is to say, he persuaded her against taking a mortgage since he felt she would soon be leaving to have children in which case the discounted rate would be lost, as it is available only to active employees.

18. This is the new trainee who took the job in which Lyn was interested. He was recruited from contacts with a fellow branch manager – Liverpool.

19. Yet, in another company, the branch manager claimed that the more extreme the oscillation of mood the better the salesperson. 'Those who never hit the depths of depression or the heights of elation generally have a mediocre performance!' Paradoxically, this criticism of inconsistency was central to the women's complaints about the office manager.

20. Indeed Allan's rapid promotion through the clerical ranks seems to be related to the prejudice of the branch manager. When his present job became vacant five years ago, Allan was a trainee inspector. It was decided that the vacancy needed to be filled by someone with experience of this office. Joan, the senior clerk at the time, was the most appropriate candidate, yet Allan, who had been with the company two years less, was appointed. Carole informed us that Joan has since resigned:

> There was all sorts of scandal about it. Everyone was very upset, especially Joan,

because she'd expected to get it. She felt Allan had barged his way in, by ingratiating himself to everybody. She would have left earlier if she hadn't married one of the inspectors.

21. This was a recurring complaint expressed by Allan. Indeed it was evident, for example, in Lyn's work after she was recently blocked from moving to the Birmingham branch as office manager.

22. Indeed, as Gamarnikow (1978:101) argues, it is even possible for some women to enter 'male jobs' or vice versa 'without these jobs losing their ideological designation as sex specific'.

23. Responding to a criticism suggested by Veronica Beechey, many people would object to lumping together such divergent theorists because of fundamental differences in epistemology and perspective. Our argument however is that despite those differences each of them has contributed significantly to exposing human anxiety and insecurity as reflecting as well as reinforcing self-consciousness, the fear of freedom, narcissism, etc.

References

Abercrombie, N. and Turner, B.S. (1978), 'The dominant ideology thesis', *British Journal of Sociology*, **29**, (2), 149-70.

Amsden, A.H (ed.) (1980), *'The Economics of Women and Work'*, Harmondsworth : Penguin.

Armstrong, P. (1982), 'If it's only women it doesn't matter so much', in J. West , (ed.), *Work, Women and the Labour Market*, London: Routledge and Kegan Paul.

Aronowitz, S. (1978), 'Marx, Braverman, and the Logic of Capital'. *Insurgent Sociologist*, **8**, 122-46.

Barker, J. and Downing, H. (1980), 'Word Processing and the Transformation of Patriarchal Relations of Control in the office', *Capital and Class*, **10**, 64-99.

Barrett, M. (1980), *Women's Oppresion Today:Problems in Marxist Feminist Analysis*, London:Verso and New Left Books.

Barron, R.D and Norris, G.M. (1976), 'Sexual Divisions and the Dual Labour Market' in D.L Barker and S. Allen, (eds), *Dependence and Exploitation in Work and Marriage*, London:Longman.

Beechey, V. (1977), 'Some notes on Female Wage Labour in Capitalist Production', *Capital and Class*, **3**, 45-66.

Beechey, V. (1978), 'Women and Production', in A. Kuhn, and A.M. Wolpe, *Feminism and Materialism*, London: Routledge and Kegan Paul.

Beechey, V. (1982), 'The sexual Division of Labour and the Labour Process:A Critical Assessment of Braverman' in S. Wood, (ed), *The Degradation of Work*? London: Hutchinson.

Beechey, V. (1984), 'Conceptualising Women's Employment', paper presented at the British Sociological Association Conference 'Work, Employment and Unemployment' at the University of Bradford.

Benet, M.K. (1972), *Secretary*, London: Sidgwick and Jackson.

Benston, M. (1969), 'The Political Economy of Women's Liberation,' *Monthly Review*, **21**, 4, 13-27.

Benston, M. (1982), 'The Political Economy of Women's Liberation' in M. Evans, (ed.), *The Woman Question*, London: Fontana.

Beynon, H. and Blackburn, R.M. (1972), *Perceptions of Work*, Cambridge: Cambridge University Press.

Brown, R. (1976), 'Women as Employees in Industry', in D.L Barker, and S. Allen, (eds), *Dependence and Exploitation in Work and Marriage*, London: Longman.

Campioni, M. (1976), 'Psychoanalysis and Marxist Feminism', *Working Papers in Sex, Science and Culture* **1**,(2) 33-59.

176   Gender and the Labour Process

Cavendish, R. (1982), *Women on the Line*, London: Routledge and Kegan Paul.

Cockburn, C. (1983), *Brothers:Male Dominance and Technological Change*, London: Pluto Press.

Collinson, D and Knights, D. (1985) " 'Jobs for the Boys' Sex Discrimination in Life Insurance Recruitment", in *E.C.O. Research Bulletin*, **9**, Spring, 24–44.

Connell, R. (1983), *Which Way Is Up?*, London: Allen and Unwin.

Coward, R. (1983), *Patriarchal Precedents*, London: Routledge and Kegan Paul.

Coward, R. and Ellis, J. (1977), *Language and Materialism*, London: Routledge and Kegan Paul.

Coyle, A. (1982), 'Sex and Skill in the Organisation of the Clothing Industry', in J. West, *Work, Women and the Labour Market*, London: Routledge and Kegan Paul.

Dalla Costa, M. and James, S. (1972), *The Power of Woman and the Subversion of the Community*, Bristol: Falling Wall Press.

Davies, M. (1974), 'Women's Place is at the Typewriter: The Feminisation of the Clerical Labour Force', *Radical America*,**18**, (4) (July-August).

Delphy, C. (1977), *The Main Enemy: A Materialist Analysis of Women's Oppresion*, London: Women's Research and Resources Centre.

Doeringer, P. and Piore, M. (1971), *Internal Labour Markets and Manpower Analysis*, Lexington, Mass.: Lexington Books.

Downing, H. (1980), 'Word Processors and the Oppresion of Women', in T. Forester, (ed) *The Microelectronics Revolution*, Oxford: Basil Blackwell.

Edwards, R. (1975), 'The Social Relations of Production in the Firm and Labour Market Structure', in R. Edwards, M. Reich, and D. Gordon, (ed), *Labour Market Segmentation*, Lexington, Mass.: Lexington Books.

Edwards, R. (1979), *Contested Terrain: The Transformation of the Workplace in the Twentieth Century*, New York: Basic Books.

Eisenstein, Z. (1979), 'Developing a Theory of Capitalist Patriarchy and Socialist Feminism', in Z. Eisenstein, *Capitalist Patriarchy and the case for Socialist Feminism*, New York: Marketing Review Press.

Elger, A. (1982), 'Braverman, Capital Accumulation and Deskilling' in S. Wood, (ed.), *The Degradation of Work?*, London: Hutchinson.

Firestone, S. (1971), *The Dialectic of Sex*, London: Paladin.

Gamarnikow, E. (1978), 'Sexual division of labour: The Case of Nursing' in A. Kuhn and A. Wolpe,(eds), *Feminism and Materialism*, London: Routledge and Kegan Paul.

Gamarnikow, E., Morgan, D., Purvis, J. and Taylorson, D. (eds). (1983) *Gender, Class and Work*, London: Heinemann.

Gardiner, J. (1976), 'Political Economy of Domestic Labour in Capitalist Society', in D. Barker, and S., Allen, *Dependence and Exploitation in Work and Marriage*, London: Longman.

Giddens, A. (1979), *Central Problems in Social Theory*, London: Macmillan.

Gramsci, A. (1971), *Selections From the Prison Notebooks*, London: Lawrence and Wishart.

Hakim, C. (1979), 'Occupational Segregation', *Department of Employment Research Paper*, No. 9.

Harrison, J. (1973), 'The Political Economy of Housework', *Bulletin of the Conference of Socialist Economists*, Winter.

Hartmann, H. (1979), 'Capitalism, Patriarchy and Job Segregation by Sex', in Z. Eisenstein, (ed.), *Capitalism, Patriarchy and the Case for Socialist Feminism*, New York: Monthly Review Press.

Hartmann, H. (1981), 'The Unhappy Marriage of Marxism and Feminism: Towards a More Progressive Union', in L. Sargent, (ed.), *The Unhappy Marriage of Marxism and Feminism*, London: Pluto Press.

Hollway, W. (1984), 'Gender Difference and the Productions of Subjectivity' in J. Henriques, W. Hollway, C. Unwin, C. Venn, and V. Walkerdine, *Changing the Subject*, London: Methuen.

Humphries, J, (1980), 'Class Struggle and The Persistence of the Working-Class Family', in A. Amsden, *The Economics of Women and Work*, Harmondsworth: Penguin.

Kadt, M. de (1979), 'Insurance—a clerical work factory', in A. Zimbalist, (ed.), *Case Studies on the Labour Process*, New York: Monthly Review Press.

Kanter, R. M. (1977), *Men and Women of the Corporation*, New York: Basic Books.

Knights, D. (1973), 'The Sociology of the Salesman', unpublished Masters, Dept. of Management Sciences, UMIST.

Knights, D. and Collinson, D. (1985), 'Redesigning Work on the Shopfloor: A Question of Control or Consent?', in D. Knights, H. W. Willmott, and D. Collinson, (eds), *Job Redesign: Critical Perspectives on the Labour Process*, Aldershot: Gower.

Knights, D. and Roberts, J. (1983), 'Understanding the Theory and Practice of Management Control', in *Employee Relations*, 5, (4).

Knights, D. and Willmott, H. W. (1985), 'Power and Identity in Theory and Practice', *Sociological Review*, February, 33, 1.

Kuhn, A. (1978), 'Structures of Capital and Patriarchy in the Family', in A. Kuhn, and A. M. Wolpe, (eds), *Feminism and Materialism*, London: Routledge and Kegan Paul.

Littler, C. R. and Salaman, G. (1982), 'Bravermania and Beyond—Recent Theories of the Labour Process', *Sociology*, 16, (2) May, 201-69.

Lockwood, D. (1958), *The Blackcoated Worker*, London: Allen and Unwin.

Mann, M. (1970), 'The Social Cohesion of Liberal Democracy', *American Sociological Review*, 35 (3).

Mann, M. (1973), *Consciousness and Action Among the Western Working Class*, London: Macmillan.

Manwaring, T. and Wood, S. (1985), 'The Ghost in the Labour Process', in D. Knights, H. Willmott, and D. Collinson, (eds), *Job Redesign: Critical Perspectives on the Labour Process*, Aldershot: Gower.

Marshall, K. (1982), *Real Freedom*, London: Blackrose Press.

Merleau-Ponty, M. (1962), *The Phenomenology of Perception*, London: Routledge and Kegan Paul.

Middleton, C. (1983), 'Patriarchal Exploitation and the Rise of English Capitalism' in Gamarnikow et al. (op. cit.).

Millett, K. (1971), Sexual Politics, New York: Abacus.

Molyneux, M. (1979), 'Beyond the Domestic Labour Debate', *New Left Review*, 116, 3-27.

Molyneux, M. (1981), 'Women in Socialist Societies', in K. Young, et al. (1981), *Of Marriage and the Market: Women's Subordination in International Perspective*, London: CSE Books.

Morgall, J. (1981), 'Typing Our Way to Freedom: Is It True That New Technology Can Liberate Women?', *Feminist Review*, 9, October.

Nichols, T. and Armstrong, P. (1976), *Workers Divided*, London: Fontana.

Nichols, T. and Beynon, H. (1977), *Living With Capitalism*, London: Routledge and Kegan Paul.

Phillips, A. and Taylor, B. (1980), 'Sex and Skill: Notes Towards a Feminist Economics', *Feminist Review*, 6,.

Pollert, A. (1981), *Girls, Wives, Factory Lives*, London: Macmillan.

Pollert, A. (1983), 'Women, Gender Relations and Wage Labour', in Gamarnikow et al. (eds), *Gender, Class and Work*, London: Heinemann.

Povall, M., de Jong, A, Chalude, M, Racape, A, Grozelier, A.M. (1982), 'Banking on Women Managers', in *Management Today*, February.

Prandy, K. (1979), 'Alienation and Interest in the Analysis of Social Cognition', *British Journal of Sociology*, 30, 4.

Reich, M, Gordon, D. M, Edwards, R. C. (1980), 'A Theory of Labour Market Segmentation', in A. Amsden, *The Economics of Women and Work*, Harmondsworth: Penguin.

Rubery, J. (1980), 'Structured Labour Markets, Worker Organization and Low Pay', in

A. Amsden, *The Economics of Women and Work*, Harmondsworth: Penguin.

Seccombe, W. (1974), 'The Housewife and Her Labour Under Capitalism', in *New Left Review*, **83**,

Sennett, R. and Cobb, J. (1977), *The Hidden Injuries of Class*, Cambridge: Cambridge University Press.

Silverstone, R. (1976), 'Office Work for Women: An Historical Review', *Business History*, **18**, (1), January.

Storey, J. (1986) 'The Phoney War? New Office Technology: Organisation and Control', in D. Knights, and H. W. Willmott, (eds), *Managerial Work; Explorations in the Changing Contents and Processes of Corporate Control*, Aldershot: Gower.

Sturdy, A. (1985) 'Contradictions of a Team Ideology', unpublished paper, Department of Management Sciences, UMIST.

Supple , B. (1970), *The Royal Exchange Assurance: A History of British Insurance 1720-1970*, Cambridge: Cambridge University Press.

Thompson, P. (1983), *The Nature of Work*, London: Macmillan.

Tolson, A. (1977), *The Limits of Masculinity*, London: Tavistock.

Vinnicombe, S. (1980), *Secretaries, Management and Organisations*, London: Heinemann.

Wajcman, J. (1983), *Women in Control*, Milton Keynes: Open University Press.

West, J. (ed.), (1982), *Work, Women and the Labour Market*, London: Routledge and Kegan Paul.

Westwood, S. (1984), *All Day, Every Day: Factory, Family, Women's Lives*, London: Pluto Press.

Willis, P. (1977), *Learning to Labour*, London: Saxon House.

Zaretsky, E. (1976), *Capitalism, the Family and Personal Life*, London: Pluto Press.

Index

Pearson, R., 50
Pelling, M., 23, 24, 25
Penn, R., 122
Perrell, J., 21
Phillips, A., 4, 96–7, 111–13, 122, 143, 147
physicians, 23–7, 28, 33–4
Picchio del Mercato, A., 98
Pinchbeck, I., 20, 21
Piore, M., 142
Podmore, D., 6, 50, 51
  on lawyers, 36–53, 147
Pollert, A, 4, 143, 144, 145, 167
pottery industry, 121, 122–35 *passim*
Povall, M. de J., 148
Power, E., 18, 19, 25
Prandy, K., 145
Prather, J., 51
pre-emptive closure strategies, 17–18, 27, 29–31
  de-skilling, 17–18,
    in medicine, 27, 29–31, 33
  incorporation, 17–18, 27, 29–31
'preference theory' in legal profession, 45–6
'pressure theory' in legal profession, 44–5
Price, R., 117
primary sector, 37, 46, 83
printing industry, closure in, 16
private woman, 2
  see also family
professions, defined, 32
  see also insurance; lawyers; medicine
proletarianisation of women, 55
  see also degradation; de-skilling
promotion
  insurance, 162–8
  lawyers, 46–8

Quandango, J., 51
Queen's Counsels, women rare as, 48

radiographers, 33
Ramas, M., 118
Read, Mrs., 21
recession, 70, 80, 109
recruiters, labour, women as, 124–7, 133–4
recruitment in insurance occupation, 153–7
registration, *see* licensing
Reich, M., 37, 141
Reid, S., 112

reproduction of job segregation, 147, 168–72
resegmentation of labour, 54, 55
reserve army of labour, 74, 79–80, 98, 143, 144
resistance, 144, 145–6
  to degradation of labour, 54
  and women in workplace, 119, 133–6
  see also organisation
restrictive strategies, 55
Richards, E., 120
riots *see* demonstrations
risk, women seen as, 47, 151
Roberts, J., 146, 161, 170
Roberts, R., 119
Ross, E., 120, 128
Rosser, J., 8, 9
  on health service, 94–116, 132, 150
Rowbotham, S., 19, 117
Royal College of Physicians, 25, 27, 28, 33–4
Royal Commissions
  on Condition of Framework Knitters (1845), 57, 59, 61
  on Labour (1892 and 1893), 62, 123
  on Legal Services (1979), 37
  on Trade Unions (1868), 54
  see also Commissions
Rubery, J., 143
Ryan, M., 137

Sachs, A., 49, 50
Saifullich-Khan, V., 132
Salaman, G., 10, 142
salary *see* earnings; wage
Sayles, L., 117
Schneider, B. E., 4
Scott, A., 19
Scott, J., 125, 128, 133
Scullion, H., 70
Seccombe, W, 142
secondary sector, 82, 140, 141
  legal profession, 37, 46
segregation, 33, 77–8
  see also insurance; technological change
Select Committee on Midwife Registration (1892), 31–2
self *see* identity
semi-professions, appeal to women, 51
Sennett, R., 161
service industries, 80–1
sex *see* gender
Shaw, H., 34

see also health service
West, J., 4, 112, 143
Westwood, S., 4, 73, 143, 144, 146
Whipp, Mrs., 34
Whipp, R., 8–9, 72
  on workplace, 117–39, 144
Whitley Council, 113
widows
  in hosiery trade, 57
  as medical practitioners, 20–1, 24
Wikler, N. J., 46
Williams, C., 4
Willis, P., 145, 148
Willmott, H. C., 1, 10, 146
Willughby, Dr., 29
Wilmott, P., 119
Wilson, H., 109
Wilson, J. H., 49, 50
Wilson, L., 64
Wise, S., 60
'wisewomen' (medical practitioners), 19,
  20, 26
witches, 19
Witz, A., 5
  on patriarchy and medicine, 14–35

Wolf, E., 120
Wolpe, A. M., 4, 73
'women's work', 141
  in hosiery manufacture, 56–60
  in legal profession, 40–3, 50–1
  in medical practice, 19–31
    passim, 51
  technical change and, 76–8, 80–5
  see also feminisation; gender
Wood, S., 1, 10, 148
Woodward, D., 51
workplace and women, 8–9, 117–39
  control, 130–3
  resistance, 119, 133–6
  skill and technology, 121–7
  wage, destination of, 127–30
Wright, E., 54
Wyman, A., 20, 21, 33

Yans-McLaughlin, V., 120, 136
Young, M., 119

Zaretsky, E., 143
Zimbalist, A., 1, 95, 96, 112